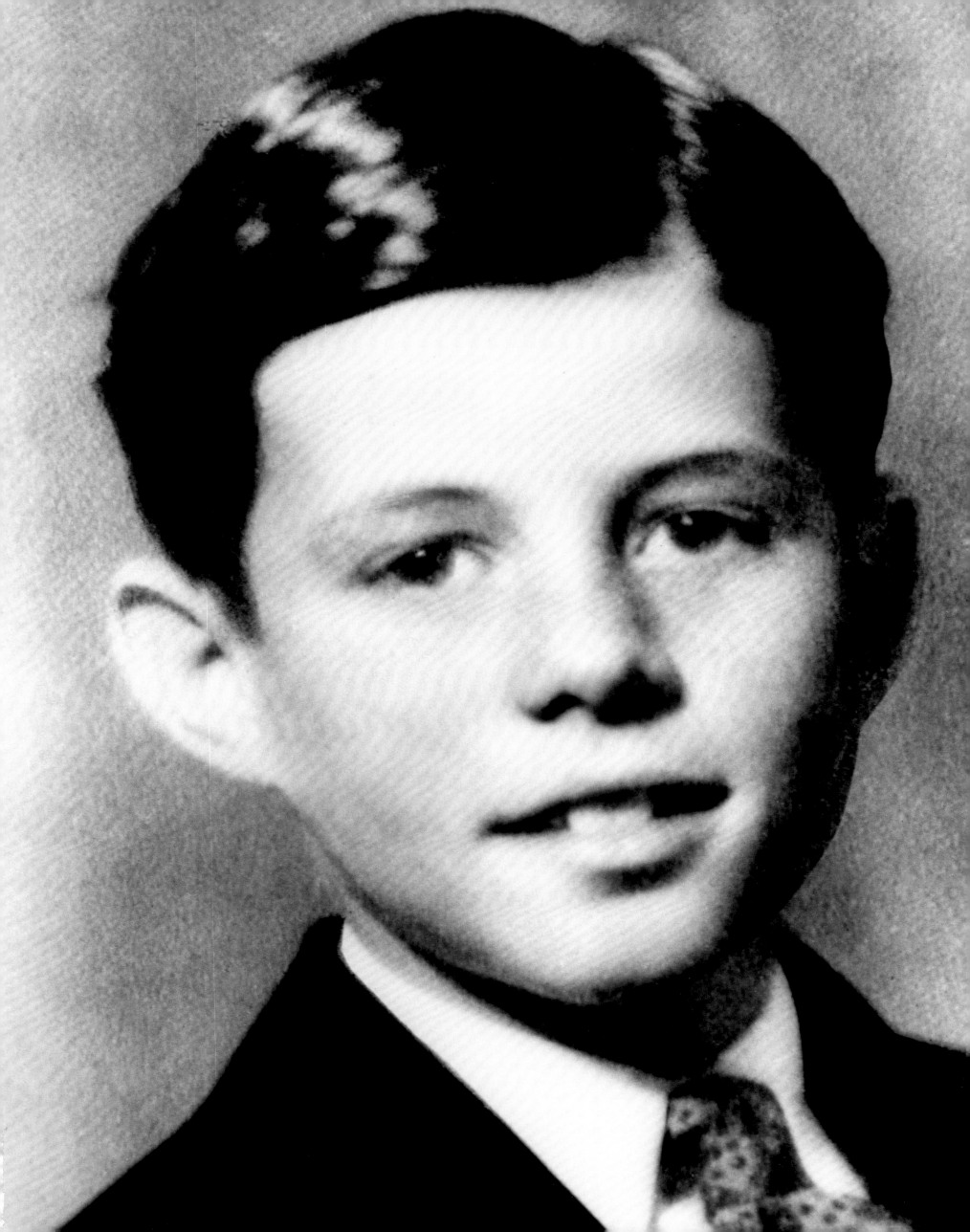

The
Day
Kennedy
Died

50 Years Later
LIFE
Remembers the Man
and the Moment

LIFE Books

Managing Editor Robert Sullivan
Director of Photography Barbara Baker Burrows
Creative Director Mimi Park
Deputy Picture Editor Christina Lieberman
Writer-Reporters Michelle DuPré, Marilyn Fu, Amy Lennard Goehner,
Mary Hart, Daniel S. Levy, Jane Bachman Wulf
Copy Chief Barbara Gogan
Copy Editors Don Armstrong, Parlan McGaw
Special Contributing Editor Richard B. Stolley
Photo Associate Sarah Cates
Consulting Picture Editors Mimi Murphy (Rome),
Tala Skari (Paris)

Editorial Director Stephen Koepp

Editorial Operations
Richard K. Prue (Director), Brian Fellows (Manager), Richard Shaffer
(Production), Keith Aurelio, Charlotte Coco, Liz Grover, Kevin Hart,
Mert Kerimoglu, Rosalie Khan, Patricia Koh, Marco Lau, Brian Mai,
Po Fung Ng, Rudi Papiri, Robert Pizaro, Barry Pribula, Clara Renauro,
Hia Tan, Vaune Trachtman

Special thanks: Megan Bryant, Karin Grant, Maryrose Grossman,
Bill Hooper, Nicola Longford, Gary Mack, David McCullough,
Farris Rookstool III, Judith Rosenbaum, Lee Statham

TIME HOME ENTERTAINMENT

Publisher Jim Childs
Vice President, Brand & Digital Strategy Steven Sandonato
Executive Director, Marketing Services Carol Pittard
Executive Director, Retail & Special Sales Tom Mifsud
Executive Publishing Director Joy Butts
Director, Bookazine Development & Marketing Laura Adam
Finance Director Glenn Buonocore
Associate Publishing Director Megan Pearlman
Associate General Counsel Helen Wan
Assistant Director, Special Sales Ilene Schreider
Senior Book Production Manager Susan Chodakiewicz
Design & Prepress Manager Anne-Michelle Gallero
Brand Manager Roshni Patel
Associate Prepress Manager Alex Voznesenskiy
Assistant Brand Manager Stephanie Braga

Special thanks: Katherine Barnet, Jeremy Biloon, Rose Cirrincione,
Jacqueline Fitzgerald, Christine Font, Jenna Goldberg, Hillary
Hirsch, David Kahn, Amy Mangus, Kimberly Marshall, Nina Mistry,
Dave Rozzelle, Ricardo Santiago, Adriana Tierno, Vanessa Wu

ISBN 10: 1-61893-074-5
ISBN 13: 978-1-61893-074-3
Library of Congress Control Number: 2013936690
Printed in China

"LIFE" is a registered trademark of Time Inc.

We welcome your comments and suggestions about LIFE Books.
Please write to us at: LIFE Books, Attention: Book Editors,
PO Box 11016, Des Moines, IA 50336-1016

If you would like to order any of our hardcover Collector's Edition books,
please call us at 1-800-327-6388 (Monday through Friday,
7:00 a.m.–8:00 p.m. or Saturday, 7:00 a.m.–6:00 p.m. Central Time)

Table of Contents

For One Brief Shining Moment

Fifty years ago, LIFE was in the midst of enjoying one of its best-ever stories: the life and times of Jack and Jackie Kennedy. Suddenly it was presented with one of its biggest stories: the murder of a President. Today, LIFE returns to both stories.

THERE ARE A FEW PHRASES THAT HAVE ATTACHED themselves to the life, times, administration and murder of John Fitzgerald Kennedy. *Camelot,* after the musical, and the lyric from that musical's lead song, used here as the title of this introduction, are two, and another is *a thousand days,* also referring to the painful brevity of Kennedy's term. The moment, historian David McCullough helps us understand in the foreword immediately following, was sometimes glorious, sometimes fraught, but for so many Americans—including those who were young at the time and who are still alive 50 years later—always shining. Kennedy and his wife, Jacqueline, shone in a new, vigorous way. That was part of the shock of his death: He looked like he would live forever.

LIFE magazine, which was at the apex of its popularity and influence when Jack and Jackie came on the American scene, was definitely complicit in the image-building. Would we choose to photograph two of the most beautiful people in the country early and often, especially when one might become (and then did become) the leader of the free world? Yes, we would. And we did. Through the years, we gave them cover after cover (Jack, 28 in all; his wife, one better at 29). LIFE was founded in 1936, and during its run as a weekly magazine, ending in 1972, there were certain stories that we considered "ours." Henry Luce said that he had not founded LIFE as "a war magazine" but that it became one during World War II, filing dispatches for Americans on a weekly basis, even from the beachheads of Normandy. Hollywood was another of our stories, with Marilyn and Liz particular friends of ours. Vietnam. The civil rights movement. The space race. And certainly, above almost all others, the Kennedys.

In that brief list there is gloss in the glamorous actresses and there is life's grit in the wars and the stories of social upheaval. The Kennedys—and in a way the Mercury 7 astronauts—fall somewhere in between. We could tour the White House with Jackie and review the renovations one week, then parse the Cuban missile crisis in those same rooms the next.

When the assassination occurred 50 years ago, LIFE was poised like no other American media outlet, print or electronic, to leap into action. We had the resources and the will, and in these pages is much of that original journalism and photojournalism, with recollections of those who were there and opinions on what it all meant going forward. The Zapruder film, first acquired for LIFE by our Los Angeles bureau chief Richard B. Stolley, is presented here, intact, for the first time ever in print, as is Stolley's detailed remembrance and also that of Abraham Zapruder's granddaughter Alexandra. LIFE photographer Allan Grant and correspondent Thomas Thompson located the Oswald family on the very evening of the assassination, and their report is presented here in full—with an explanation about why it didn't run back in the day. We have fanned out with our current reporting to include a look at the never-ending conspiracy theories and a visit with the last surviving member of JFK's so-called "Irish mafia." We have made new pictures of artifacts at The Sixth Floor Museum at Dealey Plaza in Dallas. We have interviewed or accepted writing from more than two dozen prominent world citizens, in answer to the question everyone is always asked about JFK: Where were you when you heard? We have tried to emulate LIFE's original energy and seriousness of purpose in telling this story—the assassination of a President—50 years later. If the memories of our contributors differ as to some details, the hearts of their stories beat true.

Of course, there is also the photography of Caroline and John Jr. in the White House, and of the funeral, that will take us all back in time, causing a smile or a tear. And there is a replica copy of the issue that LIFE frantically but forthrightly produced in the week after November 22, which delivers us back to the Thanksgiving season of 1963 like nothing else can.

John F. Kennedy's was a brief shining moment, followed by a brief awful moment. Fifty years later, it is worthwhile to remember both.

In 1960, Henry Luce, the founder of *Time* and LIFE, escorts presidential candidate John Kennedy through the halls of the Time & Life Building.

"A Death in the American Family"

A Conversation with David McCullough

The historian helps us understand why John Fitzgerald Kennedy still matters—
and why he mattered greatly to McCullough himself, 50 years ago.

THE PREEMINENT AMERICAN HISTORIAN OF OUR TIME IS DAVID McCullough. Some critics might put forth a second or third nominee, but we're in McCullough's camp. Twice a Pulitzer Prize winner and also the recipient not only of a National Book Award but our nation's highest civilian honor, the Presidential Medal of Freedom, the 80-year-old native of Pittsburgh has for years spent the nice months living and writing on the island of Martha's Vineyard, just across the sound from the Kennedy compound in Hyannis Port, Massachusetts.

Particularly when it comes to John F. Kennedy, McCullough is well suited to set the stage for us. It's not that he is a JFK biographer or a chronicler of the family—he isn't, at least not yet—but he has analyzed and thought for many years about the grand sweep of American and presidential history, and also, when he was a younger man, he himself was swept up by the Kennedy aura. In fact, he found his calling after having been influenced by Kennedy's deep personal interest in history. Moreover, here at Time Inc., the parent company of LIFE Books, McCullough is not only a proud alumnus, but was working for the firm when JFK went to the White House. McCullough, too, quickly went to Washington and likewise found employment in the government (albeit in a position of different scope and scale). Told that LIFE is commemorating the life and legacy of John Fitzgerald Kennedy, 50 years on, McCullough says he is happy to help, and, remembering the magazine's coverage of the time, adds graciously, "It's great you're doing this. It's wonderful. You're the right ones to do it."

McCullough is at home today on a pleasant day in late May, as rising temperatures are finally chasing away a chilly spring. He is asked to begin with the professional perspective: What is it about Kennedy? Why, a half century on, is such attention still paid to him, who after all had such a relatively brief residence at 1600 Pennsylvania Avenue?

"Well, I think there are several reasons really," he answers. "There are three things I would put at the head of the list for why Kennedy is remembered. One thing is, and this is pretty obvious, Kennedy was glamorous in a way that no President has been in the lifetimes of most Americans. He might have been the most glamorous President ever. His wife and children were glamorous. He had tremendous personal charisma. He had a phenomenal gift for using the language to lift the country's spirits, and in this he wasn't unlike FDR. I loved that he loved books, he loved culture; he was eloquent as very few leaders ever have been. In these ways, he was approaching the same type of leader as Winston Churchill.

"On the same point, he was the first President to really use television, particularly of course with his inaugural address but also his subsequent addresses and his spectacular press conferences. He knew how to use humor, a self-deprecating humor, not unlike Reagan, that was very appealing. We remember that.

"Most of us knew nothing about his private excesses, I never even heard gossip about it. Things went on that people never knew back then." So the image was intact and for some permanently so: fine-looking family man. Churchgoer, too.

That's the second thing, says McCullough: "He broke the religious barrier. This was very important; it might be hard for some people today to realize how important. And he did this by never apologizing for or dismissing the importance of Catholicism in his life. He took the issue head-on.

"And he said we would go to the moon. That was a vastly important objective he set for us." It was important, McCullough asserts, not only in terms of the cold war battle with the Soviets that had the country on edge, but in terms of America's own spirit and sense of achievement and aspiration. "He knew life was unfair and said so,"

McCullough continues, "but he was an optimist. The people liked that in him; they loved it." Sending a man to the moon would be a perfect and perfectly outrageous accomplishment—symbolic, metaphoric, but actual—for a nation forming itself in their leader's can-do spirit.

So there were those three large issues and aspects at work—the glamour and youth and vitality, the forcing of his country to overcome prejudice, the encouraging of his countrymen to join him in daring to dream—and then he was murdered. "The way he looked, he was always so photogenic," says McCullough. "He really was perfect for the hero part. And of course he had the actual heroism of his war service. So: the handsome one who was killed. The hero was sacrificed." Such a narrative as that will never be forgotten.

At this point the discussion with McCullough turns to a judgment of the man and his time in office: He had the Bay of Pigs disaster but then the successful outcome of the Cuban missile crisis, he initiated policies that would lead to the civil rights achievements of President Lyndon Johnson's term but also to the mire that would be the Vietnam War. "I don't think you could say he was a great President," says McCullough. "His time in office was a little bit too short. A good part of the time, that last year or so, he was in the soup. There was a lot of criticism. I don't think [the fault-finding] was of him personally so much as simply for the way things were going [in the country].

"Truman said that you need 50 years of time to go by in order to pass judgment, and I think that's right. You can't say he was a great President. But [Kennedy] is among our most remembered Presidents, and I think he always will be."

McCULLOUGH IS A GOOD HISTORIAN—HE'S A GREAT ONE—AND this is herein confirmed because there's an inference on the part of his listener that McCullough wishes he could give Kennedy a complete, and better, grade. As a chronicler being asked his opinion, however, he cannot; he's got a job to do.

"Whatever I say about him, I'm speaking from the bias of having been swept away by his candidacy.

"I was young, I was working for Time Inc., I had a very good job. I had been there six years, had started out at *Sports Illustrated* as a trainee, and I was a huge enthusiast for architecture and had gone to work for *The Architectural Forum* as a writer, and then I went over to *Time,* and now I was nearing 30. I had a family and we had income, but right then Kennedy began to run and I got swept up with it. I quit my job and went down to Washington having no inside [angle] on any job. I went to the United States Information Agency [a government service] and the man who interviewed me was Don Wilson, who had been the head of the LIFE bureau in Washington. Don had worked on the campaign and was very close to the administration. He knew Kennedy well. He was made number two at USIA, second to Edward R. Murrow. I didn't know Don, but Don checked my credentials back in the home office, and he hired me and put me in charge of a magazine for the Arab world. I had never run a magazine, I didn't know anything about the Arab world, I knew nothing about the Arabs, and I told him so. 'How much do you know about the Arabs?' 'Mr. Wilson, I don't know anything about the Arabs.' 'Well,' he said, 'you're gonna learn a lot.' Those were terrific times, it was so exciting."

It all trickled down from Kennedy and the energy—the vibe—of the White House: "As I say, I'm not a Kennedy scholar, but I experienced some of the effect he had on people and the country. I was so emotionally and personally involved in that story at

McCullough very much at home on the Vineyard in 1990 in a portrait made by his friend and neighbor, LIFE's famed Alfred Eisenstaedt.

that point in time, and I was so excited, and the thing was: We young, like him, were having a chance at failure. That was encouraged by him. At the beginning I was thinking, 'I'm in so over my head,' but six months later: 'Maybe I'm not in over my head, and this is my job. Maybe I can do this.' That was him.

"And we put out a very good lifestyle magazine for the Arab world—produced in Washington, translated into Arabic in Beirut—very good, if I do say so."

Certainly that particular job had to spur an interest in history in McCullough, but in fact Kennedy himself, from afar, had already done so. "I was like a lot of young writers in that I knew I wanted to write," McCullough says. "But I didn't know what. Then I learned of Kennedy's interest in history. He was a great reader of history and at one of his early press conferences he referred to Barbara Tuchman's [World War I history] *The Guns of August,* and because he recommended it, I read it, and it was at that time that I was beginning to think that I was going to be a writer for LIFE or an editor or maybe write plays or novels, but it had never occurred to me that I would be writing history. And it was at that time that I began to read people like Barbara Tuchman—because of Kennedy. That time really changed my life, because that's when I knew that's what I wanted to do. Once I got started, well, it really *was* what I wanted to do.

"Years later, I met Barbara Tuchman at a party and she told me how much she admired my work, and I thought I was about to go soaring off through the ceiling."

AS WILL BE ASKED OF MANY OTHERS LATER IN THIS LIFE COMMEMorative, McCullough is asked: "Where were you when you heard?"

"On the day he was shot," McCullough begins, and then he goes down a tangential road briefly. "Well, I should tell you, people don't appreciate this enough today: There was great worry when he announced he was going to Dallas. I really think people don't know that today. Back in that time, many people in Washington were saying, 'Oh, God, he shouldn't go there.' There really was that feeling of dread.

"I was having lunch with Don Wilson at a restaurant called, ironically, the Black Saddle, right around the corner from our offices at 1776 Pennsylvania, near the White House. And at one point an associate—I can't remember his name, it's not important—came in just as we were about to order lunch, and leaned over and whispered something in Don's ear, which I couldn't hear. And Don looked up and said, 'The President's been shot! Which President?' He couldn't accept that this had happened to his President. They had been good friends. I remember that after Kennedy was killed, Don left and went back to LIFE.

"From that moment on, we were working virtually night and day, as you might imagine, trying to put things out to explain to the world what had happened, and not only do justice to the fallen President but to tell the world something about Lyndon Johnson, the new President.

"For me, it was the most wrenching experience I had ever gone through, and I think the most wrenching experience I've gone through since—both emotionally, and [because of] the tremendous pressure that was put on us with the work.

"In a way, the work was a blessing, because for those of us who [cared about] Kennedy, it helped take our minds off what had happened.

"For us, who were excited at the time, to have the whole thing blow up like that: We were all saying, 'Oh, God!'"

But of course it wasn't just earthshaking for the young: "It was a national heartbreaker—a national heartbreaking experience," says McCullough. "It was not just a death in the family, it was a death in the American family."

The Kennedys

The United States doesn't support royalty, but if it did, the Kennedys would be royals. They have experienced the outsize triumphs, awful travails and abject tragedies of such exalted families. One of them, so obviously a prince, was elected President—our democratic version of a king—and then he was killed. The term *Shakespearean* is overused, but it certainly applies to the tale of the Kennedys.

BY ANY HISTORICAL MEASURE, IT ALL happened pretty fast, the "it" being a climb from the gutter to the Oval Office. Patrick Kennedy, an immigrant to the United States who fled Ireland during the Great Famine of the mid–19th century, was the patriarch of what grew to be certainly the most remarkable (adherents would argue, greatest) of all Irish American families. Bridget Murphy, too, was a famine refugee—from the same county, Wexford, as Kennedy. She traveled to America aboard the same ship in 1849. She would become Patrick's wife and thus the matriarch of that family. Family legend holds that aboard that boat, Patrick met Bridget, and they found they had a month to kill and much in common to discuss. By the time the boat reached Boston, they were in love.

Patrick and Bridget married, but love is spiritual currency only, and their early residence was in the slum of East Boston—they probably couldn't afford the two-penny ferry to cross the harbor into downtown. The conditions in "Paddytown" were beyond deplorable—60 percent of those born in Boston at that time didn't live to see their sixth birthday—but Patrick was fiercely determined (a great trait in the family) and became a cooper. Bridget bore three daughters and two sons in eight years (a Kennedy pace).

We need to scoot ahead: Cholera hit the Irish slums hard, killing hundreds, including Patrick. He left behind one son to carry his name, his last-born child, Patrick Joseph Kennedy. The boy, P.J., went to school under the Sisters of Notre Dame, worked in Boston Harbor, saved some money, borrowed some from his mother and took possession of a saloon in a dilapidated part of town. He worked hard, his bar prospered, he bought more properties. He married up in class in 1887 to Mary Augusta Hickey. They had four children, the first of whom was Joseph Patrick Kennedy—the Joe Kennedy you know.

Joe married Rose Fitzgerald, daughter of the legendary Boston politician John "Honey Fitz" Fitzgerald, and they had loads of children, all of whom you will see in the pages immediately following. Joe Jr. came first and was primed for greatness, John (the subject of our book) was born next in 1917, then Rosemary, then Kathleen (Kick), then Eunice (perhaps the smartest of them all), then Patricia, then Bobby, then Jean and then Teddy.

Joe Jr. was killed in the war, and John, known as Jack, was injured. Kick died in a plane crash just as Joe had. Rosemary was institutionalized by her parents after her father approved an ill-advised lobotomy. The dramas of the Kennedys would be endless.

But from it all, John—Jack—emerged. Courageous and smart, astonishingly handsome and charismatic, ambitious as his father willed him to be, he was not to be denied. And he was not denied.

He became President of the United States of America. And that was the triumphant last chapter in the remarkable Kennedy history.

Except that it wasn't.

Joe Kennedy is destined for wealth—wealth built in liquor (if not precisely bootlegging), Hollywood and other enterprises—but when Jack is born on May 29, 1917, this is the house, at 83 Beals Street in Brookline, Massachusetts. Not much more than a year later, the baby Kennedy sits in the sand of Nantasket Beach, then evolving into a working-class summer outpost for Massachusetts families, which it remains. The Kennedys would eventually move down to Hyannis Port, on Cape Cod, and the journey represented much.

Childhood

At right, Joseph P. Kennedy poses next to his car with sons Jack and Joe Jr. in Brookline in 1919. Upon graduating from Harvard in 1912, Joe Sr. had decided to eschew the family trade—politics—and go into finance. He already had some experience with successful enterprises: He had hawked candy as a kid, and in college he was an operator and part owner of a sightseeing tour bus. He continued to be a precocious titan of business and was a bank president by age 25. With their burgeoning wealth, the Kennedys were able to buy property in what would become their clan's spiritual home, Hyannis Port on Cape Cod. Below, in 1930, on the sands there, Joe and Rose's brood now numbers eight, and Teddy is soon on the way (he would be born in 1932). From left: Bobby, Jack, Eunice, Jean, Joe, Rose, Pat, Kick, Joe Jr. and Rosemary. On the opposite page, the future President poses with a pooch in the kind of portrait that families like the Kennedys could now afford to have made. Do consider: only three generations earlier, poverty.

CORBIS

JFK LIBRARY/GAMMA

Early Years

Golden boys: In September 1938, Jack arrives on the liner *Bremen,* en route to Harvard to continue his studies after spending a summer in England, where his father is the U.S. ambassador to the Court of Saint James; and in the photograph at bottom, Jack (at left) and his older brother, Joe Jr., are with Dad. We will discuss Jack further on the pages immediately following and in the remainder of this book, but for now, briefly: Joe Jr., and why it was left to Jack to pick up the torch. Joe Jr. was even more handsome than his father (and as dazzlingly so as Jack would prove to be). There is no question but that Joe, born on July 25, 1915, was the chosen one. Joe Sr., once he had come around from business and movies to the world of politics, may have had dreams of the White House for himself, but scandal and being on the wrong sides of issues—he had a bootlegger's reputation; he was seen as soft on fascism in the '30s; he was known to be anti-Semitic; he was terribly slow to come around regarding America's intervention in World War II—doomed him. So it would be Joe Jr., in every way raised to be a junior Joe, who

would be the one to fulfill the dream. Within the family, the eldest son was the designated leader, and it's a role Joe Jr. both wanted and protected. His kid brother Jack would tease him plenty, and there was a lot of tussling between the two older boys. Jack would refuse to obey Joe's commands; Bobby remembered later that the others would cower as the two brothers went at it. (The stronger of the two, Joe, would win the battles, but Jack was undeterred.) Joe might well have made it to the presidency, but the fighter pilot's plane exploded in flight on August 12, 1944, and he was dead at the young age of 29. Robert F. Kennedy Jr., Bobby's son and Joe Jr.'s nephew, once told LIFE in an interview, "That was always portrayed, in our family, not as the ultimate sacrifice, but as the ultimate extension of a life—to give yourself for our country. We were taught in our family to envy Joe."
Below: The earlier generation of Robert F. Kennedy Jr.'s family, in London in 1939, during the time of the patriarch Joe Sr.'s ambassadorship, from left: Eunice, Jack, Rosemary, Jean, Dad, Teddy, Mom, Joe Jr., Pat, Bobby and Kick.

Early Years

The photographs on this page of Jack and his sister Eunice were taken at the June 22, 1939, party at the residence of the American ambassador in London to celebrate Eunice's 18th birthday. The purpose of presenting these pictures here, as well as the one on the pages just previous, is to let our readers know: While many Americans today think the Kennedys arrived in 1960 with the President's election, this family was coming—strongly—even before World War II, and some people sensed it. Many did in England, which, although it had other issues at the time still noticed these folks. The

British were unhappy with Joe Sr.'s laissez-faire attitude toward Germany, but they were captivated by his kids. With all the merriment that the Beatles would display when storming New York a quarter century later, the young and even older Kennedys kicked up their heels in the highest style after Joe Sr. was posted by President Franklin Delano Roosevelt in 1938. Perhaps, considering these photos, a more apt cultural analogy than the Beatles, and one resonant in 2013: *The Great Gatsby,* as seen by Baz Luhrmann.

To talk briefly of Jack and Eunice and their place in the family: They both grew up

without pressure, he because there was Joe, she because she was a she. Jack had to confront no greater expectations than happiness and well-being for 27 years, and so was free to form himself as a fun guy, a fair scholar, a lover of books (he listed toward adventure stories) and a willing supplicant to the fates (oh, the hand they would deal him . . .). Joe Jr.'s domination of Jack caused the second child to become something of an anti-Joe: sloppy in his bedroom where Joe was orderly, lazy at school where Joe was industrious, carefree where Joe was intense. JFK did all of the right things, however:

COURTESY PETER HUNTER/MAGNUM (3)

Harvard, the service. He, like Joe, turned out to be a World War II hero (his valor aboard PT-109, which will be parsed on the following pages, is unquestioned, no matter how his father subsequently blared the news). Then he turned out to be an impossibly charismatic congressional candidate. Then he turned out to be an electrifying President. Then he turned out to be seen as the greatest American martyr since Abraham Lincoln.

As for Eunice Mary, born July 10, 1921, she was a smart and sensible Kennedy, but nonetheless strong and vibrant. Though Kick was her idol (everyone loved Kick),

young Eunice was caught between older and younger siblings, and found herself more often aligned with Pat and Bobby and, later, with Jean and Teddy. Her health, like her brother Jack's, wasn't always the best; she was plagued by chronic stomach troubles. But she had, like Jack, a capacity to ignore pain, and she didn't think of herself. She would accomplish much. At 26, she was working for the Juvenile Delinquency Committee of the Justice Department and saying things like "substantial efforts must be made to keep adolescents from quitting school at 14 or 15 and to give them

a chance to learn a trade or develop special skills." She was the strongest-minded of her generation and an instinctive politician (she was a great aid in 1960 during the presidential campaign). In May 1953 she married Robert Sargent Shriver after a seven-year courtship. Shriver was instrumental in forming the Peace Corps; Eunice founded the Special Olympics, which grew out of a summer camp on the lawns of the Shrivers' greater Washington, D.C., estate. Her father, Joe, once said that, had Eunice been a man, she might have been the President.

PT-109

RUE DES ARCHIVES/GRANGER

We'll talk first about the family in wartime, then specifically about PT-109. Joe Sr., Joe Jr., Kick and Jack were all directly affected by World War II. The patriarch resigned his job as ambassador when America turned from isolationism to engagement and he refused to change his tune. Meantime, he saw his two elder sons enlist and join the fight. Joe Jr. trained as a pilot at the Squantum Naval Air Station in Massachusetts in 1941 and was killed in action when his plane exploded over England three years later. Kathleen, meanwhile, fell in love with the rakish British aristocrat William Cavendish and they married before he, too, was killed in the conflict at age 26. Kick herself died young as well, killed in a plane crash on May 13, 1948.

Jack, seen here in all three pictures (above, at far right), was, like his brother, a Navy man. He rose to skipper the patrol boat PT-109, which sank after being rammed by a Japanese destroyer. Jack saved his crew, which was rescued in the Solomon Islands after he had carved an SOS message into a coconut. Jack, who had—as said—experienced ill health in his youth, would undergo many surgeries for injuries suffered during the incident, but would nonetheless be plagued by pain the rest of his life.

MPI/GETTY

The Campaign Trail

Stepping forth in 1946 at the Bunker Hill Day parade in Charlestown, Massachusetts, war hero John F. Kennedy is running for Congress. Nationwide, in the middle of President Harry S Truman's first term, the Democrats were trounced, but JFK in the 11th district did the trouncing, winning easily, and then being reelected in 1948 and 1950.

In Washington, he was an indifferent and frankly ineffective policy maker, but, as always, a riveting personality. As has been

true with many of his kin, people always knew when Kennedy was in the room.

In the photograph opposite he is seen at the 1952 Democratic National Convention, and that was a big year for him. He beat the estimable incumbent Henry Cabot Lodge Jr. in a Senate race back in Massachusetts. The outcome of that race signifies much. The Lodges were a mainline Massachusetts family reaching way, way back: aristocrats of the Bay State. The Kennedys were Johnny-come-latelies. Both Harvard men, Lodge and Kennedy had

distinguished themselves in the war. More personally, the first Henry Cabot Lodge had beaten JFK's grandfather John F. Fitzgerald for the same Senate seat in 1916. Now the tables turned. Fascinatingly, when Jack's brother Ted won the seat in 1962 in a special election due to the President's unexpired term, he defeated Lodge's son George.

But back to 1952. Now Republicans and Democrats alike were asking, "Where is this guy headed?" Joe Kennedy had a ready answer for them.

GAMMA

MASSACHUSETTS

HANK WALKER

Enter Jackie

Lorem... **L**IFE magazine had paid attention to the Kennedy family right along, but its deeply symbiotic relationship with Jack in particular—and with Jack and Jackie—began with a July 1953 cover story on the dashing senator and his gorgeous fiancée. All of the photos on these two pages, taken by Hy Peskin, are from that feature, and a cropped version of the sailboat shot was the cover.

Who was this woman, Jacqueline Bouvier, whom all of America would soon know as "Jackie"? Well, in 1953 she was, roughly, a female equivalent of her beau: Irish ancestry (on her mother's side); a bit of Jazz Age sleaziness (on Dad's side). She had been born into wealth in 1929 in Southampton, New York, to the former Janet Norton Lee and the storied Wall Street stockbroker John Vernon "Black Jack" Bouvier III. The handsome Black Jack was a hard-drinking, flamboyant womanizer, and in 1940 he and Janet divorced. Janet remarried, and young Jackie, who grew up largely in New York City and East Hampton, was subsequently raised by her mother and stepfather in McLean, Virginia, and Newport, Rhode Island—though she attended Miss Chapin's School in New York City, not far from her father's Upper East Side home. She was named "debutante of the year" by columnist Igor Cassini in 1947, then it was on to Vassar for two years, a year in France (including time at the Sorbonne) and then to George Washington University to finish up, in 1951, with a degree in French literature.

She was a horsewoman, and artsy. After graduation, she landed a job as the *Washington Times-Herald*'s "Inquiring Photographer." She became engaged in this period to a stockbroker, but that wouldn't stick. When you think about it— Harvard and Vassar, Cape Cod and Newport, Washington—it would have been inevitable that she meet the young congressman Jack Kennedy. And, considering what we all now know about JFK, it is inevitable that he would have perked up upon seeing her.

Each of them knew the journalist Charles L. Bartlett (a Yalie who would go on to win a Pulitzer), and he brought them together in May 1951. JFK was busy trying to beat Henry Cabot Lodge Jr. just then, but after he had prevailed, he got back in touch. The courtship was swift, and an engagement was announced on June 25, 1953. LIFE swooped right in, even employing some of the famous backward-running Time Inc. sentences: "The handsomest young member of the U.S. Senate was acting last week like any young man in love. To the family home on Cape Cod, John F. Kennedy brought his fiancée for a weekend of fun." Jackie was quoted as saying, "We hardly *ever* talk politics," and certainly our caption writer at the time was implying this between the lines when he or she attached to the picture at top: "Jackie tousles his hair, his political trademark. At times, Kennedy broke away from fun to get senatorial work done." Yes, at times.

President Kennedy

WITH THE KENNEDYS, IT IS HARD TO say which period might have been the happiest or most exciting. The 19th-century rise out of poverty even before Joe's birth would have to be considered, and so would the years when Joe and Rose's kids grew up so splendidly. But there were always the mitigating travails and tragedies, as we have already seen, which would prove, down the decades, to be unabating.

Certainly the late 1950s and early '60s would seem, to historians or any outsiders, constantly thrilling: "Jack and Jackie," Jack's easy second-term senatorial triumph, a bold attempt for the White House, the grasping of his nation's ultimate prize. Of course, late in this period, the patriarch would suffer his debilitating stroke, and then the great disaster that is the focus of our book would be played out in Dallas.

The Kennedys never seemed to waver in their faith that the journey was worth the cost, nor did they shrink from living public lives—lives of American fame and fortune but also dedicated service.

It seems they could not do anything either undramatically or unattractively. When Jack and Jackie wed, remember, he wasn't President—just a senator—and yet LIFE magazine and everyone else focused on aristocratic Newport, Rhode Island, that weekend. With the cameras clicking, the Kennedys certainly didn't disappoint. The 1960 presidential campaign was one of the most fraught, and interesting, in the nation's history, and the counterpoint that Jack represented to Richard M. Nixon was at the center of the discussion on a daily basis. If the electorate wanted a stark choice in candidates, as it often claims to want, it certainly got one with Kennedy and Nixon.

When Jack assumed the nation's highest office, his stirring rhetoric spurred the nation's young to a crusade of national involvement that would affect everyone's thinking. The Cuban missile crisis and the building of the Berlin Wall by the Soviet satellite would follow; and Kennedy would engage in world affairs—always dramatically. How dramatically? He asked us to send a man to the moon.

History has told us that there were many other things going on, some noble and some unsavory. President Kennedy was in pain almost constantly, between his Addison's disease and the aftershocks of the back injuries he suffered during the war. He remained stoic and good-humored; he was constantly dashing, and never seemed frail. Meanwhile, he treated his marriage vows casually. We know all this now. At the time, we were told whatever was riveting enough to hold our attention; and we wanted to believe the best. We were complicit in the fairy tale—in what would become known, posthumously, as Camelot. We were happy to know that a man like this, a family like this, a beautiful and smart couple like Jack and Jackie could happen in America. We had never seen anything like them.

And, frankly, we haven't seen anything like them since.

Only in retrospect does it seem like destiny. The Kennedys were certainly a great American family on the rise, and with such families it is said anything's possible. But for Jack there would be high hurdles to the presidency: He was too young, he was of the wrong religion, his politics were too liberal, his legislative record was undistinguished. This all would be weighed against a somewhat amorphous judgment: He was very special. He and Jackie too: They were special indeed.

JOHN F. KENNEDY LIBRARY/WNET

At left, in 1953, Senator John F. Kennedy and his fiancée, Jacqueline Bouvier, share a quiet moment in Hyannis Port two days before their high-society wedding down the coast in Newport, Rhode Island. St. Mary's parish had been established there in 1828, before the progenitors of this clan had even emigrated from Ireland, and work on the church in which Jack and Jackie would wed had begun in 1848. The Kennedys succeeded in looking like a very old family here, even though they were new. Opposite: On September 12, the happy couple kneel during their wedding ceremony. Today, St. Mary's Church is a national historic shrine, having received the designation in 1968.

Starting a Family

In London in 1947, Jack was diagnosed with Addison's disease, a life-threatening adrenal gland deficiency that causes fatigue and weight loss. On the ship home to America, he became so ill that a priest was summoned— prematurely—to give Jack his last rites. By the early 1950s, he had mastered silently bearing his many maladies and showing his public strength and vitality. As mentioned earlier, Jack challenged Henry Cabot Lodge Jr. for his Senate seat in 1952 and won; then he won the heart of Jacqueline Bouvier, every bit his match in wit, charm, intellect and, if private and soft-spoken, self-assurance. Kennedy aide and biographer Arthur Schlesinger Jr. wrote that "underneath a veil of lovely inconsequence, she concealed tremendous awareness, an all-seeing eye and a ruthless judgment." What a team these two would be! At right, the bridegroom's younger brothers (Ted at left, Bobby at right)—and a dozen other ushers—flank the couple in this photograph taken at the reception on the Auchincloss estate in Newport by LIFE's Lisa Larsen. Below: The stars of the head table.

LISA LARSEN (2)

MARK SHAW/MPTVIMAGES

ED CLARK

The early years of the Kennedys' marriage were difficult. Jackie found herself forced to apply grace and fortitude to a relationship in which she was constantly competing for her husband's attention against the demands of political life and his appetite for other women. Jackie suffered a miscarriage and then a stillbirth. Jack's chronic back problems worsened; the mere act of putting on socks or walking to the Senate chamber was for him, at age 37, excruciating. In 1954 he underwent major surgery to shore up his spine, despite a very real risk of death due to possible complications from his Addison's disease. He narrowly survived and began a seven-month recovery. All these difficulties . . . but in 1957, wonderful news, the best news: Caroline is born. The following year, Dad plays peekaboo in the Kennedys' Georgetown home (above, as captured by LIFE's Ed Clark), and in 1959, he and Mom enjoy the company of their daughter in Hyannis Port (right). Quite suddenly, all is right with the world.

The Presidential Campaign

In his run for President in 1960, Jack (right, during a debate with Republican candidate Richard Nixon; below, barnstorming with Jackie in New York City; opposite, in a Los Angeles hotel suite conferring with his closest confidant, brother Bobby, who is managing the campaign) proved himself a tremendous candidate—intelligent, eloquent and on point in explaining why his religion would not affect his policy making, cool under pressure during the back-and-forth with Nixon, charming when meeting with garden clubs and Junior Leagues. Richard K. Donahue, the last surviving member of the Kennedy coterie from Massachusetts, who were referred to as JFK's "Irish mafia," will speak to this in more intimate detail later in our pages, even as he recalls the moment when he learned the President was dead, but for now: Kennedy and company performed at a higher level than anyone might have anticipated, and their early energy and enthusiasm attracted others. Once JFK had won the Democratic nomination and started to rise in the national polls, an army of Kennedy men and women fanned out across the land. An interesting historical footnote: The vacancy sign at 1600 Pennsylvania Avenue, which afforded JFK his chance, had gone up because of the postwar (and post-FDR) two-term Constitutional limit; America still liked Ike plenty, and things might have been different had Kennedy been forced to challenge Dwight D. Eisenhower rather than his Vice President, Nixon, in the general election. Crucially as well, the two major-party rivals agreed to a series of face-offs meant to evoke the Lincoln-Douglas debates of 102 years earlier. These, though, were aired nationally. Radio audiences gave the edge to Nixon. TV audiences noted his five o'clock shadow, his perspiration—he had recently been hospitalized—and favored the more stylish JFK. Perhaps the medium was indeed becoming the message. Kennedy won 118,550 more votes out of 68.8 million.

President Kennedy
The Inauguration

John F. Kennedy, at 43, became the youngest person and the only Catholic elected to the White House, as well as the first President to have been born in the 20th century. To a nation anxious about strife over civil rights, the cold war and other issues, Kennedy's lofty inauguration-day oratory offered hope, inspiration and an appeal to every individual's greater good. "Let the word go forth from this time and place, to friend and foe alike, that the torch has been passed to a new generation of Americans—born in this century, tempered by war, disciplined by a hard and bitter peace, proud of our ancient heritage, and unwilling to witness or permit the slow undoing of those human rights to which this nation has always been committed, and to which we are committed today at home and around the world." He urged his fellow Americans to "ask not what your country can do for you, ask what you can do for your country." The dynamism of that memorable, frigid inauguration day (right—with outgoing President Eisenhower next to Jackie, at left, and Vice President Lyndon Baines Johnson and former Vice President Nixon listening, at right) was missed by none—adherent or opponent. Bottom: Jackie has a chuck under the chin for her husband moments after he has become President. Opposite: A well-known photograph by LIFE's Paul Schutzer of the First Couple, radiant at long day's end at an inaugural ball.

Storming the White House

AP

CORNELL CAPA/MAGNUM

STANLEY TRETICK/BETTMANN/CORBIS

The Kennedys did not move into their new home proclaiming "Welcome to Camelot!" But neither did they shy from declaring a new world order at 1600 Pennsylvania Avenue, with the edicts that the executive mansion should be both an international showplace and somewhere rambunctious kids could have the run of. At top left, the Kennedys pause at the door of the White House on February 4, 1961; Caroline and John are just entering their new home. (They have been in sunny Palm Beach, Florida, until now.) John Jr. was born on November 25, 1960, between the election and inauguration (and almost precisely three years before his father would be assassinated). He is a major news story—and he would remain such, especially after his father allowed (encouraged!) photos like the one of him under the Oval Office desk or gamboling in that realm with his older sister (opposite) to be disseminated to eager media outlets such as

LIFE. History tells us that Jackie sought to shield her children from the attention and to raise them as normally as possible. Jack, by contrast, had long been counseled in the political value of free and wholesome publicity, and when his wife was away for the briefest moment, he would open the doors and invite in the photographers—principal among them, LIFE's. He also hired the first-ever official White House photographer, military man Captain Cecil Stoughton, who took pictures of visiting foreign leaders but also of Caroline and John, opposite (we will learn more about him later because he was at the President's side during the fateful trip to Texas). In the photograph at bottom left on this page, President Kennedy is with his artist friend William Walton in 1961, choosing locations for artwork to be hung in his White House office. This painting reflects his keen interest in ships and sailing. Two points: The desk here also reflects that interest, as it was

made from oak timbers from the British ship H.M.S. *Resolute;* the desk was presented by Queen Victoria to President Rutherford B. Hayes in 1880, and used in one room or another by almost all subsequent Presidents. And also, if JFK did some minor renovating, his wife did much more. Jackie believed the White House furnishings—many of which had been placed in storage bins throughout Washington, D.C.—should showcase the history of the White House. As she told LIFE in 1961: "People come to see the White House and they see practically nothing that dates back before 1948 . . . It would be sacrilege merely to 'redecorate' it—a word I hate. It must be restored—and that has nothing to do with decoration. That is a question of scholarship." By the time Jackie returned to Washington after her husband's death, the Oval Office renovation was finally complete, but Kennedy's personal effects and even the desk had already been removed.

Triumphs, Travails and Tensions

AP

The cold war, which pitted the democratic United States of America and its allies against the communist Union of Soviet Socialist Republics and its satellite nations, was front-and-center or just offstage in all major issues of Kennedy's presidential tenure—from the space race to the Cuban missile crisis to the rise of the Berlin Wall to his assassination. When the Soviets launched the Sputnik 1 satellite in October 1957, it was unquestionably a shot across the bow to the U.S. Above: On May 5, 1961, President and Mrs. Kennedy follow on television the takeoff and spaceflight of American astronaut Alan Shepard, a salvo in answer to the Soviets' earlier success with the orbiting cosmonaut Yuri Gagarin. (Others watching in the office of the Chief Executive's secretary are, from left: U.S. attorney general Robert Kennedy; presidential assistant McGeorge Bundy; Vice President Lyndon Johnson; presidential aide Arthur Schlesinger Jr. and Chief of Naval Operations Admiral Arleigh Burke.)

Obviously the United States is playing catch-up, but only three weeks after Shepard's flight, Kennedy boldly declares a finish line— the moon—soliciting billions of dollars and "asking the Congress and the country to accept a firm commitment to a new course of action—a course which will last for many years and carry very heavy costs." Kennedy stresses that the outcome of the space race would impact "the minds of men everywhere, who are attempting to make a determination of which road they should take." These roads, Kennedy says, are headed in the diametrically opposed directions of "freedom and tyranny." The speech is rife with concerns that the United States is lagging badly, and that space "may hold the key to our future on earth." The President declares: "I believe that this nation should commit itself to achieving the goal, before this decade is out, of landing a man on the moon and returning him safely to the earth . . . I believe we should go to the moon."

America would go there in 1969, but in Kennedy's time there were earthly matters to be dealt with; and on the opposite page, clockwise from top left, we have three photographs depicting America's dealings with Cuba—and, by extension, Moscow: On April 22, 1961, Kennedy confers with his predecessor, former President Eisenhower, at Camp David on the topic of Cuba's posturing; ships bearing Soviet nuclear warheads cruise through the waters of the Atlantic off the coast of Cuba; Kennedy announces in October of 1962 a U.S. blockade of such ships, while his countrymen watch on department store televisions. In the event, Soviet premier Nikita Khrushchev blinks, and the Russian armaments are headed back home before Christmas. The Kennedy administration experienced policy failures, to be sure—the Bay of Pigs fiasco, a foiled attempt to topple the communist regime of Fidel Castro, being a famous Cuba-focused example—but the outcome of the hyper-tense missile crisis, with nuclear war a possibility, was an unqualified success.

JOHN DOMINIS

Above, in June 1963, President Kennedy peers over the Berlin Wall at the Eastern sector of the city on the occasion of his declaring that all world citizens who believe in freedom stand as brethren to Berliners. The cold war did not require a symbol, but it got a powerful one nonetheless in 1961 when the Eastern bloc divided the German capital—and Eastern and Western Europe generally—with a barrier featuring watch towers, barbed wire and the prospect of sudden death. (Between 1961 and 1989— when the wall was finally torn down—as many as 5,000 tried unsuccessfully to escape over it, the great majority of them from the East to the West, 191 of whom were killed in the attempt. Thousands, however, did succeed.) The cold war was made manifest throughout the world from the first day of Kennedy's administration to the last.

Meantime back home, affairs were happier if also volatile, as the Kennedy clan grew larger and stronger—and ever prouder of the man who assumed general leadership of the family after his father, Joe, suffered a stroke on December 19, 1961, that left him partially paralyzed and debilitated at age 73. Opposite: For those who study the Kennedy family tree, the President is pictured with the new generation, including, from left, Kathleen Kennedy (holding Christopher Kennedy), Edward Kennedy Jr., Joseph P. Kennedy II, Kara Kennedy, Robert F. Kennedy Jr., David Kennedy, Caroline Kennedy, Michael Kennedy, Courtney Kennedy, Kerry Kennedy, Bobby Shriver (holding Timothy Shriver), Maria Shriver, Steve Smith Jr., William Kennedy Smith, Christopher Lawford, Victoria Lawford, Sydney Lawford and Robin Lawford. In the foreground, going walkabout or just hogging the camera, is John F. Kennedy Jr.

That Day in Dallas

He had been warned not to go by those in his administration who simply didn't like Texas. He had been urged to go by his Vice President and others who either loved Texas or knew how important Texas would be to his reelection. In the event, he went.

DEALEY PLAZA. OF ALL OF THE DOMEStic place-names that resonate in American history—Concord and Lexington, the Alamo, Gettysburg, Ford's Theatre, Pearl Harbor, the Twin Towers—this is perhaps the most prosaic. It's a city park in Dallas, but a small one, nothing like the Dealey Plaza that has grown immense in the national imagination. It was born of a Works Progress Administration project in the late 1930s on the west edge of downtown because there was a bit of donated land and a man, newspaper publisher George Bannerman Dealey, lobbying for a cleanup. Main Street, Elm Street and Commerce Street came together there and, sharing a triple underpass, passed beneath a railroad bridge. Let's prettify this place, thought Dealey.

Two decades later—50 years ago—John F. Kennedy's presidential motorcade cruised down into the plaza, and the events of the next few moments bequeathed to this site—and city—the kind of fame, or infamy, none would ever seek.

Why was Kennedy in Dallas? There are short and long answers to that question, but the shortest, perhaps, is this: He wasn't well loved there. No one realized this better than the canny JFK, raised a politician on Joe Sr.'s knee, and JFK's Vice President, Lyndon Johnson, who was as representative of Texas as the state flag. "The trip was presidential politics, pure and simple," wrote LBJ in his 1971 book, *The Vantage Point.* "It was the opening effort of the 1964 campaign. And it was going beautifully."

The Kennedy-Johnson ticket had won delegate-rich Texas by only a slim margin in the 1960 election and had done poorly in Dallas. The state was growing increasingly divided between liberals (spearheaded by Senator Ralph Yarborough) and conservatives (whose figurehead was a Democrat of a different stripe, Governor John Connally). The Texas salvo in 1963, baldly in search of financial and electoral support, would include motorcades in five cities—San Antonio, Houston, Fort Worth, Dallas and Austin. Air Force One landed in San Antonio with not only JFK aboard but the road show's surprise star attraction, Jacqueline Kennedy. She didn't often accompany her husband on political trips, and this would be her first series of official appearances since her infant son, Patrick, had died shortly after his birth on August 7.

On the 21st, Jack wowed them in San Antonio, where he was cheered during the dedication of an aerospace medical center, and Jackie thrilled them in Houston, where she addressed an audience in Spanish. They arrived in Fort Worth before midnight, and then the President was up early, walking the street in the rain, greeting his fans. From there, on to Dallas, where the barnstorming tour was greeted by yet more rapturous fans at Love Field airport—and also a full-page advertisement taken out that morning in *The Dallas Morning News* by the so-called (and, in truth, nonexistent) "American Fact-Finding Committee" that read in part: "Welcome Mr. Kennedy to Dallas," a city that was victim of "a recent Liberal smear attempt" but that had risen above, "despite efforts by you and your administration to penalize it for nonconformity to 'New Frontierism.'" The ad went on to link Kennedy and his brother Attorney General Robert F. Kennedy to communists, "fellow-travelers, and ultra-leftists," and to efforts to "persecute loyal Americans."

President Kennedy had many more friends in Dallas than he had enemies. But he did have enemies, including others not at all affiliated with the American Fact-Finding Committee.

Final rituals in Washington: It was late November, and so there would be a photo-act at the White House (left) with a 40-pound turkey. Standing at center is Senator Everett Dirksen of Illinois, and in the assembly are turkey farmers and the president of the National Turkey Federation. Kennedy sent the gobbler back to its farm, saying, "We'll just let this one grow." Opposite: Jackie, the guest superstar of the Texas tour, waves goodbye before boarding Air Force One in Washington.

GOOD EATING, MR. PRESIDENT!

On these pages, the Kennedys are in San Antonio on the 21st, joined in the limo by their formal hosts in Texas, Governor John Connally and his wife, Nellie, and onstage at the aerospace center by the über-Texan, Vice President Lyndon Baines Johnson. Kennedy's relationship with both these Lone Star Staters was complicated, and probably would have been nonexistent were it not for the political circumstance of being ambitious members of the same party. Connally had supported Senator Lyndon Johnson for President in 1960, going so far as to try to undermine Kennedy's candidacy by calling a press conference to discuss JFK's Addison's disease and the drugs he took to stay alive. Nevertheless, Kennedy made his fellow World War II veteran secretary of the Navy, a post Connally would relinquish to run for governor. Connally's politics were far to the right of Kennedy's, and in fact in 1973 he would switch to the Republican side; he would serve as secretary of the Treasury under President Richard M. Nixon. As for Johnson, his problems with the Kennedys could fill—and have filled—volumes; if he didn't like Jack overly much, he liked his

brother Bobby much less. But JFK, upon
receiving the nomination at the convention in
Los Angeles in 1960, realized he needed
Southern Democratic support in the general
election in order to prevail, and offered—over
the protests of aides—the number two spot
on the ticket to Johnson, who accepted with
teeth clenched. But everyone was smiling in
San Antonio.

Houston

Today in Houston there is a John F. Kennedy Elementary School and a boulevard named for the late President; on the boulevard is a store called JFK Liquors. On November 21, 1963, when these photos were made in that city, such future commemorations for this alien being from Massachusetts were unimaginable. It's not that things didn't go well on the 21st for Kennedy; they in fact went splendidly. But if Houston feted Kennedy, no one suspected Houston loved him. The motorcade, with heavy security after careful planning, came off fine, as did the speech at the Rice Hotel, as did the dinner in honor of local U.S. congressman Albert Thomas at the Sam Houston Coliseum (right), as did, especially, the appearance at a meeting of the League of United Latin American Citizens (below), where Jackie broke out her Spanish. The Kennedys seemed to be making all the right moves in Texas, and with each city checked off the list, everyone in the entourage breathed more easily. As Lyndon Johnson, who was proudly showing off his native state (opposite, in dark glasses, with his wife, Lady Bird, at the LULAC dinner), later wrote, not without lament, the tour was going beautifully indeed.

ARTHUR RICKERBY (2)

MICHAEL QUAN/ZUMA

OWEN DAY/DANA DAY HENDERSON COLLECTION

Day one of the Texas swing wound up in Fort Worth. At about 11:50 p.m. the Kennedys checked in to Suite 850 of the Hotel Texas. Of course it was nicely arrayed (above), but the President and First Lady could not help but notice a relatively extraordinary display of artwork on the walls: not home-on-the-range paintings at all, but a thoughtfully assembled selection including modernists such as Lyonel Feininger (his "Manhattan II") and Franz Kline. This had obviously been planned—a small group of local art lovers had curated—and the Kennedys were impressed, even touched. On the morning of the 22nd, JFK made several phones calls from his suite, and it is now believed the last call he made in his life was to Ruth Carter Johnson to thank her for her and her friends' extra effort with the art. This is one of the small stories—which are not really small at all, but human—that have endured because of what happened later that day. In the run-up to the 50th anniversary of the assassination, the Dallas Museum of Art has sponsored an exhibit of the paintings; and Suite 850, in what is today the Hilton Fort Worth, is represented just as it was when a tired President and his wife, both happy with the trip so far, caught 40 winks.

Later in the morning, when the Kennedys left the hotel and walked to a borrowed convertible (right), Jackie was sporting what has become perhaps the most famous suit ever worn by anyone, ever—male or female. She had in fact already featured it numerous times on public occasions, and chose it again this day at her husband's request; it was one of his favorites. These days, everyone knows it was pink, but in 1963 most of the public didn't, because very few newspapers or magazines ran color photography. Yes, it was a Coco Chanel design—her 1961 autumn/winter collection—but no, it was not a Chanel; Jackie's was a high-end reproduction by Chez Ninon, a New York salon, using fabric and buttons supplied by Chanel. (These days, it would be called a knock-off.) Much of the rest that you think you know about the suit is true: Jackie refused to change out of it until the next morning in the White House, so people could see what had happened through the bloodstains. The suit is today in the National Archives, unwashed, having been deeded by Caroline Kennedy in 2003 and is now kept in a secret location with the provision it not be seen by the public until 2103. The whereabouts of the pillbox hat are today unknown.

CORBIS

CECIL STOUGHTON/REUTERS/LANDOV

ARTHUR RICKERBY

"Where's Jackie?" That's what the crowd in a parking lot on Eighth Street in downtown Fort Worth wants to know, and the President points, indicating that she's still upstairs and will be down in a minute. At the Forth Worth Chamber of Commerce breakfast (above, right) that follows the outdoor rally and brief speech, the main attraction is applauded by Vice President Johnson and President Kennedy—and 2,500 other distinguished guests in the hotel ballroom. The morning in Fort Worth is a constant bustle: phone calls, up and down and up the elevator, the weather starting drizzly and turning sunny for the final motorcade through downtown en route to Carswell Air Force Base, where, at 11:25 a.m., the latest plane to be designated Air Force One, a Boeing 707, will take the party for the very short hop to Dallas. It's busy and sometimes damp, this now-well-parsed morning in Fort Worth, but overall: festive. For one reason or another, probably having nothing to do with Kennedy's visit but rather with rushing the shopping season, the city's Christmas decorations are already up along the motorcade route, adding to the gaiety.

Fort Worth

CLINT GRANT/THE DALLAS MORNING NEWS

Two more photos from the rally in Fort Worth: Kennedy, accompanied by Texan politicians Senator Ralph Yarborough (above, at far left) and Representative Jim Wright, eschews a raincoat as he crosses Eighth Street from the hotel to the parking lot just before nine a.m., and then shares the love with the damp but not dampened people who have come to see and hear him. Also alongside the President all morning and throughout the rest of the day, including on Air Force One on its way back from Dallas to Washington, is Cecil Stoughton, the first photographer to be hired as an official White House documentarian and a man responsible not only for several photographs in this book (many of which first appeared in LIFE magazine, a favorite outlet for the Kennedys) but for some of the most famous Kennedy photos ever (such as John-John and Caroline playing in the Oval Office; Jackie present, as we will see later in this chapter, at the hastily assembled swearing in of Lyndon Baines Johnson). Stoughton, a native Iowan born in 1920, enlisted in the Army Air Corps even before the U.S. entered World War II and, after Pearl Harbor, was assigned to take a LIFE magazine photography training course, then helped document the fighting in the Pacific Theater. He determined, postwar, to continue with photography in the military, and in 1961 was working at the Pentagon, assigned to shoot pictures of Kennedy's inauguration. He did a good job, and it was suggested to Kennedy that it could be useful to have such a man as Captain Stoughton on hand full-time. Surely there had been photographers close to Presidents before, including several on LIFE's staff, but Stoughton was given an office at the White House. Thus was born a post that today seems as integral a part of any administration as that of the press secretary.

CECIL STOUGHTON/THE WHITE HOUSE/JFK LIBRARY/REUTERS

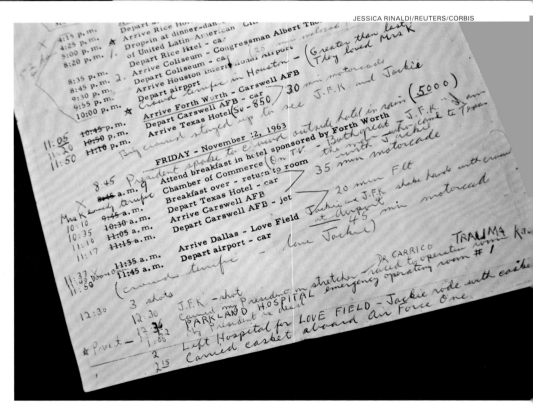

The handwritten notes are by Kennedy assistant David Powers. These photographs left and above are, as earlier ones were, by Cecil Stoughton: of the President and First Lady arriving at Love Field in Dallas only minutes after leaving Fort Worth and less than an hour before the assassination. The thorough, accurate and eloquent archivist Richard B. Trask, who has delved deeply into such subjects as the long-ago Salem witch trials and the 20th-century killing of Kennedy, talked to Stoughton before his death and writes in his book, which happens to have the same title as this chapter in our own volume: "Stoughton recalls that the press expected a hostile atmosphere in conservative Dallas, but that 'it sure didn't spin off into the Love Field crowd. My pictures show dozens of flags, hand-painted welcome signs, a lot of warmth . . . I did not feel nor see any hostility, certainly not during the whole time we were there.' Stoughton later recalled the scene as 'just a beautiful reception, a bright, warm, sunny day and thousands of people cheering—screaming like they had at Fort Worth, Houston and San Antonio.'"

Of course, there were factions not represented at the remarkably named Love Field: Those behind that day's advertorial in *The Dallas Morning News;* those in the streets with the sign that will be seen on the very next page; and, in a warehouse on Dealey Plaza, a man with a rifle.

LET'S BARRY KING JOHN

all the way
JFK & LBJ
in 64

'ALL THE WAY
WITH J.F.K.
IN BIG D

Grass Roots Dem

Glad to see you!
Jack and
Ralph

grass Roots Dems
S.M.U.

Dallas

As you can tell from the timeline unfolding in this chapter, everything was coordinated to the nth degree and was happening very fast—this was as quick a multipurpose tour as could be staged in 1963. Dallas, a city of nearly a million people then, was the largest effort, but still the schedule there would be lightning fast: an open motorcade from Love Field through downtown, winding up at a luncheon for 2,600 close friends (and others) at the Trade Mart, which was north of downtown—just beyond Dealey Plaza. As Dallas had grown in those years, it had seemed to grow more conservative and, in its expanding weave, had seen "groups" spring up or burgeon. The John Birch Society and the Indignant White Citizens Council didn't pretend to be strangers in Dallas, but whether the larger sign on the opposite page, which bade Jack and Jackie farewell from Love Field, was wielded by members of one of those organizations is uncertain. For the younger among us: The "Barry" for "bury" refers to Arizona senator Barry Goldwater, a thoroughgoing conservative, who would indeed run against (and lose to) Lyndon Johnson in the 1964 presidential election. Above: John F. Kennedy and Governor John Connally in the motorcade not long before bullets would hit the two men, fatally wounding the President. In the "Where Were You When You Heard?" chapter in our book, Jim Lehrer, then a reporter for the *Dallas Times Herald,* has a fascinating story about why the bubbletop shell was not in place on the limousine. There are also reports that, whatever the input of others, JFK himself insisted the car proceed without a roof once the weather turned from misty to sunny.

These images are not from the Zapruder film; that is dealt with extensively elsewhere in our book. There were certainly other still and film photographers paying attention to the motorcade as it proceeded into, then sped away from, Dealey Plaza. Moorman, Muchmore, Bronson and other names are attached to the evidence files, as is Zapruder. It's interesting: The Dal-Tex building, seen above with the fire escapes prominent, is where Abraham Zapruder had his offices; this photo can imply the casual stroll he had to the pergola atop the grassy knoll.

Seen through the Lincoln Continental limousine's windshield as it proceeds along Elm Street past the Texas School Book Depository at 11 miles per hour in this image, President Kennedy appears to raise his hand toward his head. Mrs. Kennedy holds his forearm in an effort to aid him. At just about this moment, the sound has registered with motorcycle police escort Bobby Hargis, who thinks to himself, *Lord, let it be a firecracker.* The picture was made within seconds of the President's being fatally shot. Governor Connally, in the jump seat just ahead of JFK, is hit, too, and shouts, "Oh, no, no, no."

In the photograph opposite, top, the Newman family is on the ground in Dealey Plaza immediately after the shooting. Who were they? At the time Bill and Gayle—who are shielding their two- and four-year-old sons, Clayton and Billy—were a struggling young

couple barely in their twenties. They had driven out to Love Field to see the President earlier, then had dashed back to town and wound up being the very closest eyewitnesses to Kennedy when the shots rang out. The father initially hoped, as had Officer Hargis, that he had heard firecrackers, then when the third bang issued he shouted, "That's it. Get down!" and he and Gayle dove and shielded their boys. The elder Newmans, now in their seventies still live near Dallas.

Above, right: An NBC cameraman stands at the left as the Newmans hug the ground in those same moments after the assault. The last of the motorcycles are rushing away at speeds that will approach 80 miles per hour, and the President's story is now moving to Parkland Memorial Hospital. Behind, in the Book Depository, Lee Harvey Oswald is on the move; on the plaza a frantic, scattered, confused and scared search ensues. Oswald, for a time, blends in to the city.

ARTHUR RICKERBY (2)

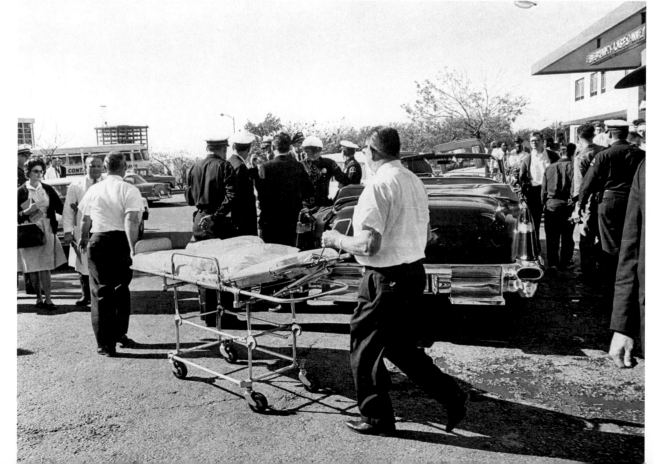

Above: Outside Parkland Memorial Hospital, a nurse is in tears. Right: The scene is jammed with cars from the presidential motorcade and people anxious for news, while hospital employees try to focus on their duties. Opposite: A bouquet of yellow roses lies on the floor of the limousine that transported the Vice President and his wife. This was and is an extremely poignant photograph, but the limousine has sometimes been misidentified as the President's. The roses tell a tale: Some of the wives had been given yellow roses at Love Field airport, but Jackie's were red. Jackie herself told Theodore White how three times that day she had been given a bouquet of the yellow roses of Texas. But in Dallas they gave her red roses. And she'd thought, *How funny— red roses.* As is recounted elsewhere in our pages, after the doctors pronounced her husband dead, Jackie spent time with the body, and subsequently put her wedding ring on her husband's finger.

THE SIXTH FLOOR MUSEUM/THE DALLAS MORNING NEWS/DALLAS TIMES HERALD COLLECTION/AP

DALLAS TIMES HERALD/AP

In the photograph at top, Hurchel Jacks (at left, in the cowboy hat), who was Vice President Lyndon Baines Johnson's driver in the motorcade, listens with others to news accounts on the car radio outside the Parkland Hospital emergency entrance. By this point, the whole world is frantically tuning in on radios and television sets, many people desperately unbelieving. Above: Johnson, flanked by Secret Service agent Rufus Youngblood (left)

and U.S. representative Homer Thornberry, leaves Parkland Hospital after the death of Kennedy and heads to Love Field airport. Above, right: The late President John F. Kennedy's casket is brought onto Air Force One—aides and agents struggling with the nearly 600-pound load on narrow metal stairs—which will fly back to Andrews Air Force Base in Maryland from Dallas. The widow Jacqueline Kennedy stands amid

members of JFK's Irish American coterie—Larry O'Brien, Kenny O'Donnell and Dave Powers are there—in the crowd at the bottom of the steps. Kennedy's staff, with the Secret Service assisting, have, essentially, spirited the body out of Parkland before a proper autopsy can be performed. There was even a scuffle inside the hospital between his staff and local officials over who had jurisdiction over Kennedy's body.

Dallas

There is so much going on in this sequence of photographs by Cecil Stoughton. First, when Lyndon Johnson had been told about President Kennedy's death at one p.m., he had been urged to return to Washington immediately in case there was a wider conspiracy functioning in Texas. The military placed the country on red alert. LBJ would not let Air Force One leave Dallas without Jacqueline Kennedy, and she wouldn't board any plane without her husband's body—and that's where the arguing with the officials at Parkland over the autopsy, which the local and state authorities had a legal responsibility to perform, came in. Johnson was taken to the airport in advance, and eventually the Kennedy entourage, having forced the point, arrived, along with the casket. Several histories indicate that Jackie was reluctant to take part in the swearing in, but Johnson was ultimately persuasive. LBJ wanted a photo record of the moment and the transfer of power. The White House photographer Cecil Stoughton urged that a Dictaphone recording be made as well, and in the stateroom of the airplane—the largest open space in the cabin—Stoughton was forced, as he told the writer Trask, to "flatten himself against the rear bulkhead of the compartment" to make the shot. He positioned Lady Bird Johnson and Jacqueline Kennedy on either side of President Johnson, and photographed over the shoulder of Federal Judge Sarah T. Hughes. The images were disseminated as quickly as humanly possible to show that the United States was moving forward in something approaching an orderly and democratic fashion.

CECIL STOUGHTON/CORBIS (2)

CECIL STOUGHTON/GETTY

UNIVERSAL HISTORY ARCHIVE/GETTY

BOB GOMEL

BETTMANN/CORBIS

An altogether extraordinary and unprecedented (and hopefully never to be repeated) scene rendered in these rarely seen photographs: The late President of the United States arriving back in Washington along with the newly inaugurated one—the 35th ceding to the 36th. In the photograph at top, Kennedy's casket is brought to an ambulance at the airport. Above: President Johnson and his wife arrive at the White House by helicopter. The autopsy on Kennedy's body was executed between eight p.m. and roughly midnight, now Eastern time, at the end of this long and awful day, at the Bethesda Naval Hospital in Maryland by pathologists who didn't even know that the tracheotomy performed earlier in Dallas had obliterated the exit wound. The rest has become part of a conspiratorial morass that has forever enshrouded the President's murder—a topic discussed elsewhere in our book.

In the photograph above: Later, a military honor guard marches in front of the ambulance bearing the late President John F. Kennedy's casket as it is returned to the White House, where it will lie in repose in the East Room, awaiting burial at Arlington National Cemetery.

Who Was Oswald?

One reason that we have been endlessly fixated on what Lee Harvey Oswald meant by his act
or whether he acted alone is that, in examining his life, there are many turns where
it's not clear where he was headed, what he was thinking precisely or what he might do next.
Also: It seems impossible to some that this particular man could have done something
so immense as the killing of President Kennedy on his own.

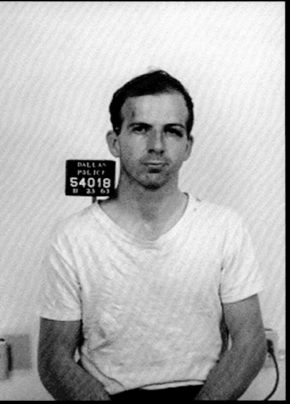

CORBIS

EYEVINE/REDUX

IN A HISTORICAL CURIOSITY (SURELY NOTHING more), many seem to be remembered by three names: John Wilkes Booth, James Earl Ray, long ago Marcus Junius Brutus, even John Lennon's killer, Mark David Chapman. They are their own subset of murderers, the assassins.

Lee Harvey Oswald was born on October 18, 1939, in New Orleans to a mother who often had to be out working; his father had suffered a fatal heart attack two months before his son's birth. Oswald and his two brothers lived for a time in an orphanage. In 1952, Lee and his mother, Marguerite, relocated to New York City, where they stayed for just over a year, then it was back to New Orleans. Lee, very much on his own through all this, was no scholar but was weirdly bookish, and over time his reading drifted toward revolutionary and socialist tracts. *Disaffected* is a catchword to describe people who, we realize after the fact, went off the rails, but it applies here: Oswald was, by the time he reached his maturity, disaffected from his heritage, perhaps his family, certainly his country. And yet he enlisted in the Marines—in 1956. His reputation during his service years has, as you might imagine, been thoroughly analyzed, and for our purposes it distills to this: He was a good marksman, and troubled. In 1958 he was twice court-martialed for possessing an illegal weapon and exhibiting violent behavior.

He finished his Marine career in 1959 and began four years of often frustrated journeys and overtures that put him on some official radar screens and that certainly informed his actions in Dallas. He went to Moscow, and there he approached Soviet authorities and said he wanted to defect. They looked at his offer and at whether or not he could be an effective spy, and then moved him to Minsk, where the KGB kept an eye on him. In that city, at a dance in March 1961, he met a lovely 19-year-old girl named Marina Prusakova; they wed barely more than a month later. The first of their two daughters, June, was born in 1962; by then Lee had decided he didn't like the Soviet Union and took his young family back to the States, where they settled in Texas.

Oswald may have become dissatisfied with life in the Soviet Union, but he hadn't gone off communism, and aspects of his personality—a hot temper, a propensity for violence—began to become part of his political profile. In 1963 he bought a rifle and a handgun and clearly saw the weapons as part of who he was (or was becoming). He had his wife take a picture of him with the small arsenal (please see the picture on page 77). On April 10, 1963, he tried to assassinate the ultraconservative retired Major General Edwin Walker, whom he considered "a fascist," at Walker's Texas home, but his shot through a window missed its mark and Oswald escaped the scene. Then there was a trip back to New Orleans and another to Mexico City, where he tried unsuccessfully to obtain entry to Cuba or even back to the U.S.S.R. Finally, a return to Dallas.

The President was due to visit Texas soon.

His was one of the strangest of all American journeys, from a toddler in Louisiana in the early 1940s (left) to a notorious assassin of a President in 1963, when, in the brief interval between deed and death, the Dallas police made the photograph above. A synopsis of Oswald's upbringing: a child with no father-figure, a latchkey kid, a boy without close friendships due to his family's peripatetic nature. No one was overly concerned about Lee until he and his mother moved from Fort Worth to New York City in August 1952, when he was 12. There, he began to get in trouble at school (truancy; said to be "beyond the control of his mother insofar as school attendance is concerned") and also with social welfare agents who sought to improve him. He hit his mother on more than one occasion and also pulled a knife on his sister-in-law.

He underwent psychological examinations between April 16 and May 7, 1953, when he was remanded to Youth House, an institution in Manhattan that served alternately as a reform school, a vocational school or a holding tank for kids undergoing evaluations. According to some reports, Lee told social workers he liked Youth House well enough, while missing his freedom (but not his mother), and yet Marguerite Oswald said that when she visited him there, he said, "Mother, I want to get out of here. There are children in here who have killed people, and smoke. I want to get out."

Anti-American

On the opposite page, clockwise from top left: Oswald wearing his U.S. Marine uniform in a photograph that was found in his wallet on the day he killed Kennedy; with Marina Nikolayevna Prusakova at a park in the Soviet Union in 1961; at center in sunglasses with fellow workers at a factory in Minsk, where he worked during part of his nearly three-year sojourn there.

In the image from a news film above, Oswald is back in the United States distributing HANDS OFF CUBA flyers on the streets of New Orleans during the trip he took there on his own while Marina stayed in Texas. You would think that between the Soviet involvement and these public political actions, he was being watched by authorities—and you would not be wrong. But he didn't represent any kind of Code Red; if he felt he was being harassed by the feds, they didn't really take him very seriously. Gerald Posner, author of the 1993 book *Case Closed,* talked with former FBI agent Warren de Brueys,

who had investigated Oswald at the time. "[I] checked with his landlady, as well as with local Cuban sources, and got negative from all of them," de Brueys told Posner. "Then I contacted our sources for Communist party activity and they were all negative. Nothing indicated he had any connections. He was just a single person, a guy expressing himself and claiming to have a Fair Play for Cuba chapter, but in actuality he was the only member . . . I thought of Oswald as a weirdo. I had several other cases at this time similar to him, where the guys had a fancy, some psychological bent, some aberration, they fancied themselves a poor man's intelligence agent. They tried to involve themselves on the periphery of things. Usually, they were disturbed people of some kind. In the final report you just say that he does not have connections that call for further investigation. You don't say in the report that the guy is a kook, even though I had decided Oswald was a nut."

Assassin

After returning to Dallas from New Orleans and Mexico City, Oswald found menial employment with the Texas School Book Depository, a warehouse on Dealey Plaza. When shots rang out on November 22, Dallas motorcycle policeman Marrion L. Baker, riding behind the presidential party, saw pigeons fly off the roof of that building. He whirled his bike, dashed into the Depository and ran up the stairs. At 12:32 p.m., he stopped a man on the second floor for questioning but was told by the building superintendent that the man, Lee Harvey Oswald, was an employee. Baker dashed on. Oswald left the building by the front door at 12:33. At 1:06, the sniper's perch on the sixth floor, shielded by boxes full of books (left), was discovered, and 16 minutes later a rifle with a telescopic sight was found stashed between more boxes near the staircase (below, held aloft by a Dallas detective later that day). When a roll call of employees was taken, Oswald was missing and a search ensued.

Even as all this was happening, Dallas police were alerted to the shooting of one of their own, Patrolman J.D. Tippit, in the Oak Cliff section of the city. This spurred a second search, and at 1:50 Oswald was found hunkering in the Texas Theatre, where he tried to shoot an arresting officer with a revolver before being subdued. (On the opposite page, top: Two views of the theater, including a sign that hardly betrays what has just happened there.) When brought in for arraignment (bottom)—initially for the murder of Tippit, shortly thereafter for the assassination—Oswald has a cut on his forehead and a blackened eye, wounds suffered in the scuffle at the theater. In custody he is belligerent, claiming he is being made a "patsy."

BETTMANN/CORBIS

LAWRENCE SCHILLER/POLARIS COMMUNICATIONS/GETTY

The Drama Plays Out

The roles could have been scripted: Both Lee Harvey Oswald and Jack Ruby were American archetypes moving on the fringes and in the shadows of mainstream society. They each seemed to represent something larger, or at least *other*.

Ruby, who had been born Jacob Leon Rubenstein in Chicago in 1911, operated the Carousel Club in Dallas; he is seen at left with a couple of his dancers. He was a man of passions, always on the watch for perceived anti-Semitism, dedicated to people and causes he believed in, among these, the Kennedys. He had moved to Dallas just after World War II and had become a mainstay in the nocturnal world of strippers and booze. People who worked with him thought he was a character. He was a certain kind of bon vivant.

Did Ruby have connections to organized crime? Was he part of a plot? Well, these were inevitable questions after Ruby murdered Oswald as he was being prepared for transfer from the city jail to the county jail on the Sunday after the Friday assassination. Nightclub owners do sometimes rub elbows with gangsters, and some of Kennedy's friends (and even Kennedy's father) had, too. But as to the killing: Ruby, like many in Dallas, was thinking of nothing but the assassination from the moment it happened; he even attended the police press conference soon after the President was killed, his revolver hidden in his pocket. Was he stalking Oswald? On Sunday, at 11:21 a.m., he shoots and kills him in the basement of police headquarters, shoving his Colt Cobra .38 into the assassin's stomach during the transfer and pulling the trigger (below) after having obtained effortless access to the building.

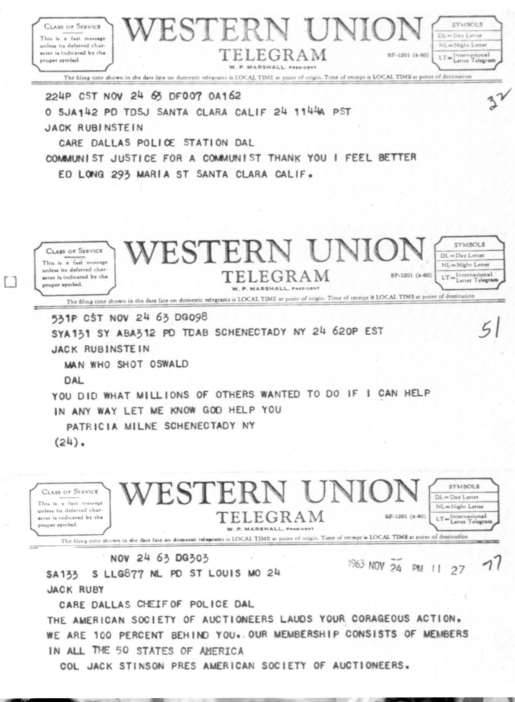

WESTERN UNION TELEGRAM

224P CST NOV 24 63 DF007 0A162

O SJA142 PD TDSJ SANTA CLARA CALIF 24 1144A PST

JACK RUBINSTEIN

CARE DALLAS POLICE STATION DAL

COMMUNIST JUSTICE FOR A COMMUNIST THANK YOU I FEEL BETTER

ED LONG 293 MARIA ST SANTA CLARA CALIF.

WESTERN UNION TELEGRAM

531P CST NOV 24 63 DG098

SYA131 SY ABA312 PD TDAB SCHENECTADY NY 24 620P EST

JACK RUBINSTEIN

MAN WHO SHOT OSWALD

DAL

YOU DID WHAT MILLIONS OF OTHERS WANTED TO DO IF I CAN HELP

IN ANY WAY LET ME KNOW GOD HELP YOU

PATRICIA MILNE SCHENECTADY NY

(24).

WESTERN UNION TELEGRAM

NOV 24 63 DG303

SA133 S LLG877 NL PD ST LOUIS MO 24   1963 NOV 24 PM 11 27

JACK RUBY

CARE DALLAS CHEIF OF POLICE DAL

THE AMERICAN SOCIETY OF AUCTIONEERS LAUDS YOUR CORAGEOUS ACTION.

WE ARE 100 PERCENT BEHIND YOU. OUR MEMBERSHIP CONSISTS OF MEMBERS

IN ALL THE 50 STATES OF AMERICA

COL JACK STINSON PRES AMERICAN SOCIETY OF AUCTIONEERS.

Not very many Americans who are regarded by a wide swath of the populace as heroes subsequently receive the death penalty, but Jack Ruby was the rarity (the telegrams at left attest to the "hero" part). In 1966 an appeals court ordered a new trial because of evidentiary miscues, and in 1967, Ruby, suffering from lung, brain and liver cancer, dies. His end comes at Parkland Memorial Hospital while he is still in custody, and of course that is remarkable: It's where President Kennedy and Oswald also died.

On top of all of the myriad connections and possibilities, there are the sometimes cruel symmetries. On Monday, November 25, there were three funerals resultant from the terrible incident: the late President's at Arlington National Cemetery in Virginia, watched on television by the whole world; Lee Harvey Oswald's in Fort Worth, Texas, witnessed by family, law enforcement authorities, a few members of the press and hardly anyone else; and Officer J.D. Tippit's in Dallas (bottom: Tippit's widow, Marie, at the services; the couple had three children, ages 13 and under, when he was killed).

All of the controversy that swirled—and continues to swirl—around the assassination has served to cloud Oswald, Ruby and, really, everyone involved, directly or tangentially. Was he this or that? Was he acting alone? Was he a hired gun? Was he behaving on principle or out of madness? As we conclude our chapter on Oswald, it is worthwhile to remember: He was cold-blooded.

Many witnesses testified to his killing of Tippit in the Oak Cliff section of town. The patrolman had received a description of the suspect from headquarters: five foot 10 inches, slim, 165 pounds. He had seen Oswald walking purposefully along Tenth Street. He slowed. They talked through the window. Tippit got out of the cruiser. Oswald shot him three times in the chest, then stood over him and fired a fourth shot to the head.

We say "Oswald" did this, but obviously there was never a trial, and so this properly should be "alleged murderer." But a few things in this case appear to be without question, and this is one. Lee Harvey Oswald's last consequential act as a free man was to murder a police officer at point-blank range.

LIFE Is on the Story

Fifty years ago, LIFE had people in place throughout the country and a big office in Los Angeles.
Our West Coast people headed for Dallas—where we also had correspondents—as quickly as they could.
RICHARD B. STOLLEY was in charge of the L.A. bureau then and still remembers the day,
and the days following. Here is his report, all these years later, of the magazine's all-hands-on-deck effort
and of how he tracked down the Zapruder film.

THE WEEKEND THAT CHANGED the world began with a shout.

"Dick, Kennedy's been shot in Dallas!"

I was in my office as Los Angeles bureau chief for LIFE magazine. The shouter was LIFE correspondent Tommy Thompson, who had wandered over to the Associated Press Teletype to find out (pre-Internet) what was happening in the world.

The AP machine was spitting out bulletins and flashes, with accompanying alarm bells, that gave the first news of the tragedy in Dealey Plaza. I ran to see for myself, then back to my desk to call my editor in New York and ask what we could do. "How fast can you get to Dallas?" was the answer.

An hour later four of us were on a (now defunct) National Airlines plane—two photographers who were in the office, fortunately with their camera equipment, Allan Grant and Don Cravens, and Tommy and I. Back then, before all the 9/11 security, you could dash on to an airliner at the last moment, which is what we did, with no baggage, of course.

The plane was crowded with other journalists, some of them carrying bulky TV cameras in their laps. I suspect we broke every federal regulation concerning in-flight safety that day, but the airline officials were understanding. Just before reaching the airport, we heard on the car radio that the President was dead, and Tommy's groan was heartbreaking. On the flight to Dallas, the pilot kept us informed, including an announcement that someone named Lee Harvey Oswald had been arrested.

Tommy, a former newspaper city editor in Houston, turned to me and said, "I know Texas cops. Let me go after him," which is what he did, along with photographer Grant, as soon as we landed. Cravens and I checked into the Adolphus Hotel in downtown Dallas; he went out to cover a city plummeting into shock, and I moved into a suite and set up an office for the other reporters and photographers that LIFE was sending in.

At about six p.m., I got a call from Patsy Swank, the LIFE stringer (part-time correspondent) in Dallas who had spent the afternoon at police headquarters. Her news was astounding. She said another reporter, knowing she worked for LIFE, had told her that a cop had told him that a local businessman had been at Dealey Plaza with a movie camera and had photographed the assassination.

Anticipating my next question, she said, "My friend couldn't spell the name, only pronounce it. *Za-proo-dur.*"

I had never been in Dallas before, so I picked up the phone book, once an invaluable asset to journalists, and ran my finger down the Zs, and there it was, just as Patsy had pronounced it, "Zapruder, Abraham." I began calling; I kept on calling every 15 minutes. No one answered. Zapruder was out trying to get his film developed, as

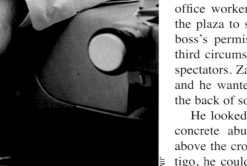

RICHARD B. STOLLEY was a young man when he began his rise at LIFE. Not only is he renowned as the guy who found and acquired the Zapruder film, but he went on to be the founding editor of *People* magazine.

I later learned.

The fact that the film existed at all was something of a miracle, the result of several fortunate circumstances.

The first was that the presidential motorcade would pass close to Jennifer Juniors, the garment company that Zapruder co-owned. An 8 mm enthusiast who had collected reel after reel of family footage, he had decided to film the Kennedy visit. But that morning, the weather was rainy and overcast. He left his Bell & Howell camera at home.

His assistant, Lillian Rogers, was upset. The rain had stopped, she pointed out, and added, "Mr. Z., it isn't every day the President comes through the neighborhood." Grumbling amiably, he drove seven miles out and seven back with the camera, the second circumstance.

Zapruder had thought about filming the motorcade from a fourth floor window in his factory, which overlooked Dealey Plaza. But at the window he realized the view was limited, and as some of his office workers strolled the half block to the plaza to see the President (with their boss's permission), he joined them, the third circumstance. It was filling up with spectators. Zapruder, then 58, wasn't tall, and he wanted to film the President, not the back of somebody's head.

He looked around and saw a four-foot concrete abutment that would put him above the crowd, but because he had vertigo, he could not stand up there without someone nearby. He found one of his employees, Marilyn Sitzman, and asked if she would help. The two of them scrambled onto the abutment, the only place on that side of Elm Street where he could film the motorcade from beginning to end. Circumstance number four. In her essay a few pages on, Alexandra Zapruder, Abraham's granddaughter, recalls this family lore just the same.

When police motorcycles came into view, Zapruder started his camera, but stopped until the presidential limousine appeared, thus saving several crucial seconds of film. Kennedy and Jackie shared the backseat, and Texas governor John Connally and his wife, Nellie, were perched on jump seats. All were smiling broadly and waving. This is when Oswald fired his first shot from a sixth floor window in the Texas School Book Depository across the street from Zapruder's factory. That bullet missed, apparently striking a tree branch or a traffic light and disintegrating.

The noise of the shot over Zapruder's left shoulder, less than 100 yards away, caused him to jerk the camera almost imperceptibly (as did the second shot and the third)—at least that's what I see in the film (though others have read more into it). At that moment, the limousine drove behind a large highway sign and vanished for a second or two in Zapruder's viewfinder. ("If I'd had any sense, I would have dropped to the ground," as many frightened spectators in Dealey Plaza were doing, he later admitted.)

When the limousine reappeared, Kennedy had both fists jammed into his throat, and Connally was slipping off his jump seat, his mouth opening in a howl of pain. This was the shot that the Warren report says passed through the President's upper back and into the governor's right shoulder, then tumbled around inside his body, inflicting serious wounds. That bullet was found later on Connally's stretcher, less damaged than might have been expected after passing through two human bodies.

The limousine's Secret Service driver and the agent beside him were disoriented, though agents in the follow-up Secret Service car—a modified 1956 Cadillac with broad running boards, nicknamed the "Queen Mary"—had turned to look in the direction of the building where Oswald was aiming for his final shot.

Suddenly the right half of Kennedy's head exploded; blood and brain matter spurted up and forward. He tipped left toward Jackie's pink-suited lap. She stared blankly, then whirled to her right and began climbing onto the limousine's huge trunk. One theory is that she was trying to retrieve a piece of her husband's skull. A more plausible explanation is that the young woman was terrified beyond imagining and wanted to escape the targeted rear seat. She later said she remembered nothing of that moment.

The Secret Service agent assigned to protect Mrs. Kennedy, Clint Hill, was standing on the running board of the Queen Mary. When he heard shots fired, he leaped onto the street and sprinted toward the back of the limousine. Reaching the vehicle, he clambered aboard as Mrs. Kennedy was on her hands and knees on the trunk, and pushed her back into the seat. At that moment, the driver realized what was

ABRAHAM ZAPRUDER was a businessman in Dallas who enjoyed taking pictures and was pretty good at it, and who, once he met Stolley in a high-tension moment, decided he had come across a man to be trusted.

Did he photograph the whole sequence? "Yes." Had he actually seen the film himself? "Yes." Could I please come to his home now and see the film? "No."

He politely explained that he was exhausted and overcome by what he had witnessed. The decision I made next turned out to be quite possibly the most important of my career. In the news business, sometimes you push people hard, unsympathetically, without obvious remorse (even while you may be squirming inside). Sometimes, you don't. This, I felt intuitively, was one of those times. I reminded myself: This man had watched a murder (of a man he revered, I discovered later). I said I understood.

Clearly relieved, Zapruder asked me to come to his office at nine the next morning. Back in at least a semi-push-hard mood, and being reasonably sure that Zapruder would have talked to other reporters after me on the previous night, I got there at eight.

He looked a little surprised, but said he was about to show the film to two Secret Service agents and agreed to let me join them. The projector was set up in a small windowless room facing a white wall that would serve as the screen. The first few frames show some of his employees who had turned out to see the President in Dealey Plaza.

Then the motorcade appeared. There was no sound except for the whirring of the projector. We watched transfixed, knowing what was going to happen, yet not having a clue as to what it would look like. The limousine was briefly obscured by the road sign, then for a couple of seconds, Kennedy clutched his throat, Connally tipped over, their wives looked puzzled.

The film advanced to infamous Frame

happening and hit the gas pedal, heading for the safety of an underpass only a few yards ahead.

Also at that moment, Zapruder stopped filming. But he had caught the entire sequence from beginning to horrific end. "They killed him," he began shouting. "They killed him." He climbed down from his concrete perch and stumbled back to his office, a block away, where his staff rallied around their stricken boss. In his office, Zapruder was "incoherent," Lillian Rogers realized. She got him seated, then took the camera and locked it in the office safe. Zapruder conferred with his business partner, Erwin Schwartz, and Schwartz later recalled his exclaiming, "I saw it! I saw his head come off!"

I, of course, knew none of this as I called his home repeatedly that Friday evening. Finally at 11 p.m., a weary voice answered. I asked if this was Mr. Zapruder, and then identified myself and LIFE. What followed was a brief, dramatic and, as it turned out, history-making conversation.

I asked if it was true that he had photographed the assassination that morning. "Yes."

313, and Oswald's bullet struck the President's head. The two agents and I responded precisely the same, with an explosive "ugh," as if we had been simultaneously gut-punched. It was the single most dramatic moment of my 70 years in journalism. The fact that we were watching the assassination only hours after it had occurred was nothing short of remarkable. I decided instantly: There is no way I am going to leave this office without that film.

ZAPRUDER HAD BEEN THROUGH A LOT, AND I WAS REALIZING JUST how much. His Friday afternoon had been unlike any other's, although everyone's afternoon that Friday had been strange. Later, I was able to piece it together.

When he had seen the head shot through his viewfinder, Zapruder had begun shouting. Within moments his experience as a media figure had begun when, on his foggy way back to his office, he was approached by reporter Harry McCormick of *The Dallas Morning News*. Zapruder told McCormick who he was but deferred any interview. Then he got back to his office, and the swarm started in earnest.

In the course of his surreal day, Zapruder (right) finds himself at one point at WFAA-TV, and as Stolley writes: He summons himself and gives a remarkably lucid account of what he has witnessed. His decorous, professional questioner is Jay Watson.

ON THE AFTERNOON OF THAT SAME FRIDAY, meantime, Dallas was in understandable chaos. While Zapruder was returning to his office shouting "They killed him," the White House press corps, riding in a bus far back in the motorcade, was trying to figure out what had happened. *Time* correspondent Hugh Sidey later told me he'd been "bored, leaning against the window" when he'd heard a noise, then a second and a third. CBS correspondent Bob Pierpoint, who had covered the Korean War, jumped up and shouted, "Those sounded like gunshots!" The bus sped up.

But instead of going to Parkland Memorial Hospital, where Kennedy and Connally had been taken, the bus went to the Trade Mart, where the President had been scheduled to make a speech. Some reporters jumped off to find phone booths and call their offices. The driver was then told to go to the hospital.

The first thing Sidey saw when he disembarked there was a young Secret Service agent in the presidential limousine, clutching a reddening pail of water, and wiping the blood and brain matter off the backseat. This tampering with evidence of the crime—the position of the brain parts could of course help determine the source and direction of the shots—was characteristic of the profound shock and paralysis that was spreading throughout the city.

When two priests came out of the hospital, Sidey approached. They confirmed Kennedy was dead, and they had given him last rites. It was still midafternoon—Kennedy was shot at 12:30 p.m. in Dallas, pronounced dead at one p.m. and Lyndon Johnson was sworn in as President at 2:38, although he was technically already in charge. At this point the new President and the remains of his predecessor were headed for Washington.

All of this had happened before our flight from L.A. landed on that dark day.

Darwin Payne, a reporter from the *Dallas Times Herald,* showed up and tried to get publication rights to the film for his paper. The situation in the office grew hectic. McCormick had told Secret Service agent Forrest Sorrels about Zapruder, and at 1:15 p.m. the two of them arrived. The pair of newspaper reporters began complaining about each other's presence, and both were asked to leave. In the office, everybody agreed that the essential next step was to have the film processed, to see what Zapruder had actually captured.

Zapruder, the business partner Schwartz and Sorrels decided to try *The Dallas Morning News* and were driven there, along with reporter McCormick, in a Dallas police car with lights on and siren screaming. When they discovered the newspaper had no motion picture film–processing capability, they went next door to the ABC-TV affiliate, WFAA-TV, only to be told it could handle 16 mm black-and-white film only. A station executive suggested the local Kodak plant and called them, and Sorrels got on the phone to insist on immediate processing. (While at WFAA-TV, Zapruder gave a brief but remarkably composed live interview on camera about what he had just witnessed.)

They arrived at the Kodak plant out by Love Field at about the same time that Air Force One took off for Washington with Kennedy's body. An hour and a half later, Kodak employees showed the original film once as a quality check, but not a second time for fear of damage. Zapruder was both relieved and sickened when he saw what he had.

Since the lab had no facilities for making copies, they drove to another company and ordered three prints of the original to be made. Zapruder and Schwartz were driven to Jennifer Juniors, had a drink and closed the office. They then took the prints back to Kodak to be made ready for projection. Their dinner was chili and beans from a vending machine at the lab.

At about 10 p.m., Zapruder and Schwartz (now in their own, not a police, vehicle) drove to Dallas police headquarters to give two prints to Agent Sorrels, who had been called away from the Kodak plant midafternoon by the news that a suspect, Lee Harvey Oswald, had been arrested.

While at headquarters, Zapruder and Schwartz were astonished to see Oswald as he was being moved in a hallway (an indication of the lax security that would have such devastating consequences two days later). Sorrels told the two men he was busy and asked them to take the prints to the local Secret Service office. One was flown to Washington, and the other was given to the Dallas FBI office.

An exhausted Zapruder finally went home to his family at about 11 p.m., and shortly thereafter, I called. Abraham Zapruder's day was not yet ended.

NEXT MORNING, SATURDAY, IN HIS OFFICE, ZAPRUDER RAN THE 26-second film for us three times. By then we could hear a commotion in the hall outside. As I had suspected, other reporters were showing up, told (like me) to be there at nine a.m. In all, two dozen or so arrived, representing the Associated Press, *The Saturday Evening Post* magazine, a newsreel and two or three major out-of-town newspapers. It seems astonishing now, but network television never appeared. TV news had only recently gone from 15 minutes in the evening to half an hour, and the three major networks were concentrating their forces on the funeral in Washington, not the crime in Dallas.

Zapruder explained to us that he was going to show his film to these newcomers. The Secret Service agents left, and I asked Zapruder if I could sit in his office, and thus be spared mingling with these potential competitors.

During the next hour or so, I introduced myself to and chatted with members of his staff, particularly Lillian Rogers. She turned out to be from southern Illinois, I was from central Illinois, and a surefire subject of interest to anyone from that state was high school basketball. I had been sports editor of my hometown newspaper, the *Pekin Daily Times,* and knew that her favorite team, Taylorville High School, was consistently one of the best in Illinois—and said so. We hit it off like old friends, something Zapruder noticed when he came into the office between showings of the film.

My brief relationship with Lillian Rogers was cited years later, long after Zapruder's death in 1970, as one of the reasons he decided to sell his film to LIFE. I had called Erwin Schwartz, to clear up some questions about that day. Schwartz suddenly asked, "Do you know why you, and not one of the other reporters, got that film?"

Surprised, I answered: "The money." Schwartz said someone would have matched or exceeded that. Our promise not to exploit the film? He agreed that was very important. Then he asked the question again, and went on to answer it himself: "Because you were a gentleman."

He cited my not badgering Zapruder to come to his house on Friday night, my treating him with respect during our negotiations and, finally, my friendly dealings with fellow Midwesterner Lillian Rogers. Some of the other reporters had treated her harshly, he said, accusing her of preventing them access to her boss. Schwartz's explanation astonished me then, and still does today.

That Saturday morning, after Zapruder had shown the film to the last reporter, he asked me to join the others in the hall. He said he realized that we all wanted to talk to him about print or broadcast rights, but "because Mr. Stolley of LIFE was the first to contact me, I feel obliged to speak to him first." In my mind, I pumped a fist. The others erupted, shouting "No, no." "Don't sign anything." "Promise you will speak to us before you make up your mind." "Promise, promise," et cetera.

Zapruder agreed, and we walked into his office and closed the door. He looked very tired, but I quickly had to determine whether he realized the value of his film. I said it was "very interesting," and that when LIFE encountered "unusual" pictures like these, we were inclined to pay higher than normal space rates, e.g., we would be willing to offer "as much as $5,000" for the film.

He smiled. Yes, he knew what he had. From then on, I would raise the bid, and we would talk, mostly about the tragic weekend. He said he was embarrassed that a middle-aged garment manufacturer, and not one of the world-famous photographers who normally travel with the President, had taken these astonishing pictures.

He also described a nightmare he had had only a few hours earlier. In it, a man wearing "a sharp double-breasted suit" stood in front of a sleazy Times Square movie theater—midtown Manhattan's Times Square was a porn mecca back then—shouting for people to come in and see the President assassinated on the big screen. Zapruder said he woke up shuddering. He told this story to his family, obviously, and it has trickled down; Alexandra Zapruder recalls it in her essay.

His message was clear. I promised LIFE would not "exploit" the film, a verb he used repeatedly during our session. Meanwhile, the other journalists in the hall were behaving badly. They pounded on the door, shouting, "Remember, you promised," and slipped pleading notes under it. A few went out to the street to a phone booth and called the office, demanding to speak to Zapruder.

He was visibly becoming more and more upset. I had reached $50,000 for the print rights, an amount authorized by my editors in New York when we had talked at midnight. I told him, truthfully, that I could go no higher without making a phone call. At that moment, as I recall, there was a particularly violent bang on the door. Zapruder looked stricken, then said to me quietly, "Let's do it."

I asked if I could use his typewriter and wrote a nine-line contract, using language given to me by a Time Inc. lawyer. Four of us signed the single page, Zapruder and I as principals, and Lillian Rogers and Erwin Schwartz as witnesses.

Zapruder handed me the precious original film. I asked him if there was a back door to the building, and I left him to face the angry and disappointed crowd in the hall. (One of the reporters never spoke to me again.)

BACK AT THE HOTEL, I GAVE THE original to a courier who flew it to Chicago, where an emergency editorial staff was closing the magazine in a temporary office set up at the Donnelley printing plant. The presses had been stopped and the regular issue all but scrapped, including the cover story on football star Roger Staubach—who is still alive, still in Dallas and whom you will hear from in later pages. In place of the Staubach cover was a somber portrait of Kennedy and, for the first time in history, the familiar red of the LIFE logo had been changed to black.

Once the editors in Chicago saw the Zapruder film, they decided to publish 31

This is a scene that could not possibly happen in this day and age. The FBI has arrived to talk to the Oswald family, but cedes control to LIFE. In this photo, taken by LIFE's Allan Grant: Robert Oswald, the alleged assassin's brother (smoking); Marguerite Oswald, the mother; Marina Oswald, the wife; and in the background, Tommy Thompson, LIFE's correspondent and Grant's word-side colleague. How fast LIFE would be ushered out of the room today cannot be imagined.

Abraham Zapruder
3009 Marquette
Dallas   501 Elm St.

570   2 vantage spots pushed earlier: ① bridge "couldn't balance"; ② signs.   obstructed by

571   "I heard the 1st shot and I saw the President leaning and grab himself
3 ?   like this (holding his left chest area)"   "But before I had a
V-5 shots chance to organize my mind, I heard a second shot and then
T/1/116   I saw his head opened up"   "I thought I heard two, it could
        be three … I never even heard a third shot."

572   "They (Police) were running right behind me, in the line of the
        shooting. I guess they thought it came from right behind me.
        … No I also thought it came from back of me … being I was here
BEHIND   and he was hit on this line and he was hit right in the head —
ME!   I saw it right around here, so it looked like it came from here
        and it could come from there."

572   "There was an echo which gave me a sound all over."
sound

572   "They claim he was hit — that the first bullet went through
Single him and hit Connally or something like that — I don't know
Bullet how that is."
Theory ?

576   "They (the FBI) told me that the time between the 2 rapid shots,
        as I understand, that was determined — the length of time it
2nd   took to the second one and that they were very fast and they
Assassin ? claim it has proven it could be done by 1 man. You
        know there was indication there were two?"

        FILM JUMPS AT Z 218-219; MEANING?

In the past 50 years, things have popped up everywhere. In the next 50, they will continue to. In preparing the book you hold in your hands, we came across these index cards in the LIFE archives. They were not written by Dick Stolley, but obviously a reporter has recorded Zapruder's testimony after the fact. LIFE has returned to this story several times since 1963, needless to say, including during the Warren Commission investigations, which involved Zapruder.

frames from it, but not grisly Frame 313, the head shot, out of deference to the grieving Kennedy family.

The pictures were also in black and white because color printing back then took time that we didn't have. (While those 31 prints were being hastily made from the original film, the film was slightly damaged, and six frames had to be removed. The damaged frames—in two places—both occurred during the time the limo was on Elm Street. All the copy prints were of course intact.)

Though the issue was going to press, the story was hardly over in Dallas. Our attention turned to suspect Oswald, who was denying any involvement in the assassination or in the murder of Officer J.D. Tippit, just 45 minutes after Kennedy's death. Oswald was calling himself "a patsy," suggesting that he'd been set up or duped.

On Saturday, Tommy Thompson called me in the hotel with exciting news. He and photographer Allan Grant had found the Oswalds—Lee's wife, Marina, and their two infant daughters, his brother, Robert, and their mother, Marguerite—and had photographed the family. Because Marina spoke almost no English, they had hired a Russian interpreter and were now planning an interview.

For several weeks, Marina and her girls had been staying in the Irving, Texas, home of Ruth and Michael Paine. Ruth was a gentle Quaker who was interested in learning Russian—and was teaching Marina English at the same time. The Oswalds had a troubled marriage and fought constantly, so Lee lived in a rooming house during the week and visited his wife and daughters on weekends. After Lee was arrested, his brother and mother went to the Paine house to comfort Marina. The pictures Allan took, only two of which appeared in LIFE at the time (for reasons Allan will explain), will also be seen, accompanied by Allan's remembrance, just a few pages on.

Tommy had other news from the house in Irving, too. He had noticed a wooden chest on the floor and asked what it was. Lee's personal papers, diary, artifacts, stuff, he was told. Could I have a look? Tommy asked. The answer was yes, but only for

$10,000. The family was desperate to hire a lawyer for the accused assassin, but they had no money, and somebody, presumably either Robert or Marguerite, came up with the idea of charging to investigate the chest.

Tommy and I talked it over. God knows what's in there, we agreed, but we surely wanted to find out. I telephoned New York and told the top editor of LIFE of the offer. The editor was George Hunt, a burly ex-Marine who had survived the Battle of Iwo Jima, had visited Jack Kennedy in the White House and was a great admirer of his fellow World War II combat veteran.

Hunt was outraged at my proposal. "I won't give a goddamn dime to that assassin," he shouted over the phone. "Alleged assassin," I reminded. Hunt was unmoved. I continued to appeal to him until he abruptly hung up on me. The matter was closed, and I told Tommy to forget it. (I did give Robert Oswald $40 to buy diapers and food

The allegations and counter-allegations of doctoring of this famous "backyard photo" of Lee Harvey Oswald with a rifle only started with LIFE, which was not in the business then—nor is it now—of doctoring (or retouching) photography—as LIFE managing editor Ed Thompson felt compelled to emphasize by telegram to the Warren Commission. It would be impossible in the space of this caption, or this book, to explain how and why this picture spawned a thousand conspiracy theories. Head to the Internet, if you must.

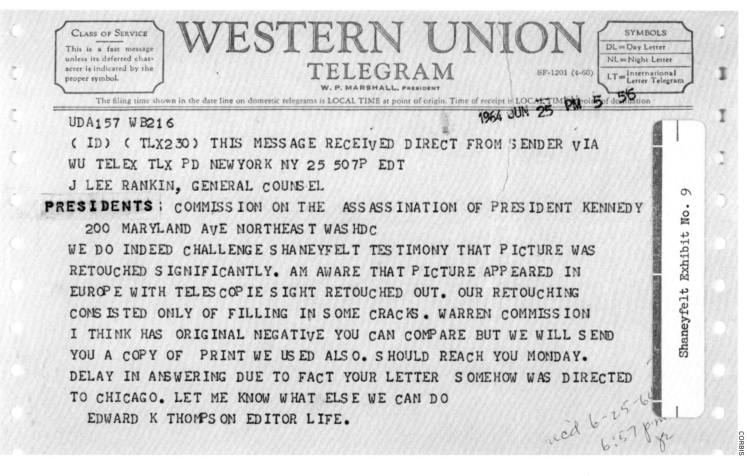

WESTERN UNION TELEGRAM

CLASS OF SERVICE
This is a fast message unless its deferred character is indicated by the proper symbol.

W. P. MARSHALL, PRESIDENT

SF-1201 (4-60)

SYMBOLS
DL=Day Letter
NL=Night Letter
LT=International Letter Telegram

The filing time shown in the date line on domestic telegrams is LOCAL TIME at point of origin. Time of receipt is LOCAL TIME at point of destination

1964 JUN 25 PM 5 56

Shaneyfelt Exhibit No. 9

UDA157 WB216

(ID) (TLX230) THIS MESSAGE RECEIvED DIRECT FROM SENDER vIA
WU TELEX TLX PD NEWYORK NY 25 507P EDT
J LEE RANKIN, GENERAL COUNSEL
PRESIDENTS COMMISSION ON THE ASSASSINATION OF PRESIDENT KENNEDY
   200 MARYLAND AvE NORTHEAST WASHDC
WE DO INDEED CHALLENGE SHANEYFELT TESTIMONY THAT PICTURE WAS
RETOUCHED SIGNIFICANTLY. AM AWARE THAT PICTURE APPEARED IN
EUROPE WITH TELESCOPIE SIGHT RETOUCHED OUT. OUR RETOUCHING
CONSISTED ONLY OF FILLING IN SOME CRACKS. WARREN COMMISSION
I THINK HAS ORIGINAL NEGATIvE YOU CAN COMPARE BUT WE WILL SEND
YOU A COPY OF PRINT WE USED ALSO. SHOULD REACH YOU MONDAY.
DELAY IN ANSWERING DUE TO FACT YOUR LETTER SOMEHOW WAS DIRECTED
TO CHICAGO. LET ME KNOW WHAT ELSE WE CAN DO
   EDWARD K THOMPSON EDITOR LIFE.

recd 6-25-6
6:57 pm 82

for the little girls, but did not ask anybody's permission about that.)

A while later, Tommy called again to say the interview was over, and he had written an exclusive portrait of Oswald for the issue. No other reporters had yet showed up. But they certainly would, Tommy assured me, and he suggested we move the family to a hotel where they could remain anonymous. I agreed immediately.

Shortly thereafter—this was all still on Saturday—the Oswalds walked into our suite in the Adolphus, clearly stunned and despondent. We quickly stashed them away in another suite under Allan Grant's name, with instructions to order anything they wanted from room service, but not to leave the suite or to open the door unless we alerted them in advance.

After getting them settled, I returned to the LIFE suite. The phone rang; I answered, "Stolley, LIFE." A harsh voice demanded, "Okay, you son of a bitch, where are they?" Startled, I asked who this was and what he was talking about. He identified himself as a Secret Service agent and angrily wanted to know what we had done with the Oswald family. I tried bluffing: "I have no idea what you're talking about."

More profanity followed, but he finally calmed down enough to explain that the Secret Service was responsible for the family's safety, which clearly could be in jeopardy with Lee accused of killing the President.

We fenced for a while, until I asked if he would promise not to tell other reporters—our worry, of course—if I revealed their whereabouts. He agreed, I told him, and to the best of my knowledge, he kept his word.

Saturday had been a tumultuous day for LIFE, and that evening we wanted to relax. Most restaurants, like most stores, had closed for the day; downtown Dallas was deserted, a ghost city. Some benefactor arranged for us to have dinner at a private club.

The club was virtually empty, but near our table was a couple we began talking to. Impressed by LIFE magazine, they invited us to their suburban home for more drinks, which we hardly needed. Everybody in Dallas seemed on edge, understandably, and their kindness was appreciated. Little did we know.

We sat in their den, the walls of which were lined with gun racks. The presence of all those weapons was unsettling given the events of the previous day, but we ignored them—everyone but Tommy, whose grief and humiliation that the President had been murdered in his home state was palpable.

He began baiting the homeowner about the guns and Texas's reputation for violence. Tommy wouldn't let up. The man was getting more and more upset, more red in the face. We all had had plenty to drink at this point, and each of us was holding a glass with even more. Suddenly the man reached the breaking point. He lurched out of his chair, screaming at Tommy, "Ah'm going to get mah gun and kill you!"

As our colleagues leaped to restrain him, Tommy smiled dangerously and said, "See, that's what I mean." I escaped to the kitchen, where the wife, too, had wisely retreated. She was depressed, but not just because of the assassination. That death had revived tragic memories of another. As occasionally happens when you're a reporter, you begin asking questions, innocently enough perhaps at the beginning, but then, suddenly, the other person bares her soul.

This was her second marriage. From her first, she had a son, a teenager reeling from the turbulence of those difficult years—from the divorce, from the stepfather, she wasn't sure. All she knew was that one evening in the past year, she and her new husband had driven home, opened the garage door by remote, and there was her son hanging from the ceiling, dead. As the mother told this awful story, she began to sob.

Appalled, I struggled for words of sympathy, and when I thought it seemly, left the kitchen and told our group it was time to go back to the hotel. We were sure the next day, Sunday, would be calmer.

Needless to say, it wasn't.

THAT MORNING, I RECEIVED a phone call from Dick Pollard, LIFE director of photography in New York. He said the editors had watched a copy of the film made from the original in Chicago the afternoon before and flown to Manhattan. Unsurprisingly, they were overwhelmed by its power and impact and had decided LIFE should buy all rights, not just print. Particularly vocal in the decision was LIFE's publisher, C.D. Jackson, the business head of the magazine (whose wartime experience in military intelligence caught the attention of conspiracy theorists when skepticism about the Warren Commission's report erupted a few months later).

I called Zapruder. He seemed relieved to be dealing with LIFE again. The battle for film and TV rights had intensified, he said; he was being hounded at home, and he clearly wanted this issue to be settled. He asked me to come, not to his place of business, but to his lawyer's office at nine a.m. on Monday. (This time I was confident enough to arrive at the requested hour.)

Then I turned to the big event of that Sunday—the transfer of Lee Harvey Oswald from the city jail to the more secure county jail, a mile away. Tommy Thompson and I were eager to see this infamous young man whose family Tommy had spent hours with and whose marksmanship I had seen on film. We decided the best place for that was not the city jail, crowded as it was with reporters and photographers who had camped out there for nearly two days, but the county jail, which we hoped would be relatively ignored by the press.

It was. Security was so light that we simply walked in, showed our Los Angeles Police Department press cards and joined a handful of reporters and a couple of TV crews. Oswald's cell was ready for him, and so were we. We waited. Suddenly a TV sound technician looked startled. He clamped his earphones tighter on his head as if to hear better. Then he ripped them off and shouted, "Oswald's been shot!" A shocked silence followed. Then we shouted back, "Where?" He replied, "The basement of the city jail."

Without waiting for further details, Tommy and I raced out to the street, looking for a cab, in vain of course. We ran up and down the traffic, banging on car windows, saying we were from LIFE magazine and asking would he or she drive us to the city jail. It goes without saying that nobody was interested in taking these two maniacs anywhere.

Finally, I spotted an open car window with a young man inside. Throwing a $20 bill into his lap, I repeated our destination. He seemed amused and gestured for us to get in. By the time we even got close to the city jail, however, police had cordoned off the area. We jumped out, thanked the driver and ran back to the Adolphus.

When we telephoned the Oswald family (at a second hotel, to which we had moved them), there was no answer. Federal agents had obviously had them under surveillance and in a matter of minutes after Lee was shot, fearing attempts on their lives too, had whisked them off to yet a third hotel, unknown to us and everyone else, on the edge of the city.

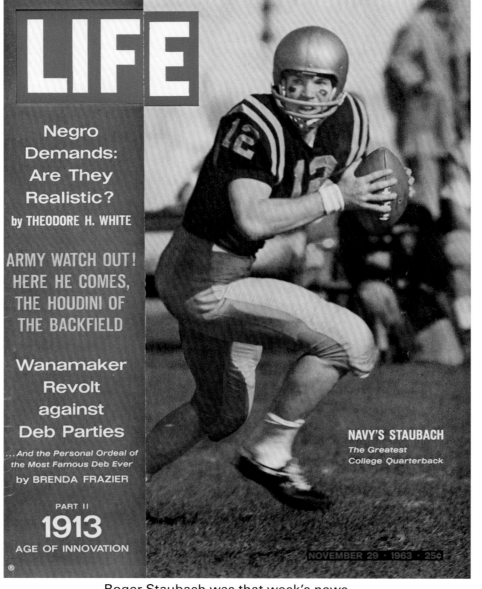

NAVY'S STAUBACH
The Greatest
College Quarterback

NOVEMBER 29 · 1963 · 25¢

Roger Staubach was that week's news . . .

The presses in Chicago, already printing the new issue, were stopped a second time, and Tommy dictated new opening and closing paragraphs on Oswald's death to his story.

Surely Monday would be less chaotic. For us in Dallas, it was. For the nation, it was the day the President was buried at Arlington National Cemetery, a devastating event that most of the tearful nation watched on television and that most of us reporters in Texas missed. That morning I went to the office of Zapruder's lawyer, Sam Passman, and to my surprise found CBS correspondent Dan Rather sitting in the lobby. We knew each other from working side by side on Southern race-relations stories.

As Rather later said, his heart sank when he saw me because he knew LIFE had "deep pockets" and he had been authorized to offer only $10,000 for the TV rights. When he was invited to an inner office to watch the film, I did not accompany him; I already knew what was there. Apparently realizing CBS was unlikely to get broadcast rights, Rather left the office afterward and within minutes was describing the film's contents by phone to CBS radio, something that Zapruder told me he had asked Rather not to do unless he wound up buying the rights. Dan later delivered the same description on television. (The story was so immense that, in retrospect, it's hard to fault him.)

My session with Zapruder and his attorney was brief. In a few minutes we had agreed on $100,000 in addition to the original $50,000, the whole sum to be paid in $25,000 annual installments. Then Passman brought up a delicate subject. In effect, he said that when word got out that a garment manufacturer named Abraham Zapruder had sold his film of the President's murder, the public response in right wing Dallas could be an anti-Semitic firestorm.

Passman suggested a way to blunt the criticism (and the tax consequences of the windfall): publicly donate the first payment of $25,000 to the family of Officer Tippit. Zapruder agreed immediately. (I was astounded that Passman would speak about such a touchy subject in front of me, but gratified at Zapruder's response. Since I had agreed on Saturday and again on Monday that LIFE would not reveal our purchase price, the donation gave rise to the myth that Zapruder had turned over all proceeds from all rights to the Tippits. It was a misunderstanding that I finally felt I could correct publicly 10 years later.)

THAT MONDAY AFTERNOON, WE NEEDED TO LEARN MORE ABOUT Oswald's killer, Jack Ruby, for the next week's story. So we visited the Carousel Club, his strip joint, where he had long welcomed off-duty cops (which helps explain why nobody in uniform stopped him when he'd walked into the city jail the day before). The club had been shut down since Friday, but we knocked on the door, said the magic words—we were from LIFE—and soon found ourselves talking to two of the dancers.

Still in shock, they told us that Ruby had ordered the closing two hours after the President's death and then had sat at one of the tables and cried. He told them, "It's awful. Just don't talk about it." They were sure they understood why their boss had shot Oswald: "Oh, that is so like Jack! He didn't want Mrs. Kennedy to have to come back to Dallas for a trial. It would be so awful for her. He thought he would be a hero." The words were simple, and as we later learned, probably true as to Ruby's motivation.

I returned to Los Angeles two days later, and never saw Abraham Zapruder again, although we talked on the phone once or twice. He went on to testify at the Warren Commission hearings, where he broke into tears when his film was referenced. "He was extremely emotional about the whole thing," his wife, Lillian (now deceased), once told me. His granddaughter Alexandra's story in this book will tell more about how this all affected him and the family.

Bell & Howell offered Zapruder a new camera in exchange for his old one, and then donated the original to the National Archives. Zapruder rarely used the new camera, however; his enthusiasm for home movies all but vanished on November 22, 1963.

He received bags and bags of mail, as many as 10 a day early on. Most of the letters were simply addressed to him, Dallas, Texas. A few called him a fool for giving $25,000 to Officer Tippit's family. More praised him. Still others asked for money for themselves. When he and his wife traveled, especially in Europe, the name Zapruder was often recognized on hotel registers.

His contribution to history that weekend has been remembered here, anew, and also captured by Hollywood. It is portrayed in a movie in the fall of 2013 titled *Parkland*—the name of the Dallas hospital where Kennedy (and Oswald) died. Oscar-winning actor Paul Giamatti plays Zapruder. Others in the cast include Billy Bob Thornton as a Secret Service agent and Jackie Weaver (who was nominated for her own Oscar last year for *Silver Linings Playbook*) as Oswald's troubled mother. (Even I made it into the script and am played by an actor named Jeffrey Schmidt.)

As the movie suggests, and his friends and family knew, and as Alexandra will tell you, Abe Zapruder, until his death from cancer in 1970, was never able to escape his unique and haunting role in the Kennedy assassination story.

Nor was I, as it turned out. Four months later, I was transferred to the Washington bureau of LIFE, where for four years I covered the man, Lyndon

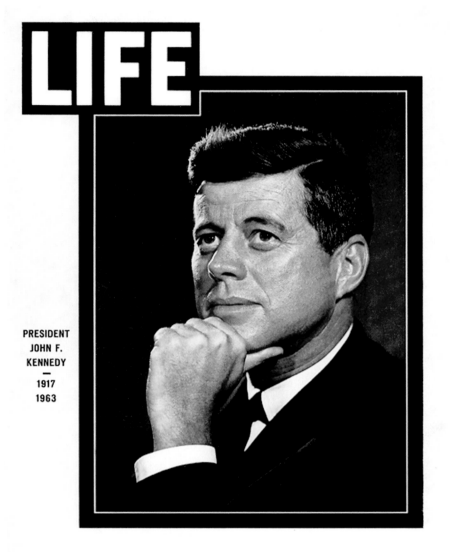

PRESIDENT
JOHN F.
KENNEDY
—
1917
1963

NOVEMBER 29 · 1963 · 25¢

. . . until he wasn't. Staubach and Kennedy were both Navy men, and Staubach had lost not only his commander in chief but a comrade in arms. His remembrances, exclusive to LIFE, end our chapter "Where Were You When You Heard?"

he calls me three obscene names—that it still makes me laugh all this time later.

Two theories identify me by name. The first is that I took the film from Zapruder's office on November 23 to a secret CIA lab outside Dallas, where I waited while the frames were rearranged to conceal the position and number of real assassins, and then I sent it on to LIFE for bogus publication.

The second theory surfaced only in recent years in a DVD and book by Brian David Andersen titled *"My God, I'm Hit,"* words which Kennedy is said to have uttered in the limousine when the first bullet struck his upper back. (A Secret Service agent in the front seat was the source of the quote, but a careful examination of Kennedy's mouth in the film during those few seconds indicates he did not speak.)

My role in this second theory is complicated. On Sunday, November 24, a man "in a trench coat and dress hat was tippy-toeing . . . in the hallway between the kitchen and living room" in Ruth Paine's house with a suitcase full of cash intended for Ruth for reasons that are murky—possibly to score an exclusive interview with Marina Oswald, possibly to compensate Ruth for her role in the conspiracy to kill the President. The book continues: "The physical description of the trench coat man . . . exactly fits LIFE Los Angeles bureau chief Richard Stolley." The man was challenged by two policemen guarding the house, who tackled him and took him to headquarters, "where he was released in a few hours with no charges made against him."

Both the CIA photo lab and the Ruth Paine house stories are complete lunacy, of course, but I suspect this 50th

Johnson, who was President only because of Dallas. I was asked to talk about the Zapruder film from time to time, usually on anniversaries. And now I remember it, and write about it, 50 years on.

Those 26 seconds of celluloid had their own history. LIFE gave first-generation copies to all relevant law enforcement agencies, but for various reasons—including a respect for Zapruder's wishes—would not sell it for broadcast, a refusal that was loudly (and unfairly) criticized.

Bootleg copies of the film began to appear, possibly coming from outside agencies. One likely source was the office of New Orleans district attorney Jim Garrison, which used the film in an unsuccessful (and ludicrous) prosecution of a local businessman, Clay Shaw, for conspiracy to kill the President. (That trial was the subject of the exciting but historically irresponsible 1991 film *JFK*.) One bootleg copy finally found its illegal way on to national television on the ABC Geraldo Rivera show *Good Night America* in March 1975.

A month later, LIFE and our parent company, Time Inc., concluded that the Zapruder family itself should properly deal with copyright issues and returned the film to the family for one dollar. In the 1990s, the federal government decided it should own the original copy of the historic film, and I was interviewed at length on the subject of compensation for the Zapruder family. In the end, they received an astonishing $16 million. The film itself is today kept in a temperature and humidity controlled container in the National Archives in College Park, Maryland.

I also was the occasional target of the deluge of conspiracy theorists who disagreed sharply with the Warren Commission's conclusion that Oswald alone, without help, killed the President (a judgment that I accepted then and now; Zapruder and particularly his wife felt the same way—she insisted Oswald was "a crackpot, a nut"—and reacted incredulously when Dallas friends recited conspiracy plots to them). My files are full of letters from conspiracy advocates asking me to comment on their beliefs or to explain my own. Most are polite, but one was so profane—in a three-sentence letter,

anniversary will produce a new crop of conspiracy theories or a replay of ancient ones, or both. I can't say I'm eager for them, but I'm ready.

For years when I looked back on Dallas, I had the uneasy sense of missing what the rest of the country endured that weekend, especially the Monday after—those hours of televised grief, of Kennedy's casket and caisson, the unruly black horse, a street full of world leaders, the veiled Jackie, John Jr.'s salute, the lighting of the eternal flame.

Those of us at work in Dallas that weekend did not have time to ponder the emotional impact of the murder nor have a place to watch its climax on Monday. When I returned to Los Angeles just before Thanksgiving, nobody wanted to talk about it. They were grieved out.

I always had the feeling that I was deprived of something crucial in my own and my nation's history. Then I was asked to help on this book. I watched the Zapruder film yet again; I looked at the still photographs from that weekend; I read the old reporting and the new. I pulled from my shelves six feet of assassination files, collected over 50 years, and went through them, page by page. I recalled my conversations in Washington in 1964 with one of Kennedy's girlfriends. I spoke to Zapruder's daughter and granddaughter and even to Marina Oswald. I immersed myself in the details of those four days. Then I sat down to try to put it all together in this narrative.

The result was a stunning revelation to me. It is best described by some favorite lines from T.S. Eliot's "Four Quartets": "We shall not cease from exploration / And the end of all our exploring / Will be to arrive where we started / And know the place for the first time."

Now, at long last, I understood what America suffered that weekend that changed the world.

RICHARD B. STOLLEY, a member of the American Society of Magazine Editors' inaugural class in its hall of fame, has been a reporter, writer, bureau chief, senior editor, managing editor and close friend of Time Inc. magazines since 1953.

The Zapruder Film

No film has been pored over, picked apart and parsed like this one. **DANIEL S. LEVY** has been poring over it in recent months and consulting with the experts, as LIFE, where select images first appeared in 1963, has prepared to present the entire film in print for the first time. Here it is, followed by commentary on the essential frames.

I T IS A HOME MOVIE AND NOT A LONG one—just 486 frames, six feet of film. Put on a scale, the whole of it weighs mere ounces. But its mass as an evidentiary thing, not to mention the burden it has borne in the unspooling of a thousand conspiracy theories, has been immense—a ponderous chain. Per image, there has never been anything like the Zapruder film.

You have read something about it already in Richard B. Stolley's reminiscence, and after this technical look at the film you will read more in Alexandra Zapruder's personal account. Here, for a moment, let's look at the film itself.

It was shot by Abraham Zapruder beginning at 12:30 p.m. on November 22, 1963, and was entirely unimportant to anyone but Zapruder and some of his staff at Jennifer Juniors until shots rang out in Dealey Plaza. Within a week, images appeared in the emergency issue of LIFE, and suddenly Zapruder and "the Zapruder film" were famous. LIFE withheld the infamous Frame 313 at that time, the image that shows Kennedy being struck by Oswald's final bullet, but the impact of the rest was immense notwithstanding. If we had known back then that all of these imagined or concocted plots and stratagems might have been forestalled by running the whole thing, in a gatefold, would we have done it? Well, we didn't have the capacity back then.

Which is not to say there wasn't a conspiracy. We don't know; a majority of Americans think there was one. Robert Kennedy Jr. thinks there probably was one and says his father felt the same. What is clear to us, after having gone over this movie time and time again all these years later is this: The Zapruder film will not bring you peace. It is not that it's ambiguous; it is the opposite of ambiguous. But people will watch it and conclude differently, despite its chemical, filmic objectivity, and there will be no persuading.

Some will say it has been faked or tampered with. Some will point their fingers at LIFE (Google on; you'll see). What can we say but what we've always said to our readers: Trust us.

We bought the astonishing thing; we have never said otherwise. We sought, long ago, to present it to the public responsibly. Today, we do the same, and we want to put the entirety of the Zapruder film out there, as LIFE and our staff think it existed right after Abraham pressed the button on his Bell & Howell movie camera.

The flip introduction to this film would conclude with something like "roll it," but we cannot be flip here. Abraham Zapruder, said his colleagues, talked about Kennedy "all the time"—he revered the man. The visit of the President was a big event for him, and nearly a third of Dallas turned out—these facts deserve respect.

As the motorcade neared, Zapruder started to run his roll of Kodachrome II, squeezing off seven seconds of film. Then he stopped because the President's car wasn't in view. Then he saw the hulking blue Lincoln Continental with the fluttering flags slowly rolling toward him, and he started again, panning from left to right as the limo slipped down Elm Street. Then he heard the sound of a firecracker, or something, but he continued filming until the car accelerated toward the triple underpass and the hospital. Later he said, "I don't even know how I did it."

T his is Zapruder's 8 mm Bell & Howell 414 PD Director Series Zoomatic camera with which he shot 26 seconds of film that, 50 years later, remains vital to American history. There were, as we have noted, other images made of the action in Dealey Plaza. Today, with cameraphones, there would be ten thousand. But Abraham Zapruder was a unique man at a unique place and time, facing an extraordinary event. And he made a permanent record.

From Beginning to End

The film has been chopped up, edited and endlessly analyzed in the 50 years since LIFE printed the first frames; you can find it on the Internet in pirated versions. But those aren't always to be trusted. Here, for the first time in print: what Abraham Zapruder filmed of the assassination of John Fitzgerald Kennedy.

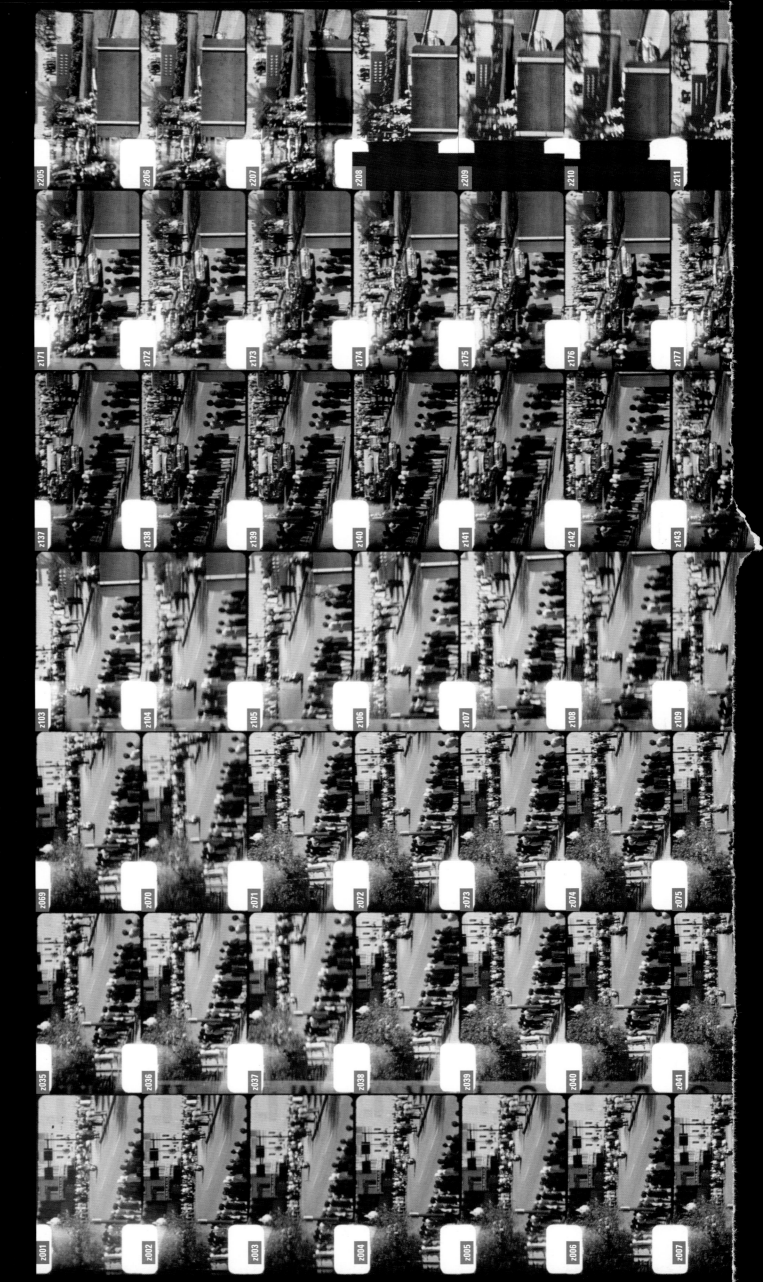

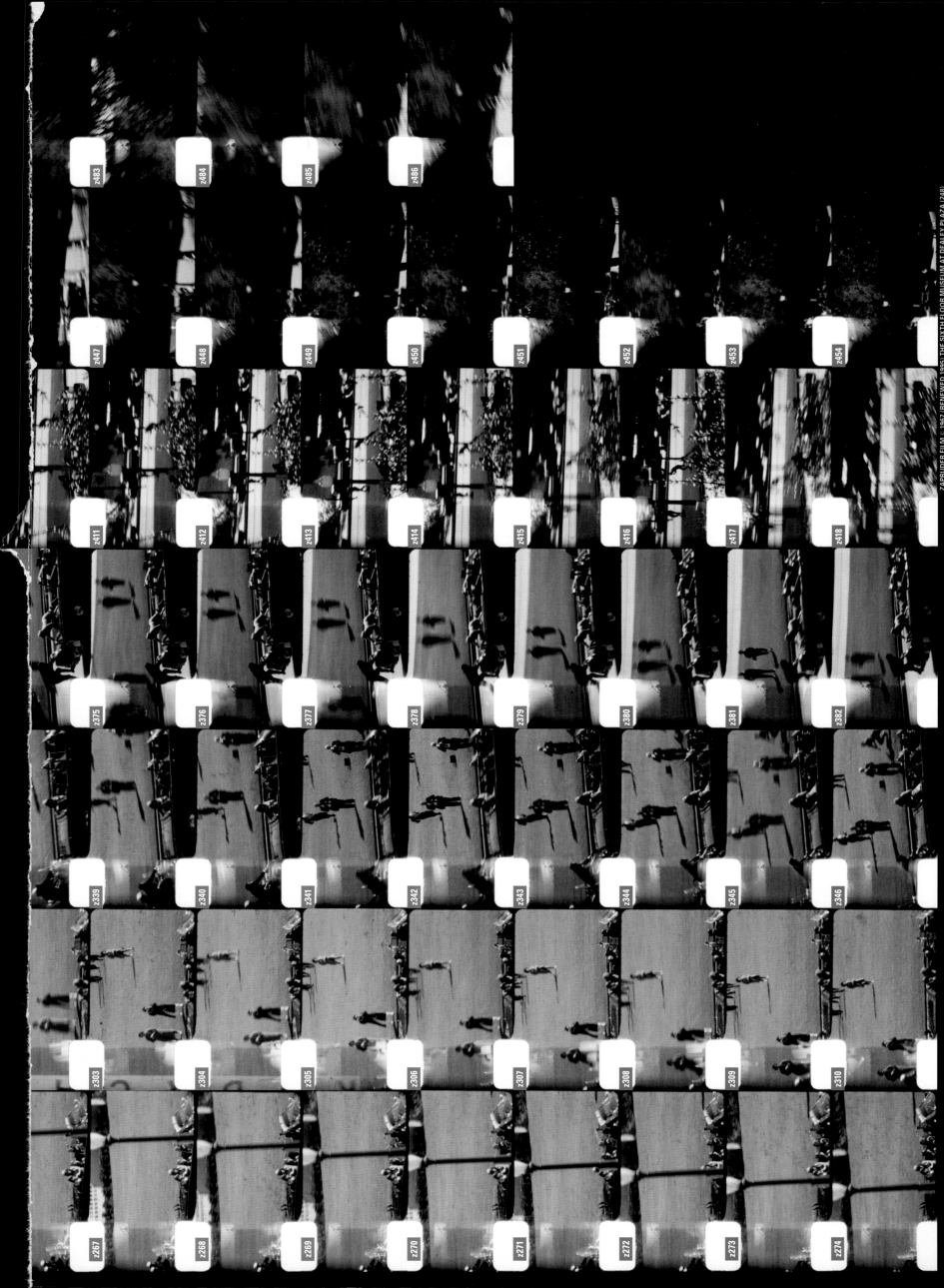

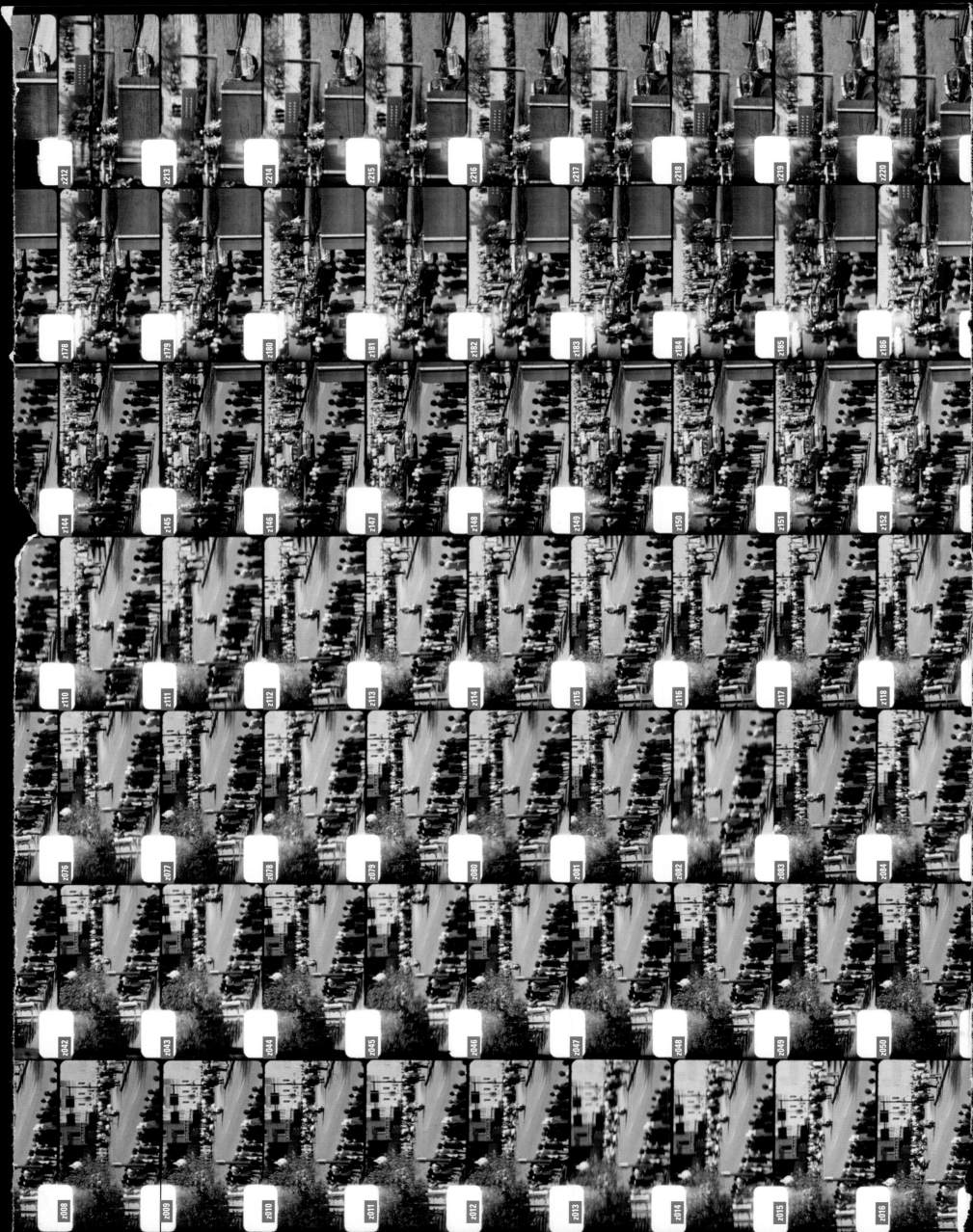

The Zapruder Film
Key Frames

Frame 17

A s you look at the selected pictures on these nine pages, it will sometimes be helpful to return to the entire film for context. (And please note: The numbers used in this presentation of the film are those assigned by an FBI investigator, not by Kodak.)

What is happening here, in Frame 17? Zapruder has started filming as President Kennedy's motorcade enters Dealey Plaza. The lead Dallas motorcycle officers are, from left to right: Leon Gray, George Lumpkin and Stavis Ellis—here making the severe 120-degree turn off Houston Street and onto Elm Street. These three men are nearly a block ahead of the President's car. The motorcycle sequence constitutes nearly a quarter of the Zapruder film.

Zapruder is using a camera with a cranked spring motor that needs to be rewound. A fully wound camera would allow for the exposure of 73 seconds—15 feet—of film. Zapruder, not knowing when the President will appear, stops filming and likely winds the camera again so that it is fully ready.

As Kennedy's car nears, the Dallas County Records Building is seen on the far right; the Purse Building, a wholesale furniture store, stands in the distance; and the Dal-Tex building, where Zapruder's firm is headquartered, is to the left. The Texas School Book Depository, where Lee Harvey Oswald had started working the previous month, is just out of the camera's view, further to the left side.

While vast numbers of people are still along Main Street to the east, the parade area ends at Dealey Plaza, and so the crowds here are thinner.

Just after the motorcade leaves Main and turns onto Houston Street, Nellie Connally turns to Kennedy and says, "Mr. President, you can't say Dallas doesn't love you."

Frame 133

W hen Zapruder starts his camera again, he of course focuses on the Lincoln Continental convertible transporting the Kennedys. The car, called SS 100 X by the Secret Service and bearing District of Columbia license plate GG 300, is a 21-foot-long dark blue whale of a car. The Ford Motor Company has leased it to the Secret Service for $500 a year, and not only does it boast a massive air-conditioning system (not that it matters on this fine day in Dallas), it also features a hydraulic rear seat that can elevate the President more than 10 inches so that he can see—and be seen— better. There are steps on the sides and on the rear bumper upon which Secret Service agents can ride. The car can be fitted with a Plexiglas—though not bulletproof—bubble top. As the weather has cleared, the President and the Secret Service have decided to proceed without the top.

The First Couple's Secret Service code names are Lancer and Lace, and in the 1956 black Cadillac behind them ride eight more Secret Service agents. Clint Hill, who is assigned to protect Jackie Kennedy, stands on the driver's side running board. Vice President Lyndon Johnson, code name Volunteer, and his wife, Lady Bird, code name Victoria, and others ride in the steel gray Lincoln convertible that follows the Caddy.

Zapruder films as Kennedy and four Dallas police officers on motorcycles—left to right: Douglas Jackson, James Chaney, Bobby Hargis and Billy Martin—make their way toward the western end of Dealey Plaza. If it is historically interesting that this is the very spot where John Neely Bryan first settled the city of Dallas in 1841, it is today more vital that Dealey Plaza is framed by two Art Deco–style structures— the Bryan Colonnade on the north and the Cockrell Colonnade at the south—and contains two long columned peristyles, pylons, reflecting pools and assorted trees. (All of these things will be mentioned in various conspiracy theories.) Bryan Colonnade, where Zapruder finds his perch, tops a gently sloping lawn, and it is this expanse of grass that Merriman Smith, the renowned United Press International correspondent riding in the fifth car behind the President, will assign a name that will live forever: "the grassy knoll." His words, written within about 20 minutes of the shooting: "Some of the Secret Service agents thought the gunfire was from an automatic weapon fired to the right rear of the President's car, probably from a grassy knoll to which police rushed."

One of the many who has come out to see Kennedy this day is Howard Brennan, a construction worker, who finds a good viewing spot on top of a retaining wall at the corner of Elm and Houston, about a hundred feet from the Book Depository. Lots of people crane for a view from the windows around the plaza, and just before Kennedy's arrival, Brennan notices someone at a window on the sixth floor of that building. Years later he will recall, "It struck me how unsmiling and calm he was. He didn't seem to feel one bit of excitement. His face was almost expressionless."

Key Frames

Frames 155, 156, 208, 209, 210 and 211

Don't look for these frames in the original film. They've been missing for 50 years.

Zapruder's Bell & Howell Model 414 PD Director Series Zoomatic camera, called at the time by *Modern Photography* magazine "undoubtedly one of the finest 8 mm motion picture cameras we have ever seen," used what is called a double 8 mm roll of film, which is really a 33-foot-long roll of 16 mm that yields two 25-foot usable strips of film. After one side of the film was exposed, the cameraman simply flipped it over and used the other side. Once processed, the film was sliced lengthwise, and the two halves spliced together and trimmed, making a 50-foot-long spool of film. The camera not only exposed the individual rectangular movie frames that would be projected onto a screen but also the areas between the sprocket holes (the rectangular openings that let the projector mechanism grab and pull the film past the projection lens). While these areas are not as sharp or clear as those in the main viewing frame, they do include an additional 25 percent of each image.

But on to the missing frames. None of the above had anything to do with their going missing—nor did any selective editing by LIFE or anyone else. LIFE was, however, culpable. After Zapruder had the film developed at the Kodak processing lab on Manor Way in Dallas, duplicate copies were run off at the Jamieson Film Company on Bryan Street. Yet when making the three copies asked for, the technician set the machine for "picture only," and the duplicates reproduced only the images in the projected area and not what was found in the perforated sections. It's worth noting: Of the three copies, only the one given to the Secret Service, which is housed at the National Archives, is wholly intact. That's Zapruder film trivia for the many who care.

Zapruder died in 1970, five years before LIFE returned ownership of the film to his heirs, and in 1999 the U.S. government took ownership of the film—after a good deal of money changed hands. But the film lacked Frames 155 and 156 as well as Frames 208 to 211. Why? These could have been important images. Part of the first sequence takes place a third of a second before the House Select Committee on Assassinations said the first shot was fired from the Texas School Book Depository building's window. The images for Frames 208 through 211 correspond with when it is believed the shooter would have been able to clearly see the President, right after his car passed under a tree. But in the film: splice lines.

LIFE admitted its role long ago, saying in 1967 that its photo lab had inadvertently ruined some of the frames. Existing records at the company do not offer any further details. Now, there *are* the prints (which don't include the areas between the film's sprocket holes)—and we have included them here in place of the missing frames in hopes of presenting the complete picture. But needless to say, such decisions have never satisfied everyone, and we doubt that they will today.

Frame 161

The Warren Commission in 1964 determined that the first shot was fired no earlier than the action seen in Frame 210. But as we know more than a decade later (not to mention, 50 years later), there was still controversy and doubt, and in 1979 the House Select Committee on Assassinations indeed reached a different conclusion—that the first shot may have issued as Frame 161 was being made. One indisputable conclusion: There is no single frame proving that *this* is when the shot went off, so assumptions are based on the reactions of those in the film, as well as witnesses' descriptions of the moment. By Frame 200, Rosemary Willis, above, in the white sweater and red skirt, turns toward the Texas School Book Depository, Kennedy briefly looks over at his wife as if something has attracted his attention. Mrs. Kennedy meanwhile looks back at him.

Governor Connally told the Warren Commission about these moments: "I thought it was a rifle shot. I have hunted enough to think that my perception with respect to directions is very, very good, and this shot I heard came from back over my right shoulder, which was in the direction of the School Book Depository, no question about it."

Frame 188

z188

Dallas residents Phil Willis, a salesman at a local Lincoln Mercury showroom, his wife, Marilyn, and her parents took Phil and Marilyn's daughters, Linda and Rosemary, out of school to see the President. Willis, who had been a young officer at Pearl Harbor in 1941, brought his Argus Autronic I camera with him. President Kennedy's limousine comes rolling along at 11 miles per hour, and as Willis takes a picture, Rosemary, the girl in the white sweater, runs along the grass to see the President. It was at this point, as the car was about to be blocked from Abraham Zapruder's view by a street sign, that Willis and others hear a gunshot. "I cocked my camera for another picture and this loud shot went off," recalled Willis later, "and the first reaction was that it could be a crank or a firecracker, but it was so loud and of such a sound it had to be [a] rifle so I became alarmed." Rosemary, a few frames on, can be seen abruptly stopping; she later remembered that at first she thought it was a firecracker, but quite quickly "I knew it was a gunshot . . . I think I probably turned to look toward the noise, toward the Texas Book Depository . . . I stopped when I heard the shot."

Howard Brennan, the construction worker who had happened to notice the dispassionate man in the sixth floor window moments earlier, also hears the rifle shot at this point, and looks back up at the building. "What I saw made my blood run cold!" he wrote years later. "Poised in the corner window of the sixth floor was the same young man I had noticed several times before the motorcade arrived. There was one difference—this time he held a rifle in his hands, pointing toward the presidential car . . . I wanted to cry, I wanted to scream, but I couldn't utter a sound." It is apparently Brennan's description of the shooter—"white male about 30, slender build"—that is first broadcast over police channels. Patrolman J.D. Tippit hears the bulletins that are issued, and whether it is this information or simply intuition that prompts him to confront Oswald on 10th Street is known only to him, and he is dead. After shooting Tippit, Oswald holes up at the Texas Theatre, where *War Is Hell!* is playing. There, he is captured. That evening, Brennan declines to identify him in a lineup. He later explains that he was afraid others were involved.

Robert Croft, a Mormon missionary, is in town briefly on his way to Denver. He has some time before his train connection and, after hearing others talking about Kennedy's visit, decides to go have a look and maybe take some pictures. In Zapruder's film he can be seen wearing a cape or raincoat and standing near Phil Willis, our car salesman. Some who have seen Croft's image have fingered him as a possible conspirator, perhaps concealing a weapon under his cloak. What Croft is carrying, though, is an Argus C3 35 mm camera. He photographs the motorcade, and later says that he had "just kind of followed the car along" as it went down Elm. One of his pictures is of the President and Jackie, who is holding the red roses she received that morning at Love Field. Croft takes four photos of the motorcade, the last of which would have corresponded with Zapruder's Frame 313 of the fatal shot— but the picture turned out blank.

Frame 210

A sign for the Stemmons Freeway stands alongside Elm Street, and starting at Frame 200 Governor Connally—and then at Frame 210, President Kennedy—are obscured from Zapruder's view. Not only is there nothing sinister about this, but even in 1963, a time before cameraphones, there were many others taking pictures in Dealey Plaza that day. Patsy Paschall, John Martin, Mark Bell, Marie Muchmore, Orville Nix, Robert Hughes, Tina Towner, Elsie Dorman—who was filming from the fourth floor of the Texas School Book Depository building—and Charles Bronson are shooting home movies, while Jay Skaggs, Richard Bothun, Hugh Betzner, Robert Croft, Phil Willis and Mary Moorman are making still pictures. Those are only the ones we know: At least three in the crowd who clearly had cameras of one sort or another have never been firmly identified, and their pictures remain unseen by the general public. So while the Stemmons sign briefly blocks Zapruder's view of the motorcade, there is some other documentary evidence of what was happening during these 11 frames—these two-thirds of a second.

z223

Frame 223

Kennedy and Connally have been hit at this point. They are emerging from behind the sign, and Jackie looks at JFK, who, onlookers note, appears to be in pain. Linda Willis, the older daughter of Phil and Marilyn, told the Warren Commission how the President "grabbed his throat, and he kind of slumped forward." According to the Warren Commission and the House committee, a single bullet traveled through JFK's upper back, out his throat and into Connally's shoulder. It then broke the governor's fifth right rib, exited through his chest, struck his wrist, fractured the bone, and ended up in his left thigh. Connally described it "as if someone doubled his fist and came up behind you and just with about a 12-inch blow hit you right in the back right below the shoulder blade." In Frames 229 and 230 in the complete film, the stricken Connally is seen flipping up his Stetson hat.

Frame 228

While the Warren Commission and the House Select Committee on Assassinations determined that Oswald was the killer of Kennedy, the House committee determined further that there was a high probability that there had been two gunmen and that the President "was probably assassinated as a result of a conspiracy." Lots of folks, including some Kennedys, agree.

Of the many conspiracy theories, 10 of which will be delineated by J.I. Baker a few pages further on, one that is intriguing and also has something of a photographic record is that of the Umbrella Man. In this sequence of Zapruder's film, the top of an umbrella can be seen rising and turning clockwise as the motorcade makes its way past the Stemmons Freeway sign. The House committee wanted to find the man holding the umbrella on a sunny day, and it released Dealey Plaza images to help identify him. In 1978, a coworker of Louie Witt

at a Dallas insurance company came forward—and so, eventually, did Witt, who was no fan of the Kennedys. Witt's esoteric Neville Chamberlain explanation (Joe Kennedy had been an appeaser of the Nazis, as had the former British prime minister, who always carried an umbrella, and so the umbrella was an anti-appeasement and an anti-Kennedy protest) didn't wash with everybody, and the theory developed that the

Umbrella Man was part of a plot by the military and/or intelligence community to kill the President—he was perhaps signaling to his colleague assassins, or even using the umbrella to fire a dart to immobilize or kill

Kennedy. Robert Cutler in a 1978 edition of the *Grassy Knoll Gazette* called Witt "a liar," and ran illustrations of what he believed such a poison-dart-launching umbrella could look like.

Frame 262

Secret Service agent Roy Kellerman, who is seated in the front passenger seat, will recall later that the last thing the President said after he had been wounded was, "My God, I am hit." Kennedy had raised his arms into a locked position in front of himself. Jackie later said that when this happened, her husband made "these terrible noises" and "he had this sort of quizzical look on his face, and his hand was up." Viewing the scene through his viewfinder and not initially comprehending what was going on, Zapruder thought Kennedy was making light of the sound of an explosion. "I heard the first shot and I saw the President lean over and grab himself like this," he said, holding his left chest area. "For a moment I thought it was, you know, like you say, 'Oh, he got me,' when you hear a shot—you've heard these expressions—and then I saw . . . I don't believe the President is going to make jokes like this."

On the film, at almost the same moment that President Kennedy recoils, Governor Connally's cheeks can be seen puffing out, further suggesting the moment when he has been wounded. "I just pulled him over into my . . . he was in my arms," said Nellie Connally of her efforts to help her husband. "I put my head down over his head so that his head and my head were right together."

In these moments lies one of the deepest divides as to what really had happened. Was Kennedy shot, as the Warren Commission and the House committee determined, by one gunman whose bullet passed through two men, or were there two gunmen whose shots individually struck Kennedy and Connally at roughly the same instant? The weapon that Oswald reportedly used was a Mannlicher-Carcano rifle, model 91/38, which he bought by mail order earlier that

year for $21.45. The Italian-made weapon was a bolt-action rifle that required the shooter to eject a spent case and load a new 6.5 mm cartridge before another shot could be taken. That takes speed and dexterity, but Oswald was well practiced with the weapon; his widow, Marina, recalled how he spent hours loading and unloading the chamber and handling the gun, even in the dark. There were between six and nine seconds between the first and last shots, which is plenty of time for someone proficient with the Mannlicher-Carcano to load, aim and shoot. But since only one bullet could be shot with each load, and tests with the weapon showed a minimum of 2.3 seconds between shots, there was no way someone could fire more than one shot faster than that and wound both men, as some

evaluations of the film seemed to show.

The point that many single-gunman theorists make: There is no evidence of bullets from different weapons. This, they say, clearly indicates the presence of just one assassin. The first bullet fired (perhaps in the frames numbered in the 160s) was never found. It most likely ricocheted off an overhead street light or a thick tree branch, and nicked a curb at the triple underpass, where it knocked off a bit of concrete that cut James Tague's cheek (Tague had been heading for lunch with his future wife and had stopped to watch the motorcade)—making him the third person to have been wounded that day in Dealey Plaza. Fragments exist of the bullet that hit JFK's head. The only intact bullet is the one that the Warren Commission and the House committee

said passed through the two men. The metal from it and the third bullet seem to be of the same type (though there is debate about this).

J.I. Baker will get into the "Magic Bullet" or "Pristine Bullet" theories—how, possibly, that bullet could not have been destroyed as it passed through two men, in the process shattering one of Connally's ribs and fracturing his wrist. The bullet was found on the stretcher after Connally was moved to major surgery in the hospital, and its presence there and not still in his body has caused some to say that it was conveniently planted. But then again, it was military grade ammo, made from stronger metal than that used in handguns; it is slightly flattened at the base, and its markings match the rifling of Oswald's Mannlicher-Carcano.

Frame 285

Another interesting character who is seen in the Zapruder film, and who will be mentioned by J.I. Baker, is the woman dubbed the Babushka Lady. The shawl-covered woman stood across the street from Zapruder, holding a camera. In 1970, Beverly Oliver claimed to be the mysterious draped maiden. A 17-year-old singer at Dallas's Colony Club, next to Jack Ruby's Carousel Club in 1963, Oliver came forth to claim that federal officials had confiscated her movie film three days after the shooting. She also stated that she had been introduced to Oswald as well as Ruby.

Frame 298

On the grass across Elm Street stand Jean Hill in a red coat and Mary Moorman in a dark blue coat. The two women not only came out to see Kennedy but also to see friends of theirs. Hill knew Billy Martin, one of the motorcycle patrolmen flanking Kennedy's car, and Moorman knew George Lumpkin, one of the three lead motorcyclists ahead of the motorcade. Moorman snapped a picture of Lumpkin with her Polaroid Highlander camera and then took a picture that closely corresponds with Zapruder Frames 315 and 316, just a sixth of a second after the fatal shot. Like a few others who photographed the shooting, Moorman licensed her picture to at least one news agency, in her case United Press International, that weekend. In Moorman's picture there can be seen, according to some, one or more figures on the grassy knoll behind the stockade fence. No such gunmen have ever been confirmed, and Hill, who was interviewed by the sheriff that day, told them that she heard five or six shots, and said, "I thought I saw some men in plain clothes shooting back but everything was such a blur." Later she claimed that she saw Jack Ruby running near the Texas School Book Depository even though his whereabouts—he was at *The Dallas Morning News*—were later firmly established.

Key Frames

z313

Frame 313

This was the awful vision that Zapruder saw through his lens and that others in the plaza witnessed. At this point one can see Kennedy being struck in the head by the fatal shot. "I saw his head opened up and the blood and everything came out," said Zapruder later. Nellie Connally did not look back when she heard this shot, but told how she could sense it. "It felt like spent buckshot falling all over us, and then, of course, I too could see that it was the matter, brain tissue, or whatever, just human matter, all over the car and both of us."

Beyond the blood, Kennedy's body can be seen recoiling in response. Supporters of a second-shooter theory point to the direction that his head moved, noting that it lurched backward as if struck from the front or the side and not from behind, where the Texas School Book Depository stands. There are different theories on why he moved to the left and backward so violently. One theory holds that an object being struck from behind by a high-powered military rifle might naturally be pushed forward by the force of the blow. In fact, Kennedy's head appears to move slightly forward for a frame or so before jerking back, and it is possible that the effect of being hit was countered by his body's own neurological and muscular response, which caused his body to move to the rear. This conjecture will surely never end. A last note: This is the frame LIFE decided not to run in November 1963.

Frames 333, 359 and 367

Roy Kellerman, who is seated just ahead of Governor Connally and the President, gets on the Secret Service radio channel immediately as the shots ring out. More than a dozen agents rode in the motorcade's first four cars; three are seen actively trying to do something. When Rufus Youngblood, who is riding in the car with Lyndon Johnson, Lady Bird Johnson and Texas senator Ralph Yarborough hears gunfire, he jumps over the seat and uses his own body to shield the Vice President. Thomas Johns, who is in the car behind Johnson's, leaps out of his car and runs forward. Clint Hill, the agent assigned to the First Lady, later recalled looking at the crowd on the lawn when the assassination

started: "The sound came from my right rear and I immediately moved my head in that direction. In so doing, my eyes had to cross the presidential automobile and I saw the President hunch forward and then slump to his left. I jumped from the follow-up car and ran toward the presidential automobile. I heard a second firecracker-type noise, but it had a different sound—like the sound of shooting a revolver into something hard." Blood, flesh and bits of bone splatter on him as he races to the President's car and hears Mrs Kennedy's anguished yell, "My God! They've shot his head off!"

Seen here, Hill is grabbing on to the car in Frame 359 and gets a foothold in Frame 367.

Key Frames

z387

Frame 387

As Hill runs, the First Lady scrambles toward the trunk of the car. Early reports indicated that she was either attempting to escape or help Hill onto the car. What she actually might have been doing was trying to grab part of her husband's head that had landed on the back of the car. When the car reaches Parkland Memorial Hospital, Dr. Marion "Pepper" Jenkins revealed years later, Jackie will hand to the doctors some of her husband's brain and ask, "Will this help?"

Hill made it onto the trunk and briefly touches Jackie's right arm as she then returns to her dying husband's side to comfort him. She weeps, "Jack, Jack, what have they done to you?" while Nellie Connally holds her own bleeding husband, saying to him "It's all right. Be still." Hill clutches the trunk and yells to driver William Greer, "To the hospital, to the hospital!"

Frames 347 and 412

Conspiracy theorists claimed that a round object at the bottom of Frame 412 is a gunman. The House Select Committee on Assassinations determined it was the back of the head of a bystander on the steps, and his "rifle" was the branch of the bush.

What is otherwise happening: Pandemonium is breaking out as it becomes clear what has happened. "I fell to the ground to keep from being hit myself," Moorman said that day. Charles Brehm, who is standing with his five-year-old son, Joe, in Frame 285 in front of the Babushka Lady, said, "I didn't know what was going on, so I just grabbed the boy and fell on him, and hoped that it wasn't a maniac around."

James Altgens, an Associated Press photographer, had been taking pictures, standing about 15 feet from the President's car when the third shot went off. "This was such a shock to me that I never did press the trigger on the camera. The sight was unbelievable." Malcolm Summers, who can be seen falling in Frame 347, told the sheriff the following day, "I hit the ground as I realized these were shots. Then all of the people started running up the terrace away from the President's car and I got up and started running also, not realizing what had happened."

z347

Frame 474

Zapruder, with his Bell & Howell, continues to follow the car as it races out of Dealey Plaza through the triple underpass and, thence, to Parkland Memorial Hospital. His lens is now pointed to the west side of the plaza, where a stockade fence separates the plaza from a parking area. Some have spied at this point in the film what looks like a man's head and shoulders through the tree branches. Also, witnesses have stated that at least one shot came from the area closer up and away from the Depository building, and that a shooter was stationed not far from where Zapruder had stood. They argue further that if someone had come to see the President that day, they wouldn't have watched from so far back—so such a person must have had an ulterior purpose.

Stabilized blowups of the area do seem to show a shape through the trees, but the action occurring here is happening so quickly, and what with the leaves being blown—well, it is simply not possible to know what, if anything, is there.

There, then: the Zapruder film. It will be dissected again, now, on the 50th anniversary of the assassination, and many will say, "This proves that . . ."

As for what the film did to and for the man who shot it, that story follows.

DANIEL S. LEVY, for years a reporter at *Time* and *People* magazines, is a writer-reporter on *The Day Kennedy Died*.

The Zapruder Legacy

The film developed a life of its own. Meantime, the man who took it and his family had to come to terms with a very strange modern kind of fame.

ALEXANDRA ZAPRUDER describes how her grandfather's film changed his life.

I NEVER KNEW MY GRANDFATHER Abraham Zapruder, who is known to the world as the author of the home movie of President Kennedy's assassination. He died when my twin brother and I were 10 months old and, although my three living grandparents were much-loved figures in my life, I felt his absence keenly. He was the missing one. My sense of him was almost mythical, formed by funny stories told about him, his expressions and catchphrases that were part of our family lexicon, a few photographs around my grandmother's house, and my father's evident sadness when his name came up. At the same time, I was dimly aware that our grandfather was important outside our family, too. I knew that he had done something big, something for which he was famous, but something that, in our family at least, no one tended to talk about. I don't know when I learned what "it" was, but I know that for most of my life, it existed in the background, a sort of shadow that I accepted without question the way that children do.

Now, as an adult, I have found myself drawn to my grandfather's story and how he so suddenly and violently intersected with one of the most important events of the 20th century. It is a story of chance and coincidence, without precedent in American history and with implications that reverberated far beyond anything anyone could have imagined at the time. In fact, over the decades, the Zapruder film has become not only evidence and artifact, but collective memory and cultural icon; artistic, literary and popular reference point; symbol of the limits of visual representation and truth; ancestor of citizen journalism and possibly even reality television; and endless source of vexing questions about privacy, ownership and the public's right to information. But while there is much to consider about the accidental legacy of the Zapruder film, I often think about my grandfather himself, the questions I would have asked him if I could, and the way he might have told his own story. (He didn't particularly want to tell it, in fact, and he might not even have approved of my doing so in this essay. Yet I imagine he would have grudgingly agreed that it is the duty and the right of children to ask questions, even questions that might be in opposition to family culture and habit.) For if, in today's world anyone can see what Abraham Zapruder saw through the lens of his camera, it is much harder to uncover and understand what it must have meant to be the man holding the camera that day, and to be irrevocably bound to a historical moment fraught with shame, loss and inconceivable horror. This essay, then, offers a glimpse of Abraham Zapruder before and after that critical moment in Dallas and how the event that changed the nation also changed his life and legacy.

A braham Zapruder, seen opposite in Dallas's Fair Park in the 1940s in a family photo supplied to LIFE by his granddaughter, was always dapper (in fact, this photograph is atypical as Zapruder often sported a bow tie). At left is an aerial view of Dealey Plaza as it existed in 1964. The Texas School Book Depository, a seven-story, 80,000-square-foot brick warehouse at 411 Elm Street, is seen here with a Hertz sign on its roof. The so-called "sniper's nest" was on the sixth floor—just below the top floor—behind the window seen here at far right. Oswald peered through his sight at the motorcade weaving through the plaza, like the traffic seen here, headed for the underpass. The grassy knoll and the wall where Zapruder positioned himself are at left. The dark car seen here in the center lane of the curving street is close to where JFK was mortally wounded. Zapruder's offices and those of several other dress manufacturers were in the Dal-Tex building, which in this picture is just above and across the street from the Texas School Book Depository.

The Zapruder Legacy

ON THE MORNING OF NOVEMBER 22, 1963, Abraham Zapruder went to work as he always did at his office at Jennifer Juniors, a dress manufacturing company located in the Dal-Tex building at 501 Elm Street in downtown Dallas. The city was alive with excitement about President Kennedy's visit. But even though his building was just adjacent to the route that the motorcade would take through the city, and even though he was an avid home moviemaker, he had not brought his camera with him. He had left it at home in part because of rainy weather that morning, and in part because he thought, pessimistically, that he would not get near enough to the President to even see him, let alone film him. As the morning wore on, the clouds gave way to warm fall sunshine. His longtime assistant, Lillian Rogers, nudged him to get the camera. "You ought to go home," she told him, "you're the one that makes the beautiful movies." He resisted. She pressured him for a few more minutes, reminding him that it was a once-in-a-lifetime opportunity. When he continued to hesitate, she gave up and went back to work. A few moments later she returned to his office and found that he was gone. Where? Home to get the camera, of course.

Most of my grandfather's home movies are unremarkable to anyone outside his own family. He shot beach scenes at Far Rockaway, family gatherings in Brooklyn, and eternal sequences of his infant daughter having a bath, eating in her high chair and learning to walk. But if these movies are of little historic significance, they have the familiarly wistful, nostalgic quality of their genre. They capture a fleeting, tantalizing peek at a life before ours, a time now irretrievably lost. They remind us that our grandparents and great-grandparents inhabited the world fully, seamlessly, exactly as we do—even if the clothes and the buildings and the cars are different—and that those lives now exist only in momentary glimpses and jerky, too-short film clips. So will it be for all of us.

For my grandfather Abe, who had come to this country as an emigrant from Russia at age 15 and who left behind poverty, anti-Semitism and a futureless fate, America had fulfilled its many promises. Like countless new arrivals before him, he had lived in a Brooklyn tenement, attended night school to learn English, and went to work on Seventh Avenue in the needle trades. Within 15 years, he and my grandmother were married and fled the tenements for an apartment in a small building on Park Place in Brooklyn. His two sisters and their husbands, as well as his parents, occupied the rest of the building. From the beginning, he had embraced his new American identity as fully and completely as anyone could. Photos of him and my grandmother from these years show a handsome young couple, always well-dressed and smiling, surrounded by the early trappings of the good life—vacations with friends in the Catskills and the Finger Lakes, around the seder table at Passover, on their honeymoon in Niagara Falls in 1933. Two children followed and, by 1941, Abe and Lillian Zapruder, with the children in tow, had left the familiar world of Brooklyn for the new frontier of Dallas, Texas, home of Neiman Marcus, to pursue a business opportunity in its burgeoning fashion industry. By 1963, two decades later, Abe Zapruder was firmly established in the middle class. He owned his own business, had seen both of his children educated and married, and was living a comfortable life and enjoying his many pleasures—playing piano and violin, making home movies, spending time with friends, traveling with his wife and tinkering around the house.

Like most immigrant Jews of his generation who had narrowly escaped life under a repressive and autocratic regime, my grandfather also embraced socially progressive ideas and liberal values. He and his family had been for Kennedy from the beginning. His grown daughter, Myrna, had volunteered in the 1960 Kennedy campaign and sold poll tax in a supermarket in South Dallas to register black voters. They joined the millions who not only supported the President's Democratic political agenda but adored his exquisite wife and family. Photos of the period show my grandmother, aunt and mother dressed exactly like Jackie, from the tailored suits and high-heeled pumps right down to the dark curled hair and pearls. And just weeks before the President's visit to Dallas, my newly married parents had moved to an apartment in southwest Washington, D.C., so my father could begin his career as a lawyer working in the Tax Division of the Justice Department under Kennedy's administration.

By the time my grandfather returned to Jennifer Juniors with his movie camera, Kennedy's motorcade was about to pass by Dealey Plaza. Nearly everyone in the office went down to watch. It took a little time for him to find just the right spot for filming. He tried out several locations and rejected them until he noticed a concrete abutment that would offer a good vantage point for the motorcade, which would swing left from Houston Street and travel down Elm. But since he suffered from vertigo, the combination of standing on the narrow ledge several feet up and looking through the zoom lens made him feel dizzy. He asked his receptionist, Marilyn Sitzman, to stand behind him and keep him steady.

The original reel of Kodachrome II 8 mm color film that ran through his Bell & Howell 414 PD Director Series Zoomatic camera begins with a minute of his young grandchildren playing outside. They are smiling and waving at the camera. Then, the film cuts to a series of choppy scenes inside his office, with Lillian Rogers mugging for the camera, trying on clothes and pretending to make him wait while talking on the phone. Suddenly, we are outside on Dealey Plaza, where the film shows Marilyn Sitzman waving to the camera and payroll clerk Beatrice Hester and her husband, Charles, sitting on a bench. The next sequence begins with a group of official motorcycles rounding the turn from Houston to Elm Street but then breaks off. When the image flickers to life again, the now-famous series of images begins to roll.

"And then I watched for the arrival of the cars, I saw the motorcycles, and then the car approached," my grandfather recalled in a 1966 interview. "As they turned I started shooting the pictures, they turned from Houston Street to Elm Street, and I was shooting as they were coming along, and Jacqueline and the President were waving, and as it came in line with my camera, I heard a shot. I saw the President lean over to Jacqueline, I didn't realize what had happened, actually, then the second shot came. And then I realized, I saw his head open up, and I started yelling, 'They killed him, they killed him!' And I continued shooting until they went under the underpass."

Amid the chaos that followed, my grandfather didn't remember getting down from the ledge or exactly what happened next. It seems that he remained on the plaza for some time, distraught and in a daze, with his camera still in his hand and the case slung over his shoulder. There, Harry McCormick of *The Dallas Morning News,* who had rushed over from the Dallas Trade Mart when he heard of the shooting, noticed my grandfather holding the camera and approached him with a few questions. When my grandfather refused to answer, saying that he would not talk to anyone but the federal authorities, McCormick promised to find the Dallas chief of the Secret Service and bring him to Jennifer Juniors.

Meanwhile, my grandfather somehow made his way back to his office. "Well, I was in a state of shock when I got back," he remembered, "and I was kicking and banging the desk, I couldn't understand how a thing like this could happen. I personally have never seen anybody killed in my life, and to see something like this, shooting a man down like a dog, I just couldn't believe." He relinquished the camera, and Lillian put it in the safe. Overwhelmed, he called my father in Washington for advice. They agreed that he would try to get the film to the federal authorities at once.

If it is one of the hallmarks of November 22, 1963, that no American who was alive that day would be unmarked by the events, an attendant phenomenon is that many very normal people, just going about their business that day, would—because of all the unanswered questions—become eternal players, famous and less so, in one of the nation's most-dramatic-ever stories. Abraham Zapruder certainly was one of those people; it is very unlikely that his name would signify today to any beyond family and friends had he not been where he was, when he was, with that camera. Many professional and amateur theorists and historians who continue to study the Kennedy assassination also know the names of not only Marilyn Sitzman but Beatrice and Charles Hester, who accompanied Zapruder that day. On the opposite page, we see the film's lead-in frames described by Alexandra Zapruder in her essay. Abraham is trying out his new toy on his friends and colleagues, making sure his take-up reel is operating properly. He tests the camera and spring by filming Sitzman beside a bench at the north pergola in Dealey Plaza. Seated on the bench are the Hesters. Zapruder then turns his attention to the motorcycles that herald the motorcade's arrival into the plaza.

The Zapruder Legacy

This is a view of the pergola on the north side of Elm Street in Dealey Plaza moments after shots have felled President John F. Kennedy and Texas governor John Connally, who are in the presidential motorcade. The man with his back to the camera in the shadows at left, barely discernible, is Abraham Zapruder, and alongside him, even harder to see, is Marilyn Sitzman. Charles and Beatrice Hester are sitting on the ground. As said earlier: They are all now being drawn, unwittingly, into a narrative from which they will never escape. Charles Hester,

for instance, will give a "voluntary statement" on "Not Under Arrest Form No. 86" later this day to the sheriff's department of the County of Dallas: "My wife, Beatrice and I were sitting on the grass on the slope on Elm Street where the park is located. When President Kennedy's car got almost down to the underpass, I heard two shots ring out. Thye [sic] sounded like they came from immediately behind us and over our heads. We did [not?] see the shooting. I immediately turned and looked at the Texas Book Depository building and did not see anyone. The shots sounded like the [sic]

definitely came from in or around the building. I grabbed my wife because I didn't know where the next shot was coming from and dragged her up next to the concrete imbankment [sic] and threw her down on the ground and got on the ground with her. Then there was utter confusion. The Police rushed toward the railroad tracks and I finally found an officer to go to the Texas Book Depository Building. The officer I contacted was Officer Wiseman of the Dallas Sheriff's Department."

Around the world, people would soon be reacting and acting. Charles Hester already had.

JAMES ALTGENS/AP

The rest of the day must have been a blur. The Dallas police and the Secret Service turned up at Jennifer Juniors, together with two news reporters. Soon after, my grandfather took his film (in the company of his partner, Erwin Schwartz, Secret Service agent Forrest Sorrels and news reporter Harry McCormick) to the offices of the *Dallas Morning News* and then to the studios at WFAA-TV to try to get the film developed. When they were unable to do it, the group traveled to the Kodak labs, where the film was processed. Agent Sorrels and Harry McCormick left to tend to other matters while my grandfather and Erwin took the film to Jamieson Film Company to have three duplicates made, and then returned to Kodak so the additional rolls could be developed. By day's end, there was the original and three copies of the film: My grandfather gave one to the Dallas Secret Service and another was put on a plane bound for the FBI in Washington, D.C. He returned home late that night with his camera, one "first-day" copy and the original film.

When he arrived home, he found his wife, his daughter and son-in-law waiting for him. It was Friday night, a time when my grandmother typically made dinner for the whole family but, of course, no one was cooking that night. His daughter, Myrna, recalled what happened next. He walked in the door, and before taking off his hat or saying a word, he got his movie projector, set it up in the den, and showed the film to his shocked wife and son-in-law. Myrna refused to watch and remained in the living room. I can only imagine what words passed between him and my grandmother in the aftermath of that moment. Then, before he could fall into bed that night, shell-shocked and exhausted, he answered a phone call from Richard Stolley of LIFE magazine. This short conversation led to a meeting between Mr. Stolley and my grandfather on Saturday morning, and, in very short order, the sale of the film's print rights to LIFE. Within a week, images from the film in LIFE would be in the living rooms of people around the country and everyone would share in the horror that it depicted. Eventually, it would become the world's memory of the assassination itself. But, in that moment in the Zapruder home, it was still my grandfather's home movie. Perhaps sharing it with his family that night was a necessary act, his only way of conveying the enormity of what he had witnessed and the awful reality of what had happened to the President and to the world that day.

Throughout the next several days, Abe Zapruder's family, like the nation, was wrapped up in grief for the Kennedy family. Myrna recalled that in her state of shock, all she could do was cry and watch television for four days straight. My parents were equally devastated. Throughout my life, I heard the story of how they, like tens of thousands of people, waited in line all night to pay their respects to the young President, filing past his body lying in state in the rotunda of the Capitol in Washington. Their experience was entirely typical of most Americans that weekend. For them, as Myrna put it, "the focus was on the loss of Kennedy, not on the film." But if for the family, the film was not the point, Myrna recalled that for her father, "it became the total point. Because the phones never stopped ringing."

Through the rest of the weekend, my grandfather felt mounting pressure to dispose of the moving picture rights to the film, as well. While no one from the federal government contacted him, or requested anything, reporters hounded him mercilessly, calling at all hours, even showing up at the house in the middle of the night. After receiving another call from Richard Stolley, my grandfather agreed to discuss the moving picture rights to the film on Monday, but not until after the President's funeral. His regular attorney was out of town, so he contacted Sam Passman, his son-in-law's uncle, for help in the matter. Sam recalled in a private family interview in 1994 that other news outlets besides LIFE were interested in bidding on the film—including AP and CBS News in the form of Dan Rather—but that "Abe was really concerned about whether he should sell it or not, whether he

should take the money and so on." His deep ambivalence about the film took shape in a nightmare he had that weekend—and that recurred for the rest of his life—in which he was walking in Times Square and saw, in front of a movie theater, a man hawking tickets to see the cheap thrill of the President's murder on the big screen.

For this reason, my grandfather was in some ways relieved when executives at LIFE decided that they did want the moving picture rights as well. He had already established a relationship with Richard Stolley, and he believed that LIFE would honor his wish to protect the Kennedy family, and Mrs. Kennedy in particular. Many people recalled this aspect of the story later. But Sam Passman may have said it best: "Abe was concerned that the Kennedy family might be harmed in some way, or might be offended, or that certain portions of the pictures would be terribly distasteful. He just didn't want to do anything that might harm them. He was really crazy about the Kennedys, he really was." In fact, he was so worried about its exploitation or misuse that he included a clause in the contract with LIFE that the film be treated in a manner "consonant with good taste and dignity." It is perhaps difficult today to imagine a time when such earnest words could be uttered in a high-stakes negotiation. But if it reminds us of a long ago time, it also suggests my grandfather's feeling of personal responsibility for the home movie he had taken and his ambivalence about sharing it with the public. For to do so was to be confronted with a painful irony: His home movie, taken in homage to the President he admired, ended up instead exposing the details of his gruesome death, robbing him of his dignity and exacerbating the grief of his young widow. It is no wonder that my grandfather forever wished that he had never taken the film.

My grandfather lived for only seven years after the assassination. In many ways, outwardly, his life eventually returned to normal. He continued to work and to travel with my grandmother. He saw the birth of four more grandchildren. He spent time with friends and he played music. But he would never fully escape the consequences of having been behind the camera that day. My father recalled that he no longer took home movies after the assassination, and that he found it very difficult to even look through the lens of a camera. My aunt says that for many months, he talked and thought obsessively about the film. Others say that he was imprinted with a kind of sadness. He certainly continued, periodically, to have nightmares of the President's murder. "The thing comes back every night," he once said.

The film continued to haunt him in other ways. Although he said in no uncertain terms that he never wanted to see it again, he was compelled to do so from time to time. He testified in the Warren Commission hearings in 1964 and in the Clay Shaw trial in 1969, where he openly wept as he watched repeated showings of the film in the presence of the press and a jury in a New Orleans courtroom. And he grew to dread the anniversary of the assassination, as it inevitably came with calls and requests for interviews from the media. In 1966, in a rare interview with radio personality Marvin Scott, he reflected on the lingering effects of the film for him personally. "Well, as I'm standing right here, I believe, I can almost see it as a picture before my eyes," he said. "It's almost three years. It's left in my mind like a wound that heals up and yet there's some pain left as to what happened." At the same time, the most lasting consequence for my grandfather was one that he never lived to see. Fifty years later, his home movie is still known to the world as the Zapruder film, forever linking him and our family name with the graphic collective memory of one of America's darkest days.

ALEXANDRA ZAPRUDER, the author of *Salvaged Pages: Young Writers' Diaries of the Holocaust,* is currently at work on a memoir about her family and its history with the famous film.

"Where Were You When You Heard?"

Everyone was frozen in space and time, and then everyone—or nearly everyone—mourned. Historian **MARTHA HODES** helps us understand what happened to us all in the crucial instant and its aftermath. Following her essay, many world citizens who vividly remember—people as diverse as Nikita Khrushchev's son and Barbra Streisand, Maya Angelou and Tom Brokaw, John Boehner and Olympia Snowe—recount the moment for LIFE.

THAT AUTUMN DAY, PEOPLE WERE AT WORK AS usual, in offices or shops, in factories and on farms. They were grocery-shopping or at home with the children, driving somewhere or walking down the street, in the barbershop or on a lunch break, in a classroom or at football practice. Meanwhile in Dallas, there came a startling blast, then two more.

How did word spread? A reporter in the motorcade used his radiophone to call United Press International, and the first news flash came four minutes later: three shots fired at the President's motorcade. At the hospital, reporters appropriated telephones, and soon the bells on Teletype machines rang out with clattering bulletins. Ten minutes after that, Walter Cronkite interrupted regular television broadcasts: The President was wounded. How fast news traveled in the mid-20th century! Everything was happening in real time, and within half an hour viewers saw Cronkite struggling to remain composed as he told the world: President John F. Kennedy was dead.

It felt like your own heart had stopped and the whole world was standing still. Drivers came to a halt and slumped over the wheel. Along the highways, car after car pulled off. Most people weren't listening to the radio or watching TV when the news came, but anyone who had heard told someone else, and that was the beginning of mourning. Passing on the news was a way not to be alone with what felt unbearable, a way to come to terms with the unimaginable. People knocked on doors and told their neighbors. Shopkeepers told their patrons. Waiters told their customers. Nurses told their patients. People went outside and told other people on the street. Overloaded long-distance telephone lines kept going dead. Principals dismissed schools. Officials lowered flags before being told to do so. People left their lunches unfinished.

Those at work ran to their cars to turn on the radio. People on the street went into bars or gathered outside appliance-store windows. College students rushed to the TV set in the student union. It was television that had captured the young President's charisma, and now it was television that made the mourning instant and communal—a pre-Internet medium that enforced communion (we gathered around the set) rather than isolation.

A little after six p.m. EST, viewers watched men unload the casket from Air Force One. The cameras stayed at a respectful distance, and the broadcasts were in black and white, but people soon knew that the President's widow was still wearing her bloodstained pink suit when she emerged from the plane. Later she made it clear that she wanted to help the world grasp what had happened—she hadn't stayed in the suit unintentionally. Helping everyone understand: That was part of the mourning, too. Before evening, quite nearly the entire nation knew what had happened, if not why. That day, and for three days afterward, the world felt like a small place, everyone telling someone something they knew, or felt.

Kennedy's mourners were Democrats and staunch Republicans. They were physicists and housewives, executives and secretaries, dishwashers and prison inmates, third-graders and nursing-home residents. But the anguish wasn't entirely universal. In Dallas, some expressed glee. In New York, a bar fight broke out between mourners and merrymakers. Some civil-rights opponents wrote nasty letters to Jacqueline Kennedy. Here and there, people vented anti-Catholic sentiments or grumbled about communism; there was finger-pointing, as Tom Wolfe will recall a few pages on.

Mostly, though, the grief *was* predominant—nationwide and even worldwide. In Mexico, a waiter brought a radio to a table of American tourists. Westminster Abbey overflowed with people and prayers. Germans recalled the President proclaiming himself a Berliner. Children in the Soviet Union placed bouquets on his photograph. Tokyo residents stopped Americans in hotel lobbies to say they were sorry. Across the globe, flags flew low and soldiers fired gun salutes. At home, everyone cried: journalists, cabinet members, soldiers, football players. Parents cried in front of their children. Teachers cried in front of their classes.

As we know from what we have already read in this book—and as many of us remember intricately from 50 years ago—on Saturday, the coffin rested in the East Room of the White House. On Sunday, Jack Ruby shot Lee Harvey Oswald on live television. The funeral was on Monday. If you hadn't traveled to Washington, you watched every minute on the screen, the coverage subdued and decorous, with no breaks for weather reports or sportscasts, and no commercials. Echoing the funeral of Abraham Lincoln a century earlier, the public filed past the body in the rotunda of the U.S. Capitol, and the immense procession included a riderless horse. In 1865 a funeral train had traveled 1,700 miles to bring the ceremonies to the people, but in 1963 television brought everything to the people. On television everyone got to see Mrs. Kennedy, composed under her black veil, holding the hands of young Caroline and John Jr. Everyone got to see the little boy, after a whispered reminder from his mother, salute his father's casket.

People knew they were witnessing history; preserving the historic moment was also part of mourning. People wrote down their memories. They wrote letters and asked the recipients not to throw them away. They cut out the gigantic headlines—KENNEDY SLAIN, PRESIDENT SHOT DEAD—and made scrapbooks. Chronicling the catastrophe was another way to try to

CBS/LANDOV

Throughout the pages of this book, and in testimony by some folks later in this chapter, it comes up time and again: The man who told many of us the President had been killed was *CBS News* anchor Walter Cronkite, who was visibly shaken as he did so (opposite). In that day and age, Cronkite was a trusted figure and a nightly presence in countless American households; he brought home how many of us felt. So did the face of this woman in New York City (above), as captured by LIFE's Stan Wayman. Across the nation, journalists and photojournalists were fanning out wherever they were stationed, trying to capture the reaction. (We'll hear from some of them— Gay Talese, Tom Wolfe, Jimmy Breslin—a few pages on.) Right: Passersby monitor developments outside a television studio in Washington, D.C.

"Where Were You . . ."

The story was in Dallas, of course, and parts of it would move to the nation's capital. But the story was so immense, so all-affecting, that it might be anywhere; as Martha Hodes points out in her essay, the grief was global. In the photograph at left, commuters head home from New York City. LIFE's Carl Mydans, who made this picture, was one of our storied photographers. He had spent time in a Japanese POW camp during World War II, and, after being released in a prisoner-exchange, went on to make famous photos of MacArthur coming ashore and then the Japanese surrender. On November 22, 1963, he was—like Stan Wayman, who had found the shocked woman on the previous page—working in the magazine's offices in midtown Manhattan. What to do? On a train heading to the suburbs north of the city, he found his photograph. Bottom row, from left: Kohei Hanami, former commander of the Japanese destroyer *Amagiri,* which rammed PT-109 during World War II, learns what has happened; French policemen read newspaper reports of Kennedy's assassination; in West Berlin, where, in a seminal cold war speech four months earlier, JFK had famously declared, "All free men, wherever they may live, are citizens of Berlin, and, therefore as a free man, I take pride in the words *Ich bin ein Berliner!*" As Sergei Khrushchev will testify just a few pages on, even behind the Iron Curtain there was regret—and also worry.

comprehend it all. Maybe tomorrow, when we open the footlocker, we will understand.

When the leader of a democratic nation dies, the citizens realize that another leader will follow. But JFK was not just our leader, he was family, too. If Lincoln had seemed like a father, Jack Kennedy was father, brother and son. Many people *loved* Kennedy—that was the word inconsolable mourners used when they wrote letters to Jackie, explaining their sorrow and outrage. Survivors of the *Titanic* sent condolences to Mrs. Kennedy. Holocaust survivors offered comfort. One housewife included her telephone number in case Jackie just wanted to talk. This was personal.

Even as patriotism deepened, just as it did more recently after 9/11, people worried for the nation. Black Americans and their allies looked back on a year of violence: the fire hoses and police dogs, the murder of Medgar Evers, the death of four little black girls in a church bombing. Was it the political atmosphere, they wondered, that had led to the assassination? Just that summer, Kennedy had spoken out for civil rights. A factor? Lincoln's mourners had revered him as George Washington; Kennedy's mourners revered him, now, as Lincoln.

Flags stayed at half-staff for 30 days, as people went back to work and school. In a controversial decision, the NFL games were played the weekend of the funeral. And children, at least, were happy to have their cartoons back on the air. A young black girl who wrote to Jacqueline Kennedy quoted Edna St. Vincent Millay: "Life must go on; / I forget just why."

As the legend deepened, people forgot the man's flaws and transgressions, and that, too, was part of mourning. A week after the assassination, Jacqueline Kennedy told LIFE's Theodore H. White how much her husband loved the title song from the Broadway musical *Camelot,* in particular the lines from the reprise about "one brief shining moment"—you will read about that a little further on. Americans were content with LIFE casting John Kennedy as the nation's knight in shining armor. If it was how Mrs. Kennedy wanted her husband remembered, it must have been what everyone else wanted, too, or it wouldn't have taken hold so quickly or resonated so deeply. Maybe the mourners embraced the legend so readily because it was a way to make sense of what otherwise felt so senseless. A President so young and idealistic, his work in the world left cruelly unfinished, all his promise now an unrealized future . . . There wasn't much room left for nuanced assessments. Out of tragedy, the people wanted an enchanted hero whose thousand-day reign could be understood as the nation's brief shining moment.

Of course deification fosters reaction: He wasn't a god, after all. This came with time: intensive criticism of Kennedy's politics, stories of all the reckless philandering, details of the pill-taking that propped up JFK's youthful vigor. If Kennedy was diminished for some, the demystification—the revisionist history of the revisionist history—simply made a hero more human to others.

Over the years came countless books and movies about the President's life and his death. Over the years, too, came the Kennedy Space Center, John F. Kennedy International Airport, the John F. Kennedy Center for the Performing Arts, and more than a hundred schools in the United States and countless streets around the world—each a commemoration, an act of persistent mourning. Each a tangible link to a moment in time, a memory etched. *Where were you when you heard?* Fifty years on, no one who was old enough to be aware has forgotten, and everyone still wants to know where you were—what your own story was.

In the pages that follow, some stories—of shock, horror and even, in instances involving men at work such as Gay Talese and Tom Wolfe, dispassion. The many faces of mourning.

MARTHA HODES, professor of history at New York University, is the author of the forthcoming book *Mourning Lincoln.*

"Where Were You When You Heard?"

All of those who were old enough to remember, still remember vividly. In a project spearheaded
by **AMY LENNARD GOEHNER,** LIFE asked more than two dozen world citizens to cast their gaze back 50 years.
Their reflections—some of them written for these pages, others offered in conversation—follow.
Their testimony is, alternately, passionate and in a few instances dispassionate, poignant or still angry.
In some cases, beginning with Maya Angelou's, that day changed the way we thought about America.

BETTMANN/CORBIS

Maya Angelou, seen here, circa 1970, in San Francisco, felt more a part of the nation after the assassination.

Maya Angelou:
My President

I WAS LIVING IN CAIRO, EGYPT, working as an editor for the *Arab Observer.* The magazine as such was not anti-American, but it wasn't pro-American either. And as I had worked for Martin Luther King and Malcolm, I was young and passionate. So if there was something in the magazine that was anti-American, it was okay with me as long as it wasn't a lie. That's who I was at the time. One of the writers brought me the news. And it just shocked me. I felt the loss. I felt my leader had died.

The only other time I remember feeling that about a non-black person was when I was in high school in San Francisco and I had a great teacher, Miss Kirwin. She received a phone call. She put the phone down and then said, "Young men and young women, in two minutes the telephone will ring. I will answer it and that will be your cue to get up and go to your lockers. Miss Kirwin's students will go to their lockers and take their belongings in silence. And you will leave the building and get onto your means of transportation and go home silently. You must ask yourself in your silence, 'What will we do now?' Because now, I've just been told, your President is dead." And that was President Roosevelt. And I had never thought of him as my President before. He was *the* President. But the way she handled the information, suddenly, he was *my* President. And he was dead. And I, with all the other students in Miss Kirwin's class, we went to our lockers. Silently. Got our belongings. Silently. Silently left the building. And went home. And when I got home I told my mother, and I wept. She asked, "Why are you crying?" I said, "Because my President is dead." She said, "Your President?" I said, "Yes, ma'am. He is my President."

And I had never thought about him in that way before. And when I heard that President Kennedy had been killed, I became an arch-American in Cairo, Egypt. My President is dead. He belonged to me then.

MAYA ANGELOU is a poet, author and historian. Her latest book, *Mom & Me & Mom,* is her seventh autobiography.

In 1977, Jimmy Carter returned the *Resolute* desk to service in the Oval Office, where it had last been used by President Kennedy.

Jimmy Carter: Inheriting His Desk

I WAS STILL A GEORGIA FARMER WHEN JOHN KENNEDY WAS ASSASSINATED. I remember climbing down from the seat of a tractor, unhitching a trailer and walking inside, where I heard the dreadful news. I went outside, wept and prayed for the future of my country.

Later, I was honored to speak at the dedication of his presidential library and remarked that, as the first President born in the 20th century, he embodied the ideals of a generation as few public figures have ever done in history.

He summoned our nation out of complacency, and he set it on a path of excitement and hope. We honored him not just for the things he completed but for the things he set in motion, the energies he released and the ideas and ideals that he espoused.

He had a vision of how America could meet and master the forces of change that he saw around him.

As a southerner, I saw firsthand how the moral leadership of his administration helped to undo the wrongs that grew out of our nation's troubled racial history.

Later, as President, I chose the same desk he had used, and benefited from his foresight in maintaining peace during the cold war and his effective attempts to reduce the threats of a nuclear disaster.

John F. Kennedy brought honor to the high office that he held.

JIMMY CARTER, who wrote the above account years ago and offers it now to LIFE, was the 39th President of the United States and was awarded the 2002 Nobel Peace Prize.

John Boehner: Everyone Came Together

I WAS SITTING IN MY EIGHTH-GRADE CLASS AT STS. PETER & Paul Academy in Reading, Ohio. It was about two or two fifteen in the afternoon. The teacher was Sister Mary Theresa. There wasn't any chaos really, just anxiety. And we all put our heads down on our desks and prayed. That's really my most vivid memory of those days, prayer. Prayed at school, prayed when we got home, went to church. It was quiet around the house for days, mostly because we were all glued to the television watching the news and then the funeral, which was on a Monday. Having the day off from school for the funeral, that's when it really hit home that this was a national tragedy.

Ours was a family of Kennedy Democrats. Not politically—we were conservative—but personally. People liked Kennedy. World War II guy, young family, optimistic. He had gotten us through the Cuban missile crisis. So that's how people took the loss: personally, like a death in the family. There was shock, but great camaraderie. Everyone came together, especially in terms of grieving for Jackie and the kids. I never thought I'd live to see another day like that.

Then 9/11 happened.

JOHN BOEHNER, representative from Ohio, is speaker of the House of Representatives.

"Where Were You . . . ?"

Olympia Snowe:
A New England Remembrance

IT'S DIFFICULT TO FATHOM HOW A DAY THAT STARTS OFF SO UNRE-
markable and even mundane can become so horrific and so profound.

I attended my classes as a junior at Edward Little High School just as I always did, and made my way home. I had lost both of my parents by the time I was nine years old, and at this point I was living with my aunt Mary. She and my uncle Jim had taken me in and were my guardians, even as they had five children of their own. After my uncle also passed away, my aunt was left to raise all of us on her own.

Arriving home, I turned the knob and opened the door, and it was as though I had opened a portal on a world that had become suddenly unrecognizable: the past obliterated with an assassin's muzzle flash. My aunt, who was born in Greece and loved her adopted country, was standing there directly in front of me, weeping with the shock and sorrow of it all. With words choked by emotion, she said, "President Kennedy was killed," and I can still picture the anguish on her face. The America we knew instantly felt like a distant and hazy memory.

I immediately ran to the television—to hear the horrific news and probably also with a desperate, subconscious craving for some kind of explanation for what was clearly an inexplicable act that was perpetrated on an entire nation. After ungluing my disbelieving eyes from the TV and spending some additional moments attempting to work through the unimaginable with my aunt, I left for the nearby library. I made the trip ostensibly to try to do some homework, but in actuality I felt deeply compelled to somehow share in the collective wave of grief that had broken over every American.

I headed directly for the librarian, Mrs. Cody. I asked her if she had seen the news—as if I had to even pose that question—and she said she had. I don't recall the details of the conversation, but we talked for quite some time, and it was comforting to be able to commiserate.

As it was for all Americans, for many days the television became a kind of lifeline connecting me with the collective grief of the country, and the nationwide yearning for answers. It was also just recently that we had lost my uncle. We were still in a state of mourning over his death, which was devastating for our family; and now with President Kennedy's assassination we were in anguish along with the entirety of America.

I will also never forget the way in which First Lady Jackie Kennedy faced those most difficult days. The way in which she carried herself and displayed strength at a time when America was reeling is something that has always stayed with me, and I've recalled her courage at moments of challenge and tragedy in my own life.

OLYMPIA JEAN SNOWE is an American politician and former United States senator from Maine and a member of the Republican Party.

Olympia Snowe, seen here in Portland, Maine, has long been a Republican, but her feelings for JFK are influenced by politics not at all.

Sergei Khrushchev:
A Memory from Moscow

IT WAS EVENING IN MOSCOW AND my father [Soviet premier Nikita Khrushchev] was at home. After dinner, he walked with his paper into the living room. The government phone rang. Evening phone calls to our residence were rare. Father was disturbed at home only in exceptional circumstances. It was the foreign minister, Andrei Gromyko. "Good evening, Comrade Gromyko," said my father, "What's the matter? What's happened?" My father listened intently for a long time, his expression changing to one of deep concern. He finally said to Gromyko in a depressed tone of voice: "Call the ambassador. Find out more. Perhaps it's some mistake. Then call me again right away."

Gromyko had told my father that there were some rumors in the press that President Kennedy had been assassinated. It took some time to hear back because communication at that time was weak, so we waited. Gromyko called back and said the President was dead. My father was very nervous. What happened? Who was behind this assassination? America can be very unpredictable, they can start the war. And there was a fear of the unknown. Remember, it was the cold war, so we thought it might have been someone very conservative and hawkish. It could have meant the threat of the war. My father felt it would be a more dangerous time after Kennedy.

He was very upset, as was I. [Sergei Khrushchev was 28 years old in 1963.] I was close to my father so I shared his reaction. He told Gromyko that we must do everything to show respect, and to send a high-level delegation. My father said he would like to go himself, but he didn't think the U.S. would be very welcoming during this time. So he told his deputy to go there and he would negotiate with President Johnson.

He said that in addition to the official protocol telegram to Johnson, he also wished to send condolences to Kennedy's widow, Jacqueline. Also he asked my mother to write a letter to Jackie. This was unprecedented. My mother had accompanied him on trips, but that was the extent of her role in state affairs. By this gesture, my father wanted to emphasize as far as possible the sincerity and personal nature of his sympathy.

My father wrote to Jacqueline Kennedy: "He inspired great respect in all who knew him, and meetings with him will remain in my memory forever."

The Soviet press was state-controlled. So the news was no sensation, no headline read, KENNEDY DEAD. To us, it was America, the Wild West, they are killing people on the streets all the time.

If we talk about the conspiracy and the theory, there are two things. We knew that Oswald had no connection with the KGB, because when he defected to the Soviet Union, they interrogated him. They found him absolutely useless to them. He tried to apply once more to the Soviet Embassy. My father's assistant, Ambassador Oleg Troyanovsky, told me when I wrote my book that the day after the Assassination, he called the KGB head and told him, "You must be prepared, 'cause the U.S. will ask, 'Who is Oswald?'" My father gave the order to share some of this information with America.

Kennedy was popular among the young people [in the U.S.S.R.]. It's difficult to say why because he was our opponent, our enemy—or adversary, to be more polite. But he and Jackie, their personalities, his youthful style . . . Many young people made their hairdressers style their hair like Kennedy.

In the spring after Kennedy's assassination, Soviet premier Nikita Khrushchev poses in Moscow
on the occasion of his 70th birthday with members of his family. From left: Galina, wife of Sergei; Sergei himself; Premier Khrushchev;
his wife, Nina; their daughter Rada; daughter Yelena; and Aleksei Adzhubei, husband of Rada.

There is a popular misunderstanding that my father thought that Kennedy was weak and too young for office, and that he could manipulate him. My father never thought this. He repeated that Kennedy's foreign policy was different from Eisenhower's. Kennedy didn't ask any advice; his style was closer to Khrushchev's, who was also the master of his foreign policy. So he respected him. The Cuban missile crisis showed that these two leaders preferred negotiations. After the Cuban missile crisis, my father repeated many times that he and Kennedy are very different, because politically they defended their treasures and their system of life. But they have one thing in common: They wanted to prevent war. My father thought that if Kennedy had been in power for the next five years, there was a strong probability that the cold war would come to an end.

President Kennedy did not have the five years that my father counted on.

SERGEI KHRUSHCHEV was a senior fellow at the Watson Institute for International Studies at Brown University from 1996 to 2012. The above account combines an interview with LIFE and excerpts from his book *Nikita Khrushchev and the Creation of a Superpower,* edited together with his permission.

John Lewis:
Civil Rights Visionary

I WAS IN NASHVILLE, TENNESSEE, WHEN I HEARD THE NEWS. I WAS AT the Fisk University campus, returning from a trial that was a result of me being arrested earlier that year for a nonviolent protest. When I heard the news, I was just so sad. I met JFK twice, and the last time I saw him was on August 28, 1963. I often think that if he had lived, history would have been so different. I truly admired him.

I will never, ever forget him. He was such a persuasive speaker; he had the ability to communicate and to inspire, and I miss that in American politicians today. He gave us hope. He was the first President to say that the question of civil rights is not just a legal issue but a moral issue. I often think and believe that when President Kennedy died, something died in all of us.

In 1963, Georgia congressman JOHN LEWIS was chairman of the Student Nonviolent Coordinating Committee (SNCC), which he helped form. He has devoted his life to the human rights struggle ever since.

"Where Were You . . . ?"

Lynda Bird Johnson Robb: The Kennedys' Kindnesses

YOU ASK HOW AND WHEN I FIRST LEARNED. I WAS AT THE University of Texas, a sophomore. I was very excited because I had gotten a ticket for a friend and me to go to the dinner that night for President Kennedy. I was going to get to go to the ranch with President and Mrs. Kennedy and my good friends, the governor and Nellie Connally. I came home at noon to eat at the dorm. I went through the cafeteria line and got lunch, and then I went up to my room and got a call from a former roommate. The way I remember it, she called me and said, "Stay where you are. I'm coming to get you." Then she came to my room and took me over to someone who had a radio. What I remember is they were saying they have a report that the President is shot. I just fell to my knees and started praying and crying. They said they didn't know about the Vice President, and there was speculation that he might have had a heart attack. I just stayed there until we heard this man in the hall. It was a women's dorm and they would notify us when a man came up. One of the dorm mothers brought this man up and he said we had to leave. I think I knew by then that the President had died.

I said, "I want to go to the governor's mansion," because I was thinking the Connallys' three children were there, and their father had been shot, so they didn't have anybody there to comfort them. I also thought it would probably be safer, they had security. While I was there I got a very brief call from my parents telling me that they were all right. They were on their way to Washington. After doing everything I could to comfort the Connally children, I went with the Secret Service over to an apartment that my parents had. We called it the Fifth Floor. It was the top floor of the radio station that my parents owned. My friend spent the night with me so I wouldn't be alone.

I do not remember hearing [from my parents] once they got to Washington—they were just so busy—until Mother talked to me about coming up for the funeral. At that point I did have the television on, and I did see Oswald shot. Having seen "pretend" lots of times, you couldn't imagine that you were seeing it as it happened: a real murder on television.

I went up the next day. I walked with my parents from the White House to the funeral. They didn't want my father to do that because they thought it was too dangerous, but he said he wanted to do it. My thoughts were just what everybody's thoughts were: *This just can't be happening. They couldn't have killed President Kennedy.* I thought so much of him and I thought he was my friend and he liked me particularly. The Kennedys had been very kind to me and [my younger sister] Luci. Mrs. Kennedy had always been very kind to me. She said in a six-page handwritten letter she wrote to Daddy two or three days after [the assassination] that she knew me better because we had shared "step-seats" together. In the Congress, when you have a joint session of Congress, each senator gets [a few] tickets. Her husband had given his tickets away and my father had given his tickets away. So we managed to get in by sitting on the stairs—I'm sure the fire marshal wouldn't have approved. Anyway, this very elegant, beautiful lady and me, sitting on these

Mark Updegrove: Remembering Liz Carpenter's Day

TO BE ACCURATE, I WAS TWO YEARS OLD, SO I DON'T REALLY have a memory of where I was when I heard. But I've talked to a few people who aren't alive anymore, a few people who were there with LBJ on that day. I didn't talk to Lady Bird, but her quote about this is the best one I've ever seen. I have it through Liz Carpenter, who was an aide to Lady Bird Johnson and to LBJ: "Lyndon Johnson arrived center stage during a national tragedy. And inevitably as Lady Bird said so poignantly at the time, 'People looked at the living and wished for the dead.'" Lady Bird Johnson always spoke poetically. I'm not sure you could capture things better than she did in that phrase.

Liz Carpenter, I did know her. She died only recently, 2010. She was witty and tart-tongued and incredibly intelligent. She was very close to the Johnsons. She was smart and she was bold—brassy—and they came to rely on her. She got things done. That was one of the things that Johnson valued in a person: "You're a can-do man" or "a can-do woman"—that was the ultimate compliment from him. Liz Carpenter was often a bull in a china shop, but she got things done.

The recording that Lady Bird Johnson made that evening, after the assassination—she used the tape recorder of Liz Carpenter's son for the sentiments she recorded that day. She knew she should get them down. She talks about how beautifully it all began. The rain had abated, the trip was going well. She reflected on how positively

step-seats. We talked and laughed, because she was actually closer to my age than she was to Mother's.

I remember asking [President Kennedy] to sign my paperback of *Profiles in Courage*. President and Mrs. Kennedy had always been very nice to my father and my mother—I never heard my father say one gruff word about President Kennedy. I [thought] of these people not just as the President and First Lady but as friends, as people I knew and loved. That was my experience . . . That's not to say that Daddy and Bobby Kennedy [got] along all the time. But there were many kind things that went on, [and] my husband [former Virginia governor Chuck Robb] campaigned for Bobby Kennedy's oldest daughter [Kathleen Kennedy Townsend, who ran unsuccessfully for governor of Maryland in 2002]. One of the things my parents told me is: "The greatest gift we can give is friendship," and likewise we should erase hurts—"Don't you carry forth old rivalries, old disagreements."

I don't remember any conversations [with my parents where they would] sit down and talk to me about [the assassination]. We were sleepwalking through this terrible, terrible tragedy. We were not thinking about ourselves or "How is this going to affect me?" We were thinking about Mrs. Kennedy and the horrible tragedy and the children. I remember that Daddy did ask me at the time—I guess it was Caroline who had a birthday coming up a few days later, and Daddy asked me to go out and buy some books for him to give her.

Afterward, as for me, I had always loved being free, I was always close to my parents, but going away [to college], being on your own, your own time schedule, learning to take care of yourself . . . When I came back, security people said we are going to have to make some changes. At night they would lock the doors, the Secret Service took up residence right by the front door. They had a room with a big plate-glass window that looked into the dorm. They put cameras on the stairs. They wanted to be sure I was safe. I'm sure they would have been happier if I hadn't gone back to school. I minded the Secret Service, [but] I recognized they had their job, and I tried to make it easier.

It was just a time . . . I don't even like to talk about it because it makes me cry. On several different occasions I have tried to talk about it with my children. It's just very hard.

We all wish that November 22, 1963, had not happened. I remember Daddy wrote Mrs. Kennedy handwritten notes—10 times more than I have of any handwritten things [from him]. Because he was a man of the telephone—he called. Luci and I don't have his handwriting. But this year I was reading for the first time the love letters that Daddy and Mother had sent back and forth. And he handwrote Mrs. Kennedy many notes.

LYNDA BIRD JOHNSON ROBB, the former First Lady of Virginia, is the elder daughter of Lyndon Baines and Lady Bird Johnson.

A portrait of President Lyndon Baines Johnson and his family made on November 30, 1963, showing (from left) Lynda Bird, Luci Baines, LBJ and Lady Bird.

YOICH OKAMOTO/AP

the trip was being received by Texans and Americans at large: the auspiciousness of how the day began. And then the shots ring out, the motorcade rushes to the hospital and after waiting for news in a small cubicle, Lady Bird Johnson hears "The President is dead," and she realizes how everything has changed.

Liz Carpenter penned the speech during the flight from Dallas to Andrews Air Force Base—the speech LBJ would give after landing. It's only 58 words, but I think it's one of the most underrated speeches he ever gave. The last lines are the most resonant—"I ask for your help and God's." A wonderful speech. We have it here at the library, and you can see the slight revisions he made to Liz Carpenter's words. It had been "God's help—and yours." And he penciled in "your help and God's."

MARK UPDEGROVE is the director of the Lyndon Baines Johnson Presidential Library in Austin, Texas, and author of *Indomitable Will: LBJ in the Presidency*.

Liz Carpenter's typed version of the 58-word speech Lyndon Baines Johnson would deliver at the Andrews Air Force Base on November 22, with the President's handwritten changes.

> This is a sad time for every American. The nation suffers a loss that cannot be weighed. For me it is a deep personal tragedy. I know the nation, and the whole free world, shares the sorrow that Mrs. Kennedy bears.
>
> I will do my best. That is all I can do. I ask God's help -- and yours.

Bob Schieffer: An Unexpected Caller

I WAS THE NIGHT POLICE REPORTER AT THE *Fort Worth Star-Telegram* and President Kennedy was coming to Fort Worth, where he was spending the night before that fateful day. There is nothing like being a reporter at a place where a big story is happening. More than 10,000 people turned out at night to see Air Force One land. I got off work at three a.m. So, I was sound asleep the next day, and my brother woke me up and said, "You'd better get to work. The President's been shot." And I was just in a complete fog. I got dressed. I went to work.

Just as I got to town, it came over the radio that the President was dead and people were lined up all around the *Star-Telegram*. These were the last of the "extras" days. People were lined up to buy souvenirs of the paper. Every time a new development would come up, they'd stop the presses and reprint the front page, and then start churning out more of these extras.

I made my way through the crowd [to the newsroom]. I was just trying to help out and answer the phones. One phone call came in and a woman said, "Is there anybody there who could give me a ride to Dallas?" I said, "Well, lady, we don't run a taxi here and besides, the President's been shot." And she said, "Yes. I heard it on the radio. I think it's my son they've arrested."

It was Lee Harvey Oswald's mother. I quickly put aside that part about "We don't run a taxi service." I said, "Tell me where you live and I'll come get you." I told her to hang up the phone and not answer it if it rang again. I knew it was a matter of time before someone else figured out she lived on the west side of Fort Worth. I suppose the reason she had called the *Star-Telegram* was because when Oswald defected to the Soviet Union, she was living in Fort Worth, and another reporter had interviewed her.

I went with the automobile editor, Bill Foster. We went out to the west side and there, standing on the curb, wearing this white nurse's uniform, was this little woman: gray hair, great horn-rimmed glasses and carrying a little blue travel bag, like you'd take to the gym. Bill drove and she got in the backseat with me and I interviewed her on the way. She was on the verge of hysterics, almost immediately saying that people would feel sorry for his wife and give her money and wouldn't remember the mother, that she'd die penniless. She was obsessed with money.

So we get to Dallas, and in those days we never told people who we were. We didn't lie if they'd ask us if we were reporters. If they wanted to assume we were police, we let them assume that. As a police reporter, I always wore a snap-brim hat so I'd look like Dick Tracy. I got to the police station, and the first uniformed police officer I saw, I said, "I'm the one that brought Oswald's mother over here. Where should we put her?" They actually found a little office in the burglary squad. So we went back there, and it was a great help for us because we were still putting out these extras and I would go out in the hall where the rest of our reporters were and I'd gather the information and then phone it in using that phone. People today don't realize what a big deal it was to have a phone. The other reporters had to go across the street. This was working out very well. About dark she said to me, "I wonder if they'd let me see my son?" And I said, "I'll go find out."

I went to the chief of homicide and said, "She'd like to talk to her son." He said, "We probably ought to do that." Again, it was so informal in those days, no PR, no *Miranda* decision where you had to advise people of their rights. I always dealt directly with the cops on the police beat. We were ushered into this holding room off the jail. I'm thinking, *My God, I'm going to get to hear this guy talk to his mother or maybe I'll get to interview him.* Finally a guy standing over in the corner said, "Who are you?" I said, "What?" He said, "Are you a reporter?" I said yes. And he said, "Son, you get your ass out of here, because if I ever see you again, I'm gonna kill you." He was an FBI agent just doing what somebody should have done. I had been in the police station at least six hours and nobody had asked me who I was. I excused myself and that was the end of the story.

I later went to Vietnam and I'll never forget that. And 9/11. But the Kennedy assassination: I never felt again the way I felt, until 9/11. When the assassination happened, we were terrified. We didn't know if it was the beginning of World War III. We'd never had one of these horrific events like this. Fort Worth was the base where the strategic bombers were.

They closed off the borders to Mexico. No one knew what this was about. I covered the story for about a week, then went back to the police beat. A couple of weeks later and I was covering this awful car wreck involving a family. I was looking at the victims of the crash, waiting for the justice of the peace to come. I was looking at these bodies and I realized I had no emotion at all. I just had none. I was like a dog watching TV, I could see some lights but it didn't have any impact on me whatsoever. It was months before I began to have any emotion about anything. I kind of decided that when you cover a story like that, there's something inside of you: You just use it up. You have to wait till you regenerate and it comes back. And it took a while. You ask why do I remember that day in such detail? I can remember it like it was yesterday. When you're covering a story, well, we're trained as journalists to cover stories about other people. But when it's your friends or happens in your hometown: You are a part of the story in addition to trying to cover the story. I just think you don't ever forget that. I'll never forget it. It just has some impact on your brain and psyche. It's etched in there, like getting a tattoo. You don't wash this off. It stays with you. I still don't understand it; over the years people asked if I thought someone else was involved. I've never seen evidence that convinced me that others were involved. I'm convinced that Oswald pulled the trigger and was a cold-blooded killer. Just an amazing time.

I always tell people, "That was the biggest story I almost got." What an adventure. I look back on that and I sometimes wonder if it really happened. The fact that she would call the paper was odd, but people were always doing things like that. People would walk in off the street, and if they didn't like a story they'd go right up to the city desk and complain. The guy who sold papers on the corner, if he didn't like a headline he'd raise hell with the city editor and say, "I can't sell this paper with this kind of headline. Put some news up there." So the fact that someone would call the paper and ask for a ride, we were part of the community, people had the damnedest requests.

So to this day I cannot let a phone ring past one ring. I grab the phone. My wife gets so mad. I will never look to see who's calling. Every time I go to speak to a journalism class, they ask me, "What's your advice?" I say, "Answer the phone. Be the one closest to the phone. That's where stories come from."

BOB SCHIEFFER, a native of Austin, Texas, grew up in Fort Worth and is a longtime television journalist and anchor with CBS. In 1963 he was a 26-year-old reporter for the *Fort Worth Star-Telegram*.

The President's motorcade on November 22, just ahead of *Dallas Morning News* photographer Tom Dillard's car. Dillard immediately looks toward the Book Depository after shots ring out.

Robert MacNeil: Oswald Himself, in Passing

THERE HAS NEVER BEEN ANOTHER STORY I COVERED AS MOMEN-tous as that—personally for me, for the nation, for the world. It made what had seemed inconceivable from then on conceivable. Anyone who is 60 or older—the youngest having been, say, 10 in 1963, children then—remembers for the first time in their lives seeing grown-ups, teachers and parents cry. The attacks of 9/11 would compare, because they traumatized America and transfixed the world, but I was only a spectator, watching my television in Manhattan a few miles north of Ground Zero. I wasn't a participant, as I had been with JFK.

As I wrote in my book, *The Right Place at the Right Time:*

In 1963 I was traveling with Kennedy as the number two White House cor-respondent for NBC. It was my first big presidential trip, the first time with my name on a White House manifest and linen labels saying "Trip of the President" on my luggage. The morning of November 22 in Fort Worth, the reporters stud-ied advance copies of the speech JFK was to deliver at the lunch in Dallas. It was a spirited attack on his conservative critics: "In a world of complex and continu-ing problems, in a world full of frustrations and irritations, America's leadership must be guided by the lights of learning and reason; or else those who con-fuse rhetoric with reality and the plausible with the possible will gain the popular ascendancy . . . There will always be dissident voices raised . . . We cannot hope that everyone, to use the phrase of a decade ago, will 'talk sense to the American people.' But we can hope that fewer people will listen to nonsense." It was sig-nificant that Kennedy had cho-sen to attack the spirit that had made Dallas seem such a nest of extremists.

The Chamber of Commerce breakfast looked like any other political banquet. There was only one seat vacant at the head table and the entire room began twisting and muttering,

Robert MacNeil reports for *NBC News* from Dallas in November 1963.

"Where's Jackie?"

When Jackie was announced, the cameras whirred and followed her through the crowd until she emerged in the lights at the end of the head table, resplendent in a suit the color of strawberry ice cream, with a pillbox hat. She was cheered all the way to her seat.

Capitalizing on his wife's new verve and zest for politics, JFK began his speech: "Two years ago, I introduced myself in Paris by saying that I was the man who had accompanied Mrs. Kennedy to Paris. I am getting somewhat the same sensation. As I travel around Texas, nobody wonders what Lyndon and I will wear!" That brought the roof down. I remember saying to the locally based cameraman Moe Levy, "Well, even if nothing else happens, we've got a story with Jackie."

By the time we got outside and into the press bus, there was bright sunshine. As we waited for the motorcade to begin, several reporters argued about how to describe the color of Jackie's suit. They settled on pink. Most reporters don't like to be caught too far away from the pack on details like that.

We were seven minutes behind schedule leaving for Dallas. Our press bus ran straight up to the press plane.

When we arrived in Dallas, we ran for the press buses. We could just see the presidential limousine, which was seven cars ahead. The crowds were sparse on the outskirts of Dallas. We were all watching for some kind of demonstrations but didn't know quite what to expect. The route was thick with policemen. But indications of opposition were pretty innocuous. It began to get monotonous and I was a little drowsy from the heat. My eyes grew tired from searching ahead for something to happen.

I don't remember at just what stage it happened, but during this half-drowsy phase I found myself wondering what I would do if someone shot the President. How would I get to a phone? Where had that thought come from? Even with our premonitions about Dallas, such an explicit idea had never occurred to me. That premonition: I don't know where that came from.

Just as we turned the corner onto Houston Street, I looked at my watch. I know it was roughly five minutes fast, and it said something like 12:36 when we heard what sounded like a shot. I said, "Was that a shot?" Several people said, "No, no." And others said, "I don't know."

Then there were two more explosions, very distinct to me. I jumped up and said, "They were shots! They were shots! Stop the bus! Stop the bus!"

The driver opened the door and I jumped out. I couldn't see the President's car but I really started to believe that there was shooting because on the grass on both sides of the roadway people were throwing themselves down and covering their children with their bodies. I saw several people running up the grassy hill beside the road. I thought they were chasing whoever had done the shooting and I ran after them. It did not enter my head at that moment that Kennedy had been hit. I was thinking, it must have been some crazy right-wing nut trying to make a demonstration by firing a gun off. He couldn't have been trying to hit Kennedy. With several policemen, I climbed a wooden fence at the top of a grassy slope.

I figured they knew what they were chasing. It soon became clear they didn't and I thought I had better look for a telephone.

I ran into the first building I came to that looked as though it might have a phone. It was the Texas School Book Depository. As I ran up the steps and through the door, a young man in shirtsleeves was coming out. In great agitation I asked him where there was a phone. He pointed inside to an open space where another man was talking on a phone situated near a pillar and said, "Better ask him." I ran inside and asked the second man, who pointed to an office on one side. I called the NBC Radio news desk in about 10 seconds.

I filed my report: "Shots were fired as President Kennedy's motorcade passed through downtown Dallas. People screamed and lay down on the grass as three shots rang out. Police chased an unknown gunman up a grassy hill . . ."

A small crowd had begun to gather outside the Book Depository. A little boy of about eight was telling a policeman, "Mister, I saw a man with a gun up there in that window." Pointing above our heads, another man corroborated that. It was the first I knew that the Book Depository had any connection with the shooting. And I still did not realize that the President had been hit. Just then a woman ran up crying hysterically. Seeing my White House press badge, she asked dementedly, "Was he hit? Was he hit?" I said, "No, I'm sure he wasn't." And then it began to dawn on me that what I thought so impossible could have happened. I rushed over to a policeman who was listening intently to his motorcycle radio. "Was he hit?"

"Yeah. Hit in the head. They're taking him to Parkland Hospital."

It was about a year and a half later that I got a call in New York from William Manchester, who was writing *The Death of a President*. He said he had gone carefully over the ground to find out who had been in the Book Depository before and right after the shooting. He had seen a statement I had made to the FBI. He had traced my call through the telephone company to 12:34, four minutes after the shooting, and he was convinced I had spoken to Lee Harvey Oswald. I had no way of confirming I had.

Then Manchester asked if I knew about the statement Oswald had made to the Secret Service. Oswald had told them that as he left the Book Depository, a young Secret Serviceman with a blond crew cut had rushed up the steps and asked him for a phone. Since no Secret Serviceman had entered the building, Manchester concluded that Oswald had mistaken me for one. I could only say that it was possible. I am blond. My hair was very short then and I was wearing a White House press badge he might have mistaken for a Secret Service I.D.

In *The Death of a President*, Manchester wrote that at 12:33 p.m. Oswald "Leaves Depository by front entrance, pausing to tell NBC's Robert MacNeil he can find a phone inside; thinks MacNeil is a Secret Service man."

It is titillating but it doesn't matter much. Far more important to me as a reporter was why I had not had the wits to stop and talk to the people lying on the grassy knoll. They had seen the whole thing. And I had run by these people, fixated as I was about chasing a gunman, because I didn't believe Kennedy had been shot.

However much violence I had witnessed around the world in those years, it was still inconceivable to me that this could happen to Kennedy. I suppose unconsciously I thought him invulnerable. It was not until Monday, three days after the shooting, that my private emotions caught up with the professional drive that had preoccupied me.

I decided on Monday, the day of the funeral, to do a piece for the Huntley-Brinkley report back at the grassy knoll. People had come and put flowers there, some with notes attached. While we were filming, an old man sat down near us and turned on his transistor radio. Over it came the broadcast of the President's funeral in Washington. It was when I heard the lament played by the bagpipes of the Black Watch Regiment, marching in the funeral procession that I really understood, with my feelings, what had happened. I sat there in the sunshine with tears running out of my eyes, aware of how much the salt in them burned, because crying was such an unaccustomed thing to do.

LIFE asked MacNeil if, looking back on his long career, he had ever cried again while covering a story. MacNeil responded: "I am 82—men tend to weep as easily as girls! Recently I watched an airline commercial showing a young woman soldier, African American, in uniform, boarding a flight. An elderly white man stood back to let her pass, then saluted her and caught her shy smile of thanks. That's the kind of stuff that makes me cry now."

Robert MacNeil is a former PBS news anchor and, in 1963, was a 32-year-old reporter for NBC. The above account combines an interview with LIFE and excerpts from his book *The Right Place at the Right Time*, edited together with his permission.

Jim Lehrer: If Only It Had Rained

I WAS A REPORTER FOR the *Dallas Times Herald*, the afternoon newspaper. I was assigned that day to cover the arrival of the Kennedys at Love Field and stay at Love Field and report their departure. The Kennedys were only going to be in Dallas for two or three hours.

That morning, I got to Love Field around 9:30, they were due around 11 or 11:30. I went to my spot. The *Times Herald* was not known for spending a lot of money, but in this case had made an exception and paid to have an open telephone line for me to

Jim Lehrer working at the time for the *Dallas Times Herald*.

use when the Kennedys arrived so I could talk to the rewrite man downtown. I had the telephone set up on a table right inside the fence where Air Force One was going to arrive. The Kennedys were going to arrive at the same time as our main deadline.

It had been raining that morning. After I had been at Love Field a while, the rain had stopped and it looked like it had cleared. The plane was coming from Fort Worth, which is only a 20-minute flight.

With about 20 minutes to go, I was checking the phone to make sure it worked. The rewrite man, his name was Stan Weinberg, said to me, "I'm gonna be writing under deadline here. Is the bubble top gonna be up on the presidential limousine?" We all knew about the bubble top. We'd written about it in advance stories, that if the weather was bad, the bubble top on the back of the car would be up, so the Kennedys wouldn't get wet. So I said I couldn't see it because there were six or seven cars that were waiting to be part of the motorcade. They were down a ramp and I couldn't see. So Stan said to me, "Would you mind going down there and see?" I said fine. So I put the phone down and went down the ramp.

I was a federal reporter, so it meant I knew the local Secret Service agents. The agent in charge of the Dallas office, a man named Forrest Sorrels, was standing at the head of the ramp. I came up to him and I could see the cars were lined up. I saw the presidential limo two or three cars down, and I saw, in fact, the bubble top was up over the back of the car. So I said to Mr. Sorrels, "Look, rewrite wants to know, is the bubble top going to be up?" So he looks up at the sky and he yells at another Secret Service agent who's got a two-way radio, "Check downtown. See if it's clear downtown." The other agent was saying something in the radio and then he hollers back to Mr. Sorrels, "Clear downtown." So then Sorrels says to the agents, "Okay, lose the bubble top." And so they start taking the bubble top off and I go back to rewrite and say, "All right, the bubble top's gonna be down."

The Kennedys arrive, and they leave. I did my reporting to rewrite, then I went into the main building to wait. Just as we got inside, we got the word that there had been shots fired. I ran to a telephone, got to the city desk and they told me to go to Parkland Hospital. I got there just as they announced that Kennedy was dead. And then they told me to go on to the police station. I got there just as they brought in Oswald. And I stayed there the rest of that day and night.

About midnight, the police station in Dallas was a chaotic place. There were reporters from all over the world, law enforcement people, local cops, FBI agents. It was jammed. There was this kind of eerie, not only sound, but feeling: that a helluva story was going on. And there was profound sadness.

I had gotten word they were having a meeting upstairs in the police chief's office. I went up there, the door was closed, someone outside said there are officials in there in suits. So I just stood outside the door and waited.

Finally the door opened, and the men came outside, five or six of them. And one of them was this Secret Service agent. He saw me. He came over to me and there were kind of tears forming in his eyes. And he said, "Jim, if I just hadn't taken down the bubble top."

I was blown back by that. I thought, 'My God, what if I hadn't asked the question?'"

Jim Lehrer coanchored PBS's evening newscast with Robert MacNeil for 20 years, then continued on his own with *NewsHour*. His new novel, *Top Down*, is loosely based on his experience of the day JFK was shot.

"Where Were You . . . ?"

Gay Talese: The Contrary Story, Unwritten

NINETEEN SIXTY-THREE. AT THAT TIME, I was a reporter at *The New York Times*. I generally was writing about crowds. I'd be covering, typically, the Saint Patrick's Day Parade, riots in Harlem, crowds—there were a lot of them in '63, '64. It was a reporters' paper, it wasn't a writers' paper like the *New York Herald Tribune*. And so, in '63—with the *Tribune,* a sinking beautiful ship it was, but still afloat, and still dancing on that ship were people like Jimmy Breslin and Tom Wolfe and a lot of others who were also good writers—I was one of the few on the *Times* that had any freedom at all. Granted, it wasn't as much as Breslin and Wolfe. I mean, they would make two sentences out of one, but *The New York Times* was a reporters' paper, really an editors' newspaper, where the *Tribune* was a writers' newspaper. I only bring this up because of what will happen.

Wolfe and I knew one another socially, and we were competing reporters in a way because he had the same kind of assignments I did. And when the President was shot, I knew even before going in to the paper, when I heard it on the radio, I thought: That's going to be my assignment. When I walk in, it was my assignment. The editor said, "What's the reaction in New York?" The other assignment would be the President—political. Tom Wicker was at work. Mine would be: If an astronaut was shot off, the crowd on Cape Canaveral, the beach on Cocoa Beach. If Mickey Mantle was coming close with Maris in trying to top Babe Ruth's record, I wrote about the crowd reaction. I covered the riots in '64. I covered the civil rights march on Selma.

So here we are back in '63, and I knew I'd be covering [the reaction to the assassination] because I had covered the Saint Patrick's Day Parade. I wrote scenes. The editor said, go, get the reaction, [so] I just walked down the street. *The New York Times* was at 229 West 43rd Street in those days. It was between Eighth Avenue and Times Square. I'm working, I think, well, I'll go down and get on the subway and I'll start off at Wall Street. I'll just go way the hell down to Wall Street. And maybe Little Italy or go to Chinatown, take another subway, come up the West Side. Maybe I'd stop at the Garment Center, 34th Street, Herald Square, and maybe then I'll go up to Harlem, 125th Street. My plan was that. But it all halted when I saw Tom Wolfe. I knew him socially, we had dinner a lot. I knew him as a fellow reporter and I admired him and I liked him. He's a likable guy. So I saw him on the street. He was coming up from 41st Street, the *Tribune* offices. I said, "Hey, Tom, what are you doing?" I said, "You're covering the reaction?" He said, "Yes." I said, "Why don't we share a cab?" They didn't want you to take taxis. They were too expensive, especially to go all the way downtown.

I think we took a cab. Now, we could have taken a subway, but I'm not sure. If we took the subway, then we took the subway right there on 42nd Street. I don't remember. But what I first thought when I saw Wolfe: *Ah, he'll split the cab with me.* So we went off.

Downtown, we walked from Canal Street to what would be Little Italy, what would be Chinatown, or maybe someplace in between that didn't have a neighborhood identity name. And I would sometimes hear from car radios or radios the news of this atrocity in Dallas. But I didn't see, except for the radio sounds, I didn't see anybody cry in the street, I didn't see anybody in a loud voice saying, "Oh, my God, what are we going to do now?" or "What a terrible thing." Nobody.

Myself? No, I wasn't affected by it. It was work. It's the worst thing about us reporters—and I don't know if it's still true, but I can tell you about my generation—Wolfe and I are about the same age, both came up in the '50s and '60s—and I'm just trying to think: Did I ever feel badly about anything? I just have to take a minute . . .

Everything was a story. I mean, your book is going to be glowing and raving and all that. But, no: You didn't, you couldn't feel sorry for a guy that's so privileged and so rich. I know he had an older brother who died, and I was affected by that—I grew up with it, had been young enough. I remember that with John Kennedy on television, I was very proud to be an American. He was wonderful in those news conferences; he could speak the language. A wonderful picture: good-looking, a rich guy, with a beautiful wife, and he's emerging out of the Cuban missile crisis as the guy who humiliated the Russians, so he's on top of the world. I mean, how could you feel sorry for the guy?

But I wasn't writing about myself. What I'm looking for: I want to write about what I see. So I'm looking on the street, and I guess I wasn't even aware of what Tom Wolfe was doing because he was with me. We walked together. From time to time, we heard the radio. But on the street: nothing. I remember moving up to the Diamond District and the west 50s, I remember going further uptown to Yorkville on the subway, getting out, running around, finally working ourselves back to Times Square. I just didn't see anything. And I thought, *Well, that's interesting,* because either the ordinary life so dominates the emotions of people—their ordinary life, whatever happens, they're so into themselves, I don't mean to be critical—but I didn't see much. I didn't see anything.

I went back to my paper, Tom went back to his paper. I only know what I said to my editor, Mr. Adams, the day city editor. I said, "It seems like there's no great sign of anguish out there. I just didn't see people crying in the streets or I didn't hear anything that is quotable." I listen, I'm an eavesdropper. But I told the editor: "I can write *that,* you know." Sometimes it's not the story you think you're going to get. I thought I would see people like when you have the German army enter Paris in 1940, or even pictures of the Yankees losing and somebody's screaming or crying—Mickey Mantle struck out!—or some auto accident. People reacting with horror or reacting with sadness or tears. I didn't see it. I'm getting all kinds of interpretation, which may have been true interpretation: Shock, it hadn't set in. I walked in to the paper at five p.m. maybe, and our deadline, I think, was seven, and I said, "I can write this no-reaction."

And he said, "No, I've got so many stories." He didn't need me. They didn't want a contrary story. Mine would have been a nonstory, or the contrary story.

GAY TALESE is the author of *The Kingdom and the Power, A Writer's Life* and other books.

Tom Wolfe: The Contrary Story, Written

Tom Wolfe, dressed characteristically in the mid-1960s. After the assassination, he writes what his editors determine people didn't want to read.

THE *TIMES* HAD SENT GAY OUT TO DO A MAN-on-the-streeter, and the *Herald Tribune* had dispatched me (and others). This was immediately after the assassination, early afternoon, as I recall—hours before the name Lee Harvey Oswald had come into the picture. By coincidence both Gay and I had picked out the Chinatown–Little Italy area to start with.

We both wrote long stories. [Wolfe wasn't aware that Talese had been called off writing.] Not one line of either story made it into print. I don't know what happened in Gay's case, but mine was a real piece of the Human Comedy. I talked to a host of locals, Chinese, Italian, Jewish, Ukrainian, Russian, Moravians even . . . you name it. Put together, their reactions were a laugh and a half . . . *leg-slappers* is the word. Each neighborhood ethnic group blamed another one for Kennedy's assassination. The Ukrainians blamed the Russians, the Russians blamed the Jews, the Jews blamed the Chinese, the Chinese took the broader view and blamed the Russians, the Ukrainians and while they were at it, all peoples they thought had been "contaminated" by the alcoholic sponginess of the Slavic Weltanschauung, such as, they thought, the Moravians, thanks to their short common border with the Ukrainians.

I wrote this long story, and I thought the *Trib*'s editors would crack up over it. Late in the afternoon I was deputized to do a rewrite of all our man-on-the-streeters, which consisted of a mile of copy paper pasted together to create a single grand account. But my story was not there! . . . Had to be a mistake! . . . So I wrote my crazy Italians, Jews, Ukrainians, etc., back into the story, me being the rewrite man *for everybody's* man-on-the-streeter.

The first edition comes out, and I hungrily read my rewrite, which is on the bottom half of page one with my byline—and not a line of my own copy is there!—and *I'm* the one who did the rewrite!

This was my introduction to the Victorian Gentleman. The Victorian Gentleman is the Press in America (on TV, too) whenever any solemn event makes the news. The Gent, in the persons of copy editors, city editors, managing editors and *the* editor, takes over and will allow only *seemly sentiments* to appear in print. In this case, the only people the Gent was going to let in were anguished men pressing their cupped palms against their temporal fossae and little old women collapsing in front of St. Patrick's Cathedral.

TOM WOLFE is the author of *The Bonfire of the Vanities, The Right Stuff* and other books.

In these editions of *The New York Times* and the *New York Herald Tribune* that hit the streets on November 23, there is not a word by either Talese or Wolfe. Within days, there will be other stories by them, joined by Breslin's notable piece on the gravedigger.

Jimmy Breslin: The Story That Ran

VOTED FOR HIM. IRISH CATHOLIC! VERY IMPORTANT TO US. R.C. Roman Catholic. And he was smart, which is a [expletive] sin in that business. Terrific voice. Spoke terrifically and he looked good. He was the best. Absolutely the best.

I was in Selma, Alabama, when it happened—Selma, which had been a very bad place for a while. [My editors at the *New York Herald Tribune*] told me that Kennedy got shot. And I don't know how I'm going to do something, but I tried to think of what to do. There would be 5 million people on that story, and I said, [expletive] that, I'll go to the guy who's burying him. And I go to whatever the place was: I called ahead at [Arlington National] cemetery and they told me this one guy is gonna do the digging for the grave. So I went to the guy's house, I go to him before he left. Good for me. He finished his breakfast, and I was talking to him. I went out with him to the grave.

Now the clock was running against us, too. I knew I'd have to beat the clock. I talked to him for a while and then took a run and went to Washington, to the office that we had there. And I wrote a column on the gravedigger. I knew I had it, 'cause I'm never comfortable doing what everyone else is doing. I'm much more comfortable being totally freaking alone: That's what I try to do every time out. Because going out

with the mob is a waste of time, a terrible waste of time. What are you gonna get out of it? Supposing I didn't go there that day? What would I have done? With the 2,000 others, writing the same freaking thing. But alone with the guy: You're alone, and there's nobody else, and you don't know what's going on in the main story. But what you turn in: It's the main story. Which it was. It was about life and death. I always hope for something very big. It's some break when they're like that.

I went back to my house, which was in Forest Hills, Queens. I got back there, and then I went to Queens Boulevard, Pep McGuires bar.

It was a bad problem with [Kennedy]. Too smart. Very unconcerned about getting hurt.

Jesus Christ. That was some loss.

JIMMY BRESLIN of the *New York Daily News* was, like Tom Wolfe, on the staff of the *New York Herald Tribune* in 1963. His column about the affection and respect shown the late President Kennedy by Arlington National Cemetery's gravedigger, World War II veteran Clifton Pollard, is one of the most celebrated in his long journalistic career.

"Where Were You . . . ?"

Judson Hale: Nonsense, or Ominous?

NOVEMBER 22, I REMEMBER EXACTLY WHERE I WAS. I WAS WITHIN 10 feet of where I am right now. I was correcting page proofs of the January issue of *Yankee* magazine. In those days you would telephone in the corrections, that's how we did page proofs. You would call and say, "Page three, fourth line down, should be a *t* in t-h-e." And we're printing in Pittsfield, Massachusetts, that's where we printed—at Sun Printing there. And I was talking to a guy named Cliff, and I heard in the background up here in this office somebody say, "Somebody shot the President." And I remember I said, "Wait a minute, Cliff. Hold on. Somebody shot the President." And I'll never forget his reaction, it was so negative and so awful, and I still to this day don't understand what he meant. He said, "Oh, they got him, did they?"

That was where I first heard it. And then we heard, a few minutes or a half hour later, that he was killed.

I do have something else I can tell you about *The Old Farmer's Almanac* to do with this. The month of November—and I'll tell you, we got more letters on this than any weather forecast—the month of November, many people came to believe we had predicted the Kennedy assassination in the 1963 *Old Farmer's Almanac*. The reason they said it was that, for November, covering the whole month, it says—I'm reading this to you, I hauled it out this morning—"Two full moons this month, guard against crime." And then you go to the 22nd, which was a Friday, as we all know. And I'll read you what it says right next to it, it says, "Night is coming on, and murder perhaps."

We got a lot of letters about it.

Ben Rice—he's long, long gone—I used to confirm his calendars in those days, and I asked him about that, and I said, "Ben, we've gotten quite a few letters about that, 'Night is coming on, and murder perhaps.' We have the 'two full moons, guard against crime' in this Kennedy assassination month. Ben, what did you mean by that?"

He said, "I didn't mean anything by it. I just felt always that way about a November, particularly one with two full moons." He was the one who wrote it: Ben Rice.

I'll say Massachusetts was closer and probably more affected than here in New Hampshire, which was pretty conservative back then, but we—my wife, Sally, and I, as lifelong Democrats and total admirers of John Kennedy—were devastated. I remember saying to Sally—my father had died the year before, and I remember saying to Sally—"I think I feel worse today than I did a year ago when my father died." That's how bad I felt.

I think that, in my lifetime, it's the one historic event that affected me the most. My mother and father would probably have said Roosevelt's death, and I remember being very somber then, too, but I was a kid—12 years old or something. I remember everybody being so sad, but it didn't hit me personally, the loss. Kennedy hit me personally—me and Sally. That weekend was a weekend like no other, Oswald killed live on TV . . . Maybe for those who had been alive when Pearl Harbor occurred, that could have been something equivalent. But for me, that was the number one historic event—and so sad, of course.

Now the Kennedys have the young congressman again. I find myself rooting for him.

JUDSON HALE, longtime editor of *Yankee* magazine and the annual *Old Farmer's Almanac,* was managing editor of *Yankee* that day in 1963 and now has the not-entirely-emeritus title editor-in-chief. He lives in Dublin, New Hampshire.

James Carville: More Silence than Anything

I WAS IN THE OLD STUDENT UNION AT LSU MY SOPHOMORE YEAR AND somebody said, "Somebody shot Kennedy." I looked up and it was on television. People started gathering around. I remember having to stand on a chair to see what was going on. The first thing I thought was some right wing group had shot him. People were kind of numb, looking stunned. There wasn't a lot of commentary. I would have remembered if people had sobbed uncontrollably. More silence than anything. People had been getting ready for Thanksgiving holidays. Football season. People were in a good mood 'cause Thanksgiving holidays were coming up, a joyous time in my part of the world. Then silence.

I think after Walter Cronkite took his glasses off, everybody pretty much dispersed.

I didn't know how to digest it. Presidents didn't get shot back then. Maybe people remember when Reagan got shot less because he lived. It didn't have the same effect. Kennedy was in a car, he was with his wife. The whole image of Johnson taking the oath on Air Force One.

And Kennedy was so different from Nixon, or Eisenhower. He talked different, the country was enamored with the whole family, Hyannis Port and the compound. His wife was glamorous. There was a whole interesting, fascinating construct around the guy.

JAMES CARVILLE, a professor of political science at Tulane University, managed Bill Clinton's 1992 presidential campaign.

Nathaniel Philbrick: Buried Memories

I WAS BORN HERE IN NEW ENGLAND—IN BOSTON LYING-IN Hospital—but when I heard [about Kennedy], I was in second grade in the Squirrel Hill neighborhood in Pittsburgh, Pennsylvania, and back in those days you'd go home for lunch. I went to Linden Elementary School, and my brother and I had gone home for lunch, and we were walking back up Linden Avenue toward the school when someone told us. And I just remember what the day looked like. And then we went to school, and what memory I have is sitting in class and watching TV. It was unusual, watching the TV in the school. It's just something kicking around in the dendrites, that memory, so obviously it made an impression.

But I think it was through the adults that I realized this was momentous. It's a funny thing: When you're a kid, you're really just learning about life, and clearly this was a formative experience since I do remember that day. That's a part of it: learning to interpret the magnitude of events. And it starts to creep into you from others. Something that becomes one of those things that define your youth. I remember, later, Bobby Kennedy's death. My mom was a big Bobby Kennedy fan—Kennedy bumper stickers and so on—and she would write poems, some of them for the local paper. I remember there was a dead robin in our backyard, and she wove that in. And for me, that there . . . It's kind of tied up with whatever it was that was happening to me when John Kennedy died.

It's funny, it's all kind of coming back, talking to you. One of my first memories was in Burlington [Vermont] during the Kennedy election campaign and my dad took me to see him. There's kind of a green there in Burlington, and [Kennedy] was on the balcony of a hotel, and I was on my dad's shoulders, and I'm sure that was one of the reasons it represented such an emotional wallop when I heard that he was dead. It's not till now that I even remembered I had seen him in life. It's interesting how memory works, especially how early memory works: It seems to be a slide show, with scenes, not really a narrative. But it is a narrative.

Myself, I feel like an adopted New Englander, having lived on Nantucket now for 26 years. The Kennedys are a big part of the mystique of New England here. There are stories on the island about how Jack and, I think it was, Bobby sailed a Beetle Cat all the way from Hyannis Port to Nantucket, and then they had the temerity to walk into the yacht club in bare feet. *Not allowed*—and they were kicked out. Just on a personal note: Back when I was a competitive sailor in college, I would teach sailing in the summers, and one year I was asked if I were willing to work at the Kennedy compound in Hyannis Port, and teach the Kennedy clan sailing, manage their fleet. For a variety of reasons I didn't do it—an interesting road not taken. All of this comes back now when I think of him.

It's interesting that their family has really come to define the Cape. They're responsible for the whole outer beach being preserved. And now as someone who's studied New England, the Pilgrims and all that, it's interesting that the Kennedys, who define so much up here, are really nouveau—very shallow roots, and just in a generation or two they created this legacy. I find that wonderfully refreshing, because New Englanders have a tendency to look at their *Mayflower* pedigree and look at that as the definition of being a New Englander, and here is a family that really through the extraordinary accomplishments of just two generations coopted that heritage. I think that really speaks to what this country is all about.

Also: Jack himself. I did this book called *The Last Stand,* about Custer. Custer will never get older than 36. Custer was beginning to lose his hair and would have gained weight, and if he had lived would have become a pompous old man. None of the flash of the Battle of Little Bighorn would have happened. There is . . . Well, being cut down young does leave you in your prime, all of the human imagination that goes with that.

Here on Nantucket we're a fairly small community, particularly in January and February, when all of the funerals seem to happen. And it's the people who die young that still often fill the church, and it's the ones who've lived on and on and on who get their family and friends. It's different. You've lived a full life and you've seen it through and you've fulfilled your potential—even if no one ever fulfills all of the potential they might wish—and it's a life. But someone cut down, someone so vibrant and handsome and in the vortex of his life, dying so suddenly and tragically, it's something we don't forget.

NATHANIEL PHILBRICK is author of several acclaimed histories, including, on New England subjects, *Bunker Hill, Mayflower* and *In the Heart of the Sea,* the true story of the whaling boat that inspired Melville's *Moby-Dick.* He lives on Nantucket, in Massachusetts.

A crowd gathers around a radio shop downtown in New York City. Similar communal gatherings sweep the country.

"Where Were You . . . ?"

David M. Shribman: The Never-Ending Afternoon

I LIKED GEORGE "BUD" SAMILJAN AS A BOY AND ADMIRE HIM AS A MAN. BUT I'LL NEVER socialize with him again—never—and we both know why. He and I are tied by tragedy, and divided by tragedy.

November 22, 1963, was a splendid afternoon in the beach town where we both grew up, and when the dismissal bell rang at 2:10 at school, he and I set out to walk through Orchard Circle and up Humphrey Street en route to my house on Stanley Road. We were pupils in Dorothy Rich's fourth-grade classroom, and the Stanley School was one of those timeless places on the New England coast, and not only because the clock on the outside of the brick building was stuck, much like the clock atop the old vicarage in Grantchester immortalized by a splendid poet and soldier who died young, Rupert Brooke. This was a Friday and we were free of school and there were snacks to be had at home and a weekend ahead to be enjoyed. We were halfway home when the police lady who stood at Salem Street hurried to us. "The President's been shot," she screamed, the volume intended to impress us with the urgency of it all, though the words were startling enough. "Get home immediately."

We did, and there at home was my grandmother, a worrywart on her best days, a portrait of panic on this day. Her son—my uncle—had been on PT-111, in John Kennedy's squadron, and though ordinarily she had no patience for Democrats, Kennedy was a special case and had enjoyed special favor. In his 1952 Senate race, Representative John F. Kennedy, onetime commander of PT-109, had stopped in her hometown of Salem and had spoken to her about the son she had lost in the Pacific during World War II. That meant the world to her, because that son—and of course her other, surviving son, my father—meant the world to her. And so on this day the one loss mixed with the other so profoundly that a nine-year-old could sense it, so poignantly that a 59-year-old cannot forget it.

That terrible afternoon I sat in front of the television in a room we called the den and watched the black-and-white images flicker by, not knowing that those images would remain with me forever; following the news with remarkable attention, not knowing that the news would become not only my avocation but my vocation; thinking about the President whose administration I barely understood, not knowing that the years 1961 through 1963 would mark me like no others.

I am stuck on those three years, stuck like a broken record. I have long agreed that in life it is not very important how old you are, but it is very important when you were young. (It was on this weekend that Daniel Patrick Moynihan said to Mary McGrory that while they might laugh again, they would never be young again.) So the lessons of the Kennedy years, the triumphs and the tragedies, have stuck with me, with a stubborn vividness, far more so than anything from the years of Jimmy Carter, Ronald Reagan, George H.W. Bush, Bill Clinton, George W. Bush and Barack Obama—all of whose presidencies I witnessed firsthand as a reporter. I knew every one of those men, and Gerald R. Ford too, and yet it is Kennedy, whom I never met, I feel I know best.

In Massachusetts, he was the measure of us. When my brother Jeff and I fought sometime in the fall of 1960—a six-year-old beating up on a four-year-old, not exactly a championship prizefight—my mother, who wasn't even a natural-born citizen, called us aside and said: Look at those Kennedy brothers. One of them is running for President and the other brother is helping him, not fighting with him. My earliest political memory is the Kennedy inaugural address, an occasion for our Canadian mother, who emerges in this tale as a bit of a political opportunist, to urge us to ask not what she could do for us. Hardwired into my brain is President Kennedy's American University speech, which of course I never heard but whose words I know by heart. ("I am talking about genuine peace, the kind of peace that makes life on earth worth living, and the kind that enables men and nations to grow, and to hope, and build a better life for their children.") Somewhere in the recesses of my memory is the Kennedy Trade Mart speech, which I also never heard, because no one ever heard it, as it was to be delivered later that afternoon in Dallas. (Words to remember, even so: "We, in this country, in this generation, are—by destiny rather than by choice—the watchmen on the walls of world freedom.") And I cannot count the times I have told my kids that they should take on some challenge not because it is easy but because it is hard. (They know nothing of JFK's Rice University speech of 1962 that set America on a trajectory to the moon, but they have heard its theme many times.)

All these years later—a husband, a father, a newspaper editor, above all a premature but recondite old-timer, maybe even a relic—I still am drawn to John Kennedy, not so much for what he did but for what he represented. If, as Kennedy said in an unforgettable phrase, Winston Churchill "mobilized the English language," then it can be said that John Kennedy mobilized the American idiom in service of American idealism. His eloquence was a fire that truly lit the world, and anyone of my turn of mind knows exactly why that phrase shapes my thoughts, even now, even after so much time, even after so much revisionism, even after so much cynicism.

I've grown up and perhaps grown old, but never have outgrown the agony of that afternoon, which I remember better than I remember yesterday—because it has, to me, always been part of the present, never the past. And so I never invited Bud Samiljan home to play again. I bump into him every decade or so and we unfailingly exchange a warm hello, and maybe a handshake. But that's it. No reminiscences, no promises to get together sometime. Because we won't get together sometime. We never will. We are tied, and divided, by that afternoon. The shock of his death, the notion that I don't want to repeat that day.

DAVID M. SHRIBMAN is executive editor of the *Pittsburgh Post-Gazette* and the *Pittsburgh Press*. He grew up in Swampscott, Massachusetts, and won a Pulitzer Prize when covering Washington, D.C., for *The Boston Globe* in 1995.

The coming together to listen to or watch the news spreads around the globe. Here, on November 25, a French family gathers in front of the television, which is adorned with photos of the late President, to watch the funeral.

President Kennedy's body lies in state in the Capitol rotunda.

Tom Brokaw: The Future Deferred

Tom Brokaw at the time was hardly the news anchor he would become, but he found ways to work the story as best he could.

I WAS IN THE NEWSROOM AT KMTV in Omaha. I had been there about a year. I was a noon news editor. The [Teletype] bell began to rattle, both wire services. I went over to the UPI wire and read that astonishingly effective description by Merriman Smith. I tore the copy off and ran downstairs to our studios. In those days, NBC would hand back programming to the local stations, so we were not on the network. I interrupted a garden show to announce from the announcer's booth what had happened and then ran back up and got some more and continued to do that kind of relay.

I was operating with two tracks in my mind—as a journalist and at the same time I was terribly affected by the news. I thought John Kennedy would represent for a long time the kind of President that we would have [going forward]—the demographic cultural shift from very serious, older men to this dynamic younger guy.

I was a child of the '50s. For my generation—I was born in 1940—the pathways were clear. Everyone I knew at college in those days got a job. We were a relatively small generation because we were born just before the war. Life seemed filled with possibilities for us. In fact, life *was* filled with possibilities.

We lived in a part of the world where television wasn't readily available until, for me at least, 1955. Suddenly these masters of that medium, the Kennedy family and the way they ran the campaign, made it a vicarious experience for those of us who were living out there on the Great Plains in the middle part of America. He presented something that we were only able to read about: this enormous wealth, a compound on Cape Cod, the hobbies of sailing and skiing, golfing. That was pretty much reserved for the wealthy class in America in those days. So it seemed at once distant and glamorous, but also something we could share vicariously because of the way it played in our living rooms.

My parents were lifelong Democrats and Harry Truman aficionados. They were a little skeptical about Kennedy's age and about his Catholicism. They were skeptical of his wealth, and that represented a generational shift, as well. I wanted to be part of that, as I think a lot of my generation did. We didn't want to stand in line and wait our turn anymore. We wanted to do what they were doing. Our parents, who had been so tempered by the Great Depression and by the war and had real working-class suspicions about the wealthy, were not as enthusiastic. It was a generational thing: Here was a young man—and he had served in the war. He didn't have a button-down shirt and the double-breasted suits. We could identify with him from a generational point of view. I think his greatest legacy is that he represented that generational change in which he seemed to speak to people who were younger than he was as well as the people who were his age and older, and say to the younger people, "You can have a role in the destiny of your country, as well." That was a pretty remarkable change. Before that, they were expected to stand in line. And wait their turn. Kennedy said, "We're going to need everybody." And he personified that with his youthful energy and the way he lived his life.

And I think he represented hope. Life could be better for all manner of people in America, not just for those who were politically connected.

As I raced out to the local strategic air command headquarters [on the day Kennedy died] to see what kind of alert they were on, I remember vividly thinking, *This is gonna change us. This is gonna make us a different place.* Surreal: It completely shattered my consciousness about what life should be about.

My wife was teaching school [that day]. I don't remember what we were doing on Friday night, but the whole weekend was consumed by it. We were in church on Sunday morning when the pastor came back out after delivering the sermon, and with a shocked look on his face said, "They've just shot Lee Harvey Oswald. What are we coming to in this country?" So I raced back down to the station, but there was not much we could do about that in Omaha. I guess it was Sunday night when Meredith and I, still dazed, realized what we'd just been through, and the uncertainty of it all.

TOM BROKAW was the managing editor and anchor of *NBC Nightly News* from 1983 to 2004. He is also the author of the best-seller *The Greatest Generation* and several other books.

"Where Were You . . . ?"

Bill O'Reilly: Being Irish Catholic Helped

I WAS IN BROTHER DIODATI'S RELIGION CLASS at Chaminade High School in Mineola, New York. The principal came on the loudspeaker and said the President's just been shot, and then they put the CBS radio report on. Everybody was a little bit confused 'cause we didn't know whether the President had died.

I went home and my parents were watching the TV news. My parents weren't demonstrative. There wasn't any histrionics. They were sad, didn't attempt to engage me in conversation on it. Because my maternal grandmother is a Kennedy, he was revered in my family. It became a fairly emotional situation. [Being] Irish helped, Catholic helped. All of that. I at 13 didn't have an emotional connection to him, but certainly my parents did and everybody in the neighborhood did. It's almost like Pearl Harbor was for my parents' generation. There wasn't anything that was close to the impact of that. The '50s were a tranquil time and nothing really happened. There hadn't been an assassination since [William] McKinley. And then all of a sudden 1963 comes along and you have this huge national tragedy. And there was

mystery surrounding it, and there was anger—all that played into it. When 9/11 happened, everybody knows where they were—Pearl Harbor, Kennedy.

I wrote *Killing Kennedy* because most people just don't know what happened. There are all these crazy conspiracy theories that people made a lot of money on. We just wanted to make it very clear what happened, who was responsible, and to tell people the truth about the Kennedy administration. Americans, particularly younger Americans, should know about icons like Lincoln and Kennedy. I wove in as much emotion as I could, which is why I wrote about the death of his baby and the heroism of Jackie—to show people they are real people, not somebody made up. The man was not a good President in the beginning. He was a flawed individual. He became a good President and he changed his whole outlook on life. I don't have a lot of philosophical points to make, and I don't like to do speculation, [but] Kennedy changed after the death of his baby. He became a totally different person, a totally different President. People can change and life dictates that. Some people

never do, but everybody gets the opportunity. And he did. Unfortunately, the change was brief because a gunman cut him down.

What might he have done? He would have been reelected, no question about that. Vietnam might have been altered, though he was adamant he wasn't going to give in to worldwide communism, which is why the Cuban missile crisis went our way. Not so sure he would have been a dove on Vietnam, but it would have been handled differently than what Johnson did. Otherwise, it's impossible to say.

Do I think we'll ever see the likes of him again? Sure. There are great men and women all over the place. It's just a question of them having enough courage of putting up with the crap they'll have to put up with in public life. We live in a very vicious media culture and good people don't want to put themselves in that zone. And I don't blame them.

BILL O'REILLY is the host of the Fox News program *The O'Reilly Factor*.

Dan Rather: Born in Texas, Working in Dallas

I WAS IN DALLAS, IN CHARGE OF CBS NEWS ON-SCENE COVERAGE OF the President's trips. The memory often resonates in odd moments and places. For example, frequently when I gaze at the moon. Generally, the echo in my mind's ear is some version of, *What might have been? What would our country and history have been like if he had lived?*

Because of the sudden and tragic ending, the Kennedy years are but of one brief shining moment in the broad sweep of American history. But what a moment. The

hope and promise of the first President born in the 20th century opened up new vistas for all Americans. The hammer to the heart which was the assassination makes the moment more poignant and meaningful for those of us who lived through it. It is a moment for the ages.

DAN RATHER, a native of Houston, Texas, is anchor and managing editor of AXS TV's *Dan Rather Reports* and is the former news anchor for the *CBS Evening News*.

Dan Rather outside the Texas School Book Depository in Dealey Plaza in 1967.

In the summer of 1963, the season before the assassination, Tony Bennett and his wife, Sandy, at home in New Jersey with sons Danny and Dae.

Tony Bennett: The Kennedys Mattered

REMEMBER I WAS AT THE LATIN CASINO IN PHILLY. I WAS VERY INTO the Kennedys at that time; I still am. They treated me so beautiful there, when I would see them in Cape Cod. I knew the mother, a sensational lady—the mom treated me wonderful. Jack—I knew him as much as anybody knew him. He was great, so handsome and exciting, bigger than a movie star. He meant a lot to us. So I heard, and I just couldn't believe it. Surreal? That's how it was for me. It affected me that much, to where I couldn't remember what I was doing. A very strange time. I remember it just felt like the Declaration of Independence had ended. I'm always getting in trouble because I'm a liberal Democrat and always saying things, but this seemed so destructive. And then with his brother Bobby. The Kennedys mattered, they were important. I'm still in touch; I became great friends with Ted, and I'm getting together with some of the family soon—the annual JFK Profile in Courage Award at the library in Boston. I'll see Caroline. The story of that family, goodness . . .

TONY BENNETT's singing career spans seven decades. He is an Army veteran and longtime civil rights activist.

Garrison Keillor:
As I Remember, Brahms

A SWEET SUNNY DAY IN Minneapolis, on the university campus, warm for November, and I was walking with my girlfriend Mary Guntzel out of Scott Hall, where she'd been practicing organ in the basement, playing Bach chorales, and I overheard someone saying that the President had been shot.

Next door to Scott was Eddy Hall and the studios of KUOM, where I'd been hired in September, at the age of 21, as an announcer, a jump up from my job washing dishes in a cafeteria. The two of us hustled over and through the back door into a hallway where the AP Teletype stood in a closet, and I opened the door and saw the early bulletins—very fragmentary, incomplete sentences, the machine stuttering, then stopping, scrolling down a few lines, then stuttering again.

Shots had been fired, the President had been hit. Blood was seen. The motorcade was heading for a hospital. The President was seen lying facedown in the backseat of the limousine. We stood watching the keys banging out the lines. I walked into the KUOM office and was stunned by how quiet and unperturbed it was, people at their desks, everything ordinary, and into the music library, where the announcer Russell Walsh was listening to the on-air monitor—something symphonic, Brahms I think—and I said that the President had been shot in Dallas and we had better make an announcement. When I went back to the Teletype, the AP said that the President had died of a gunshot to the head at one p.m. I tore it off and took it back to the news studio, and Russ faded the Brahms and I said, "We interrupt this program to bring you an important news bulletin," a line that I must've heard someone say on the radio when I was a kid, and I gave the news and the Brahms came back up. KUOM played somber music the rest of the afternoon, and all of us sat in the lounge and watched Walter Cronkite and Dan Rather. Most of us were smoking and nobody said much. I stepped outside and the campus felt empty. Couples walked past in silence. I went back to my apartment and watched TV for the next three days.

GARRISON KEILLOR, writer and humorist, is host of the American Public Media radio show *A Prairie Home Companion*.

Art Garfunkel and Paul Simon, circa 1964.

Art Garfunkel: Eyes Unfocused

H AVING A HANDSOME PRINCE AS OUR PRESIDENT, we sensed—I did—that it was all too pretty for realpolitik. I was in architecture school at Columbia in New York in 1963. There, in Avery Hall, among the drafting tables, the day was suddenly suspended. Eyes went unfocused among my classmates.

"The party's over," is what we felt that afternoon. But through the years, I have come to question what power means to each President. Was confrontation with the Soviet Union unavoidable? Through time, I ask myself: Did John Kennedy lead us up a path of prudence? Doesn't the awesome sobriety of the presidency require the nation to look beyond the charisma?

Am I being a spoilsport? I'm sort of chopping at his legs a little bit, but what I'm doing here is not just idolatry. With years gone by, mine is a shaded response. Yes, we all loved him. He was a big star. I remember hitchhiking in Europe feeling we Americans were lucky sons of guns: We have such a likable hero in the White House. Our nation is touched. But so what?

Did Paul and I talk about him? Not really. Our dialogue was always jokes; hip, inside fooling around. We did not speak for a generation. We were not a political act. We spoke for the thoughtful museum-going kind of girl, not for the nation.

ART GARFUNKEL teamed with his schoolboy friend Paul Simon in the late 1950s to form what would become one of the most popular singing duos in history.

Mikhail Baryshnikov: Unfathomable from Afar

AT THE TIME, I WAS A YOUNG MAN OF 15 LIVING IN SOVIET-occupied Latvia. Even at that age, I understood the historic brutality of the Soviet regime and was perfectly aware that Joseph Stalin, our dear "Father of the Nation," had quietly killed more than 20 million of his own people. But to think that in the United States—the free world—a young, progressive, vibrant, charismatic man like President Kennedy could be brutally murdered in front of the entire nation was completely unfathomable.

Half a century later, the principles and aspirations set forth by President Kennedy—his unwavering dedication to social service, responsibility and freedom—continue to resonate and inspire many of today's political figures. And even when faced with great tumult, JFK's legacy remains a guiding light in the storm.

MIKHAIL BARYSHNIKOV has danced with the American Ballet Theatre and New York City Ballet, among other troupes, since defecting from Russia in 1974.

Dick Van Dyke: Forgotten Songs

IT WAS DURING THE TIME OF *THE DICK VAN DYKE SHOW*. I WAS RETURN-ing from lunch with a couple of cast members and found our assistant director John Chulay slumped over and crying on the sofa in the living room set. He had a radio. The only TV set around was the prop model. John said, "President Kennedy has been shot." We sat by the radio until the President's death was confirmed, then canceled the show and went home.

I had forgotten that I was scheduled to record an album that night. Thirty musicians were rehearsed and were waiting at a studio. Canceling wasn't an option. To do so would have cost a fortune. With tears in our eyes we recorded 10 songs.

I don't recall the titles. Only the crying.

DICK VAN DYKE is an actor, dancer and singer who has won a Tony, a Grammy and four Emmys in his seven-decade career.

The Dick Van Dyke Show on television, which costarred Mary Tyler Moore, was a cultural touchstone that helped define the energetic, postwar Kennedy era in America.

Mikhail Baryshnikov in the 1960s.

Plácido Domingo: Songs Unsung

MY WIFE, MARTA, AND I HAD MOVED to Tel Aviv in 1962, just after we were married, to join the Israel opera company, our first professional engagement outside of Mexico. In September 1963, the company put on a new production of Mozart's *Don Giovanni*. I was singing the role of Don Ottavio and Marta was singing Donna Elvira.

On the evening of November 22, we were about to perform when one of our cast members—an American soprano—came rushing backstage in tears, almost hysterical, with the news that President Kennedy had been assassinated. The cast included singers from many different countries, but this came as an incredible shock to everyone. Of course we canceled the evening's performance.

I was only 22 years old at the time, but that moment remains tragically unforgettable—for me, and for so many millions of other people around the world. John Kennedy, with his youthfulness and intelligence, had seemed to us a symbol of hope for the world, and he was removed from the scene long before he had managed to achieve most of the goals that he might otherwise have accomplished.

PLÁCIDO DOMINGO, a native of Spain, has sung an unprecedented 140 different roles in his 50-plus-year career as one of the world's foremost operatic tenors.

Alec Baldwin: The Mothers Cried

I WAS AT MY FRIEND'S HOUSE ON A COLD LATE-November day on Long Island. We were five-year-olds, outside playing, and our mothers kept running into the house, ashen and crying, to watch the TV.

Kennedy, in my view, was definitely killed by a conspiracy, probably of rogue CIA and military factions that wanted a full-scale escalation of the Vietnam War. They likely felt Kennedy had let them down in Cuba, viewed him as a threat to U.S. national security and orchestrated his murder. The fact that JFK's assassination has never been honestly investigated is a shameful sin that will haunt this country forever.

ALEC BALDWIN is an award-winning actor, host of the NPR podcast series *Here's the Thing* and a columnist for *The Huffington Post*.

RALPH MORSE

New Yorkers in Times Square listening to a car radio for news of the assassination.

"Where Were You . . . ?"

James Earl Jones: All Men Are Created Equal

I WAS DOING A PLAY CALLED *NEXT TIME I'll Sing to You*. We were in rehearsals, preparing to go into previews. It was a play about a hermit and we were playing young people who were celebrating a hermit's life. Estelle Parsons, Harris Yulin were both in it. We had a break and I went round the corner to get a hero sandwich. While I was waiting for the sandwich to be made I heard that the President had been shot. I walked back to the rehearsal hall. We all gathered, the director and everybody involved. They said they were suspending rehearsal and the preview. The stage manager came to me and said, "Jimmy, the suspected shooter wasn't a black guy." And that surprised me—that that should come to his mind as important for me to know. It was an odd thing for him to say. And an odd thing for me to hear.

We just all gathered together as best we could. I remember going home and just watching TV—watching it unfold on TV. And not doing much else. It was nothing like I had ever experienced, or would.

I thought of the President in the same light as, then, Pope John and Martin Luther King. I thought, well, when men have done all they can do for

a cause, then it's not that they're dispensable, they are free of that responsibility. I just thought the President has done all he can. In my mind, he was free already of the responsibility of doing more to advance society.

It became a more bitter reality [with] all the other assassinations that followed. The certain hopelessness and realization that there were forces at work that were really, really evil. Something we'd have to someday deal with and confront.

But that moment, there was something equalizing about what it did to all of us. The director had no more influence, the stage manager, the actors or the man making the hero sandwich. We were trying to figure out how we were supposed to deal with this, trying to sense our own reactions, and nobody was putting on airs, nobody was being a tough guy, nobody was separate. We were all somehow strangely equalized. Which was one of his missions, JFK. No one was more important than anyone else at that moment. Because the important person was dead.

JAMES EARL JONES is an actor who has won numerous awards for his work in theater and film.

James Earl Jones as Othello in 1964, in a production featuring Julienne Marie.

Praying in New York City.

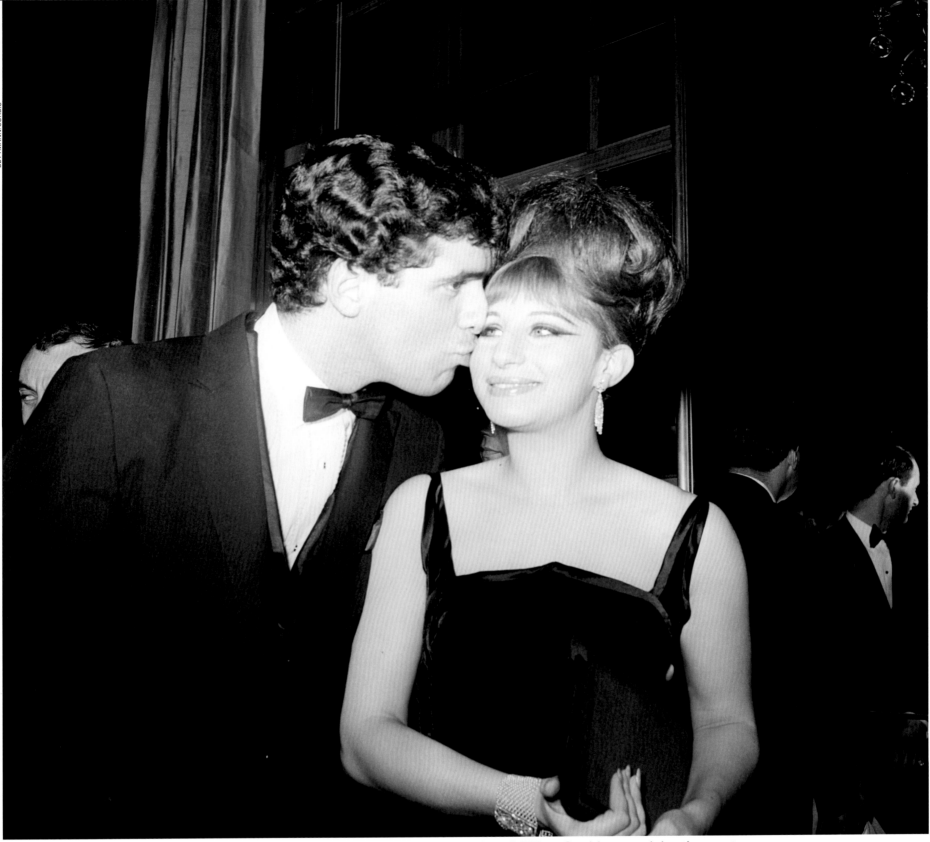

Barbra Streisand receiving a kiss from her husband, Elliott Gould, at a celebration party for the cast of Broadway's *Funny Girl* at the Rainbow Room in New York City.

Barbra Streisand: The Necklace

I HAD JUST GONE TO PICK UP THE FIRST serious piece of antique jewelry I ever bought—a beautiful Victorian choker. It was a lot of money for me to spend, but I was doing *Funny Girl* [on Broadway], so I could afford it. In the shop, we heard that the President was gone. I was so stunned and devastated that I got in a cab to go home. Driving through Central Park, I suddenly passed Elliott Gould—my husband at the time—sitting on a bench. How did he get there? It was like out of a dream. I stopped the cab and ran back to him and we just held each other.

I never could wear that necklace.

BARBRA STREISAND, an Oscar-, Tony- and Emmy-winning actress and a Grammy-winning singer, has been active in political affairs for decades.

Elliott Gould: The Husband's Remembrance

I WAS WITH A FRIEND WALKING TO A REHEARSAL that Barbra was in for the original stage production of *Funny Girl*. When we got there, we were told that the President had been shot and rehearsal had been canceled and everybody had left. I was concerned for Barbra. I didn't know where she was going. The street was chaotic. It was catastrophic what had happened and people were reacting and responding.

I was looking for Barbra. I saw her in her cab and I was able to run the cab down. My remembrance is more than just "ballpark" because there *was* a cab and it was unbelievable, in that chaos and with that traffic, and nobody knowing where they were going—I saw her in the cab. How Barbra recalls it is so beautiful. I know nothing about jewelry. As I remember it, it wasn't a dream. It was real. I'm sure we held each other.

There couldn't have been a conversation. There were no words. There were no words. It was like part of our spirit was killed. That's how deep it was. Barbra and President Kennedy were friendly. She was one of his favorites. The first time I voted, ever, was for John Kennedy. He meant so much to us. It was like a part of us was taken away. One of the most important parts of us—what President Kennedy represented to us.

When it comes to Barbra and me, it's so deep and we're part of one another's fiber. And President Kennedy was a part of us. I'll start to cry now. I didn't know how choked up I would be just talking as a singular solitary person. But when it comes to us, it's so deep . . . I care for Barbra so. And our stories are slightly different, but I felt that you would want both sides of it.

ELLIOTT GOULD, an Oscar-nominated actor, met his first wife, fellow Brooklynite Barbra Streisand, when they appeared on Broadway in the comedy *I Can Get It for You Wholesale*. They were married from 1963 to 1971.

"Where Were You . . . ?"

Beau Bridges: A Call to Duty

ON NOVEMBER 22, 1963, I WAS IN LOS ANGELES, PICKING OUT Christmas cards to send to friends and family. I was 21 years old, and serving in the Coast Guard Reserve. I had joined up right out of high school when President Kennedy put up the blockade on Cuba. The President had truly inspired me and a whole generation of young people. He seemed to be the first President in my lifetime that was more committed to worldwide humanitarian concerns rather than his own political survival.

I felt at this time that our biggest problem as human beings was an unwillingness to accept anything that was different: a different haircut, a different color skin, a different religion, a different culture. President Kennedy was a man who was poised to lead us into a future that was defined by respect: respect for ourselves and for our fellow man. He was a true peace warrior. I admired his leadership during the Cuban crisis. He stood firm but chose a path that avoided all-out war. His assassination was a shock and for a long time made me lose all hope for a brighter, more peaceful world. [Then] in 1968, the assassinations of Martin Luther King and Robert Kennedy affirmed for me the fact that my beloved country was a violent place and with the proliferation of guns and ignorance, not a very safe place.

Since then, there have been other leaders that have stepped forward to pick up and carry the torch of peace and love that was snuffed out so suddenly on that sunny day in November 1963. One of those people is our current President, Barack Obama. He has been courageous in his attempt to stand up to those who do not seem to recognize the need for compassion and patience as we deal with the complex problems of the world. JFK's legacy of peace, justice and equality for all is still alive today.

BEAU BRIDGES, veteran of eight years as a Coast Guard reservist,
is, as an actor, a three-time Emmy winner who has appeared in nearly 200 films and
television shows, playing roles up to and including a unicorn and Santa Claus.

In 1963, Beau Bridges was beginning his run in the TV show
Mr. Novak, playing a student whose teacher was young and idealistic—
as Bridges was himself.

A sailor salutes as the late President's casket passes by during the funeral procession in Washington.

Willie Mays: Hopeful

IT WAS OFF-SEASON FOR BASEBALL AND I WAS going to play some golf. I was just leaving, walking through the door. I'd left the radio on and heard a voice cut into the broadcast. It caught my attention. I backed up to listen.

The news didn't seem real. The man said President Kennedy had been shot. My heart filled with so much sadness and fear. How could they shoot the President? I started to cry. I stood there and listened as hard as I could. Maybe I had heard it wrong.

But I'd heard it right.

I had been invited to the inauguration, but couldn't make it. I always thought that I would have another chance to meet President Kennedy. I never did. But I have met many members of his family and that has been a wonderful thing in my life. They have gone forward and done great things with their lives.

Now, thinking back, there is still sadness and regret but even hope. I was sad for my country on that November day in 1963, but I see these young ones coming up and I have hope.

WILLIE MAYS, native of Alabama, is one of the greatest baseball players ever. In 1963 he batted .314 for the San Francisco Giants.

Billie Jean Moffitt (later, Billie Jean King) of Long Beach, California, in the mid-1960s.

Billie Jean King: A Special Date

I WAS CELEBRATING MY 20TH birthday. I was a student at what is now California State University, Los Angeles (then called Los Angeles State College). I had just walked out of my geography class and was headed to see friends at the tennis courts. As I got closer to the courts, my friends shouted to me that Kennedy had just been shot. It took a while for me to comprehend what they were saying. I think we were all stunned. We left the courts as a group and went back to the locker rooms, where we just hung out and talked. It was definitely a surreal moment and it took us some time to fully understand the impact of what we were hearing.

For my generation that day was a pivotal moment in history, and every year when my birthday rolls around, I still look back on where I was and what happened to our President and our nation that day.

BILLIE JEAN KING, an athlete, coach and humanitarian from California, won 39 Grand Slam tennis titles. In 2009 she was awarded the Presidential Medal of Freedom.

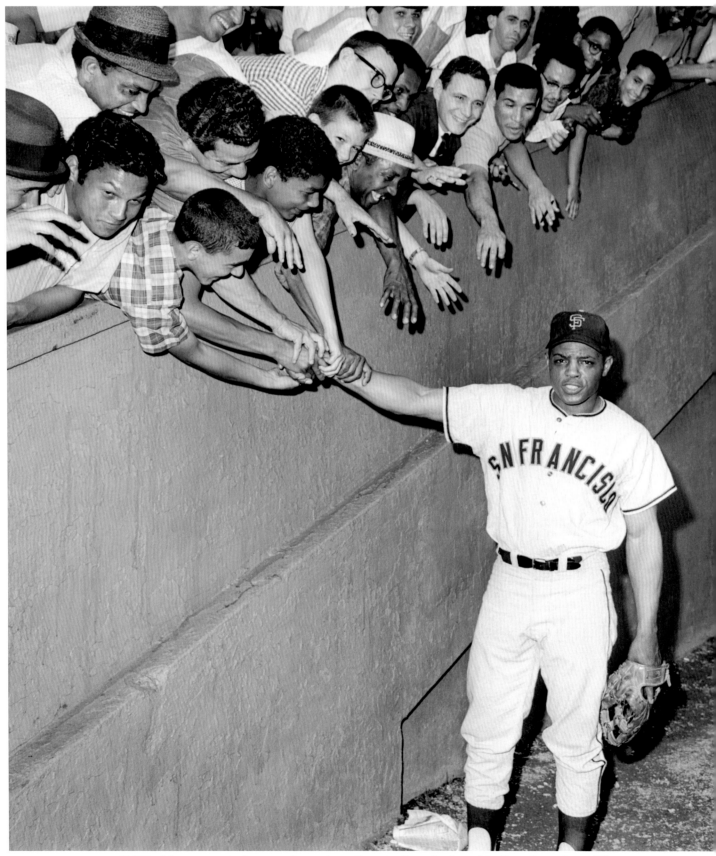

Willie Mays greets fans as he enters the stadium before his San Francisco Giants play the New York Mets in a 1962 game.

Roger Staubach:
Our Commander in Chief, Navy Guy

I WAS IN MY ROOM AT BANCROFT HALL AT the Naval Academy getting ready to go to my thermodynamics class. As I'm walking down Stribling Walk to class, the buzz was all over that the President was shot. And I said, "I hope he was just wounded." Then it got worse as we were walking down the walk. And when we got to class our teacher said, "He's not gonna make it. And you can either stay here in class and we'll go through the motions or you can go back to Bancroft Hall." So most of us went back to Bancroft Hall and they had a ceremony that night. The academy really felt very close to the President, being commander in chief and also because he was a Navy guy.

Our team had had a chance to meet the President. He was in our locker room after the '62 Army-Navy game. My first Army-Navy game, and here I have the President of the United States in the locker room! Because he was a Navy guy, we felt more akin to him. I think he felt more akin to us, also. Even though he had to switch sides at the game, I heard he whispered he'd rather stay on the Navy side.

Robert Kennedy was at some of our games. The Kennedys really loved our Navy team, especially the '63 season, when we had a great team and I'll bet [the President] was really looking forward to the Army-Navy game. He was well-loved by many in the country of course—very charismatic, that smiling face of his, very popular. Jackie Kennedy was popular, the whole Kennedy clan—but as I say, at the Naval Academy we definitely had a kinship with President Kennedy.

In November of 1963, we had been getting ready to play the Army-Navy game again. And so we met as a team and Coach Harden said, "We don't really know if the game's gonna be played." So we didn't practice. And then we got the word that the Kennedy family wanted us to play the game on behalf of the President.

The game had been postponed a week, and that day was an emotional time. With the President being assassinated, the game became secondary. We didn't have any pep rallies or any of the craziness you have before the Army-Navy game. That all was shut down. But all the emotion that everybody had kept inside came out at the game. It turned into a heck of a game. Army ended up on our two-yard line at the end, and we ended up winning, 21–15.

We wound up playing in Dallas that season. It's kind of ironic: In the Cotton Bowl in January, we played the University of Texas. We had a great season. We had beat Army, and now we were getting ready to play in Dallas—but in the heart of all of that, you just can't get over that the President was shot and killed here. It sure puts your priorities in perspective. I still see him smiling in the car, going down the streets of Dallas. Seeing that smiling face of his . . . and all of a sudden you realize he was shot and killed.

I worked downtown there in the off-season in the '70s [when I was with the Cowboys], right near where he was shot. It's still eerie even today when you go right to the area. It's still a weird feeling.

I think the city took a real hit, undeservedly. It's a shame Oswald was shot. When Ruby shot Oswald, that really put a wrench in things, and even to this day, it's amazing: not being able to have a final reason for what happened. I believe Oswald was the single shooter. But what made him do it? All of that mystery is a shame. He just happened to pick Dallas. The city took a heavy hit on it.

They still think of the assassination, here in Dallas, of course. The city has recovered, certainly. It's a great city, there's a lot going on. It's a vibrant city—that's why

Navy quarterback Roger Staubach in late 1963 with the Heisman Trophy. He had already caught the attention of LIFE's editors.

my family stayed here after I finished with the Cowboys. But the assassination is still a major topic of conversation as far as how people think of "Dallas, Texas." We're trying to do something on the 50th [anniversary] here, and I think I'm going to be involved in trying to help. The Cowboys have been given a bit of credit in making people aware that Dallas isn't just the city that shot the President.

Of course, it's a moment in history you would like to forget, but you can't. You wonder what he might have done, if. He was there for the early stages of the Vietnam War. I spent a year in Vietnam, and we had 58,000 killed over there. Our veterans weren't respected for fighting over there, that's how unpopular that war was. President Kennedy had his hands on the beginning of the war, but you just don't know if he would have continued to escalate it.

The LIFE cover? Yes, I was on the cover. I saw the magazine. I guess it was Friday when they were shipped out, before they immediately pulled it back. A number of them survived, and I got a copy, with that date, November 29. I have the copy with President Kennedy on the cover, too.

ROGER STAUBACH won the Heisman Trophy in 1963 and was slated to be on LIFE's cover before the assassination brought our presses to a halt. A graduate of the United States Naval Academy, he spent four years on active duty, and played 11 seasons with the Dallas Cowboys.

AMY LENNARD GOEHNER, a veteran of Time Inc. magazines, has served as a writer-reporter at LIFE Books for the past year.

Remembering the Moment, and the Times

ALWAYS KNOWN AS A MILL TOWN, THE CITY OF Lowell, Massachusetts—a jewel of the nation's 19th-century industrial revolution—has been forced to reinvent itself more than a few times since its mill days. Forty minutes' drive northwest of Boston, this diverse parish of 100,000, sitting at a sharp bend in the Merrimack River, is today a tough city, a sometimes troubled city and an often vibrant city, with a bustling university, a brewpub scene, a Red Sox Single-A minor league ball club and a well-regarded theater company that sometimes sees its productions noticed in *The Boston Globe*. A driving force behind the theater company is Nancy Donahue, philanthropist and mother of 11, grandmother of many more, who is involved in just about everything in town and is, at 83, a dedicated pickleball player (it's a tennis variant). She has been married for 60 years to Richard K. Donahue, who, like his brother Joe, is a lifelong lawyer in this town. Everyone in Lowell knows who the Donahues are, and most of them know that Dick and Nancy have lived "up on the hill" in the Belvidere section for just about forever. "Dick was in the Irish mafia," some of the old-timers will tell you. "He was with JFK."

Yes, he was—and he's the last of them able to tell the tales. Asked if any of his old comrades remain with whom he might reminisce, either by phone or maybe over a single-malt at the Last Hurrah at the Parker House in Boston, he says simply, "No. None."

Donahue was, back in the day, a politically inclined eager-beaver barrister who, even then, was amused by the rough-and-tumble traditions of Massachusetts politics that extended back to James Michael Curley, Honey Fitz and beyond. "When I was buying this house, well, there were these rivalries," he recalls with a smile. "This was the O'Dea house. I was on the other side. When this house was for sale, they wouldn't sell it to me. I knew this guy, and I had to buy it through a straw. That was 50 years ago."

He is sitting in the library of his fine house on Belmont Avenue on the sunny afternoon of the day when the John F. Kennedy Library will bestow its annual Profile in Courage Award on Gabrielle Giffords. He sits on the board of the library's foundation, having been involved with it since its inception, but: "I'm stepping down tonight. It's time." Donahue is 86 now, walks with the aid of a cane (his pickleball days, if there were any, are behind him), but he is as sharp and sly and wry as they all must have been in the late 1950s, when these sparkling satellites coalesced in an orbit around the sun that was John Fitzgerald Kennedy.

"I started with him right here in Lowell when he was a congressman. I was one of the local leaders in the campaign against [Henry] Cabot Lodge Jr. [for U.S. Senate in 1952]—which of course was a race Kennedy won at a time when he shouldn't have won, when he wasn't particularly well known. I was recruited. What had happened was, I had just won a tremendous victory—in the school committee." Donahue pauses here, acknowledging the humor with a half smile. "It was the result of a drunken wedding, with everyone telling me I should run and I said, 'Yes, I think I should.' And they said, 'Well, the election's Tuesday.' And that victory got some national attention—'national' being statewide. And at the time Kennedy had people out looking for people to work for him. I heard from them, and with this guy being Irish Catholic and all, I was anxious to get on board."

Donahue's recruiters and his two future friends/mentors/bosses in the Kennedy camp were Larry O'Brien of Springfield

and Kenny O'Donnell of Worcester—"they were sort of my godparents in politics"—who would remain with JFK until the end; they were with him in Dallas, a trip O'Donnell helped arrange. This Hibernian faction, which included Dave Powers, who would later coauthor a Kennedy memoir with O'Donnell entitled *Johnny, We Hardly Knew Ye,* warred with another group in the Massachusetts Democratic Party in the 1950s, and to hear Donahue tell it, both sides relished the battle. "I got involved in the fight for control of the state party, and control of the mechanism in the state party was a big deal. It was a fight with us against the McCormacks, and we won. And of course they accused us of cheating and all that, but anyway, that eventually went away and it all kept me in closer contact with Kennedy."

It is put to Donahue: "They called you guys JFK's Irish mafia."

"I don't know about that. That was after the fact—later."

"Do you know who came up with that?"

"No, I don't. Well, actually, I do know, but I can tell you—it wasn't one of Kennedy's favorite expressions."

"I can imagine."

"He didn't like that idea at all."

"With you guys—was he your friend? Were you friends with Jack Kennedy?"

"Sort of," Donahue says, and then pauses. "He was a great guy to be friends with, but he wasn't a friendly guy. Does that make sense? He was very thoughtful. Later, he took almost all the people who worked for him to Ireland. A wonderful time. He was very thoughtful.

"So at some point, it became clear that he was going to run for President," Donahue continues. "Now, before that, he had had that untoward campaign, which I did not participate in, for Vice President [in 1956]. It would have been a terrible thing, because they weren't going to win, and they would have said the whole thing was sunk because Kennedy was an Irish Catholic. But he didn't get to run anyway. Then he started to run for President seriously, and Larry was sort of the architect of it—and that I worked on."

Donahue remembers in particular going to Wisconsin and then West Virginia during a primary season that was quite different from today's extended, nationwide, multimillion-dollar campaigns. "There was one primary that we wanted to win, and it was in [rival] Hubert Humphrey's backyard—Minnesota was the next state over from Wisconsin. In those days we had a headquarters with a broken-down door. We had a few tables set up. And I remember sitting on a bench working opposite Mrs. Kennedy, who was sitting on a bench. She was so fastidious. She checked this, and checked that. She would write and correct and write again. She was a real hard worker. A lot of the relatives liked posing for pictures, but she was really working. And we won. We went into Humphrey's backyard and we won.

"Now, there are all kinds of mysterious stories about West Virginia, but what I'll tell you is the truth. We went down to West Virginia with a certain assurance that we were gonna blow 'em away, because we'd had a poll done by the illustrious pollster and it said we were way ahead. But he hadn't asked about the Catholic thing, and when that landed, it landed like a lead balloon. You have no idea about the bitterness of the non-Catholic vote.

"It was a relatively short campaign—five or six weeks. And we started hitting back with the [PT] 109. I would get a call, 'They're murdering us here with the Catholic stuff.' And I would say, 'Hit 'em with the 109.' West Virginia had the greatest percentage of gold-star mothers, really proud of what

O'Brien, O'Donnell, Powers, Donahue and company: Several of the best and the brightest from Massachusetts were on Kennedy's team even before he won the White House. One member of JFK's so-called "Irish mafia" is the last named, Richard K. Donahue, and he's the last survivor. **ROBERT SULLIVAN** visited with him at his longtime home in Lowell, and asked what it had been like—50 years and even longer ago.

Entertaining the Donahues at the White House, as JFK did not long before leaving for Dallas, was quite like welcoming any of the extended clan of Kennedys: a lot of Irish American bonhomie, great hair and a lot of kids in tow. In this period, the President was balancing the competing personalities—and cultures—of his policy intelligentsia and the Massachusetts crowd that had brought him to the dance. Dick Donahue of course had no idea that, when he resigned, he was leaving just before the lights would go out.

Remembering the Moment, and the Times

Opposite, top: On May 11, 1960, in Charleston, West Virginia, Democratic presidential candidates John F. Kennedy and Hubert Humphrey shake hands after the primary, which Kennedy has just won. Humphrey bows out of the race after this defeat, but Lyndon Baines Johnson will press his suit until the convention in Los Angeles—though West Virginia is a crippling blow. Bottom: The widow Jacqueline Kennedy visits her husband's grave in December 1963 with, from left, former White House staffers John J. McNally, Larry O'Brien and Kenny O'Donnell and sister Lee Radziwill. Above: Caroline Kennedy and Dick Donahue at the Kennedy Library. When both returned for the annual dinner this year, Caroline offered moving remarks in introducing the Profile in Courage honoree, Gabrielle Giffords, and came as close as she has in 50 years to speaking publicly about her father's death: "Our family is still suffering from the heartbreak of gun violence. No one should have to lose a husband, a wife, a father, a child, to senseless murder. But as our honoree has shown, out of that pain and tragedy, we must find the strength to carry on, to give meaning to our lives, and build a more just and peaceful world."

their sons had done in the service. That started to help.

"Now, the greatest speech I ever heard [Kennedy] give, and I have said this before, was on television in West Virginia. It doesn't exist, because in those days they erased the tapes. But he said that he was not disqualified for the presidency because of his baptism. He was not disqualified from being an American because of his baptism. Kennedy was magnificent that time. You could really feel his greatness."

Kennedy did win West Virginia, a crucial victory over Humphrey and Lyndon Johnson in the primary season. Whether his victory had anything at all to do with Joe Kennedy's solicitation of mob pressure on the unions, well, that is a point Donahue doesn't raise—filed under, perhaps, "all kinds of mysterious stories." In his view, "the 109" and Kennedy's forthrightness in addressing the religion issue carried the day, and led to a big blowout for the stalwarts. "Right on the eve of the election, the hotel had been filled with Kennedy staffers, but the campaign thought that we were going to lose, and most people left—back to Washington or wherever, so they wouldn't have to be there. But those that stayed, well, it was very closely contested with Lyndon, and when we won, I still think it was my biggest thrill in politics. Everyone there cut loose."

Donahue returned home, if briefly. "I left West Virginia, and I had to come back and practice law. I saw the debate with Johnson. That was pure Kennedy: wanting to tell the world how important it was that Lyndon continue to lead the Senate. He always used a silky knife, not a sloppy knife. Everyone knew exactly what he meant.

"And then I was a delegate to the convention. No, I was not involved in any of the discussions that led to Johnson being put on the ticket, and anyone who says they were is lying, because we had such bitterness against Johnson. I thought it would be [Missouri senator] Stuart Symington or someone like that. But that [decision] was all Jack. Bobby was so against it. But Jack knew he needed the Southern Democrats, and he made the decision himself. He was a smart politician." Donahue goes on to say, later, in circling back to Johnson: "After the assassination, some of our people just destroyed themselves. So bitter. They blamed Johnson, which was nuts. He didn't pull any trigger. They faded away in their anger. I unfortunately saw a lot of guys I had great respect for lose it. There was a lot of drinking going on, and they fell apart as a group."

But before the team split in remorse and recrimination, there would be triumph—the greatest triumph. "When he was elected, I was at what they called 'Bobby's House' at the Cape. Bobby, Kenny, Larry, Sargent Shriver. And it was long ago, so very different than today. We had a television in what was called the family room, and we had a phone on the sun porch. What we were getting out there was quite different than what the television was saying. Much more subdued, and we knew it was close. And finally [Jack] said, 'Well, I'm going to bed and you all go home,' and we did. And the next day, when things sorted themselves out, when Kennedy came into the room, we all stood up. Well, we never stood up for the guy. But now we did.

"I was getting my introduction to the way Washington government works. That morning, this fellow, who suddenly shows up, says to me, 'Good morning, Mr. Donahue.' He was with the Secret Service, and I'm thinking, 'How does this guy know my name?'"

What, Donahue is asked, was your role in the administration? He leans back in his chair and smiles. "Well," he says. "I ran the government." He laughs lightly.

"What happened was: Kennedy decided to give me a job. I was put in charge of appointments, and I was doing that with Kenny O'Donnell. I started with that, and instead of coming back to Lowell, I had to go back to Washington. My role never really changed. When Kennedy found you were being tasked with something, he thought about you that way. *Oh, this needs to be assigned, that's Donahue.* I soon learned: You did what the President thought you were doing. 'Have Dick take care of this guy.' Because, you know, you may think that you run the President. But the President runs the country."

The Massachusetts Democratic party had been fractious, and so was the White House; famously, the academics (Arthur Schlesinger Jr., Ted Sorensen) were suspicious of the Irish Catholics from Massachusetts, and vice versa. Donahue is asked about the infighting, and he smiles quickly before answering with what—he wants it known—is a joke, whether or not it's true: "Well, it was a working group. People worked hard. But, yeah, sure [there were rivalries]. Luckily, those bastards have died."

Donahue was not in Dallas. O'Brien, O'Donnell and Powers were, but Donahue had handed in his resignation to return to Lowell and his law practice one week before; the gracious letter from the President respecting Donahue's wishes, framed on a wall of the Belmont Avenue house along with other mementos, is dated November 19, 1963. It refers to working together again in the future.

"They had a nice goodbye party for me on the boat, the *Honey Fitz,* just a week before he died," says Donahue, who would go on to a tremendously successful career as a lawyer, even unto becoming the president and COO of Nike. He retired from practicing law in 2010.

So he wasn't in Dallas that day, he was in Lowell.

"I was right out there, raking leaves, when I heard."

He stops. "No, that's not right. That was later. I was having lunch at the Yorick Club with Kenny O'Donnell's brother. Some reporter from the *Globe* was in town looking around for me, for a story on what's it like to be back in Lowell after being in the White House. The Yorick Club did have a TV screen. That's where I heard. Later, I was raking leaves.

"I have to say, in retrospect, I was lucky to have just resigned. I had the luxury of weeping by myself and with my family."

ROBERT SULLIVAN is the managing editor of LIFE Books.

LIFE Stays on the Story

When a team of journalists deploys, there are orders from the boss or conversations among themselves: "You do this, I'll do that." As LIFE editors and photographers flew from Los Angeles to Dallas on the fateful afternoon, Richard B. Stolley was determined to make his way to Dealey Plaza, and thus did he find the Zapruder film. His colleague, staff photographer **ALLAN GRANT,** accompanied by reporter Thomas Thompson, would see if maybe, just maybe, the Oswalds could be found.

ALLAN GRANT (2)

NEW YORKER ALLAN GRANT WAS OUT in Los Angeles working with Richard Stolley and the rest of LIFE's L.A. bureau in 1963. "He was very handsome and glamorous," Stolley remembered when Grant died in 2008 at age 88, "two virtues that made him popular in Hollywood." True enough: In 1962, Grant enjoyed a shoot with Marilyn Monroe that is today famous, since it appeared in LIFE's August 3 issue of that year. She died on the 5th. Grant also fashioned memorable pictures of such as Richard Nixon hosing down a roof fire at his rented house in Los Angeles in 1961 and A-bomb tests in the Nevada desert. Asked by fellow LIFE photographer John Loengard what kind of shooter he was, Grant answered forthrightly: "I would say a good one, for starters. I stayed [at the magazine] for a long time. I was very versatile; I did everything."

A valued professional, then, who flew commercial to Dallas on November 22. "Every journalist in the country seemed to be on a flight to Dallas that day," Grant later remembered. "The aisles of my flight were cluttered with heavy video cameras, tripods, lights." Just after 11 a.m., as the airplane was about to take off, one of the pilots came on the intercom, as Grant recalled: " 'Ladies and gentlemen' he said, then took a deep breath, 'We have just been informed that President John F. Kennedy has died a few moments ago, I'm so sorry.' His voice choked up, then faded

into the hushed silence on the airplane." Stolley, Grant and Thompson recovered as well as they could during the flight; they had work to do. "When we landed we contacted the Dallas bureau of LIFE and were told of the capture, in a movie theater, of Lee Harvey Oswald . . . The corridors of the jail were swarming with photographers and reporters . . . all trying to get the same shot of Oswald being moved from one room to another a few yards away . . . Knowing LIFE could always pick up that shot from one of the news photographers, I left the county jail.

"[Thompson] had spent his youth in Dallas and managed to get the address of a rooming house where the suspect lived. There we found a red brick house with a rather friendly talkative housekeeper who showed us the closet-size room she rented to a 'Mr. O.H. Lee' for $8 a week. She showed us the phone in the rooming house and told us of the phone calls made by the strange man to Irving, Texas, a small town between Dallas and Fort Worth. She said he always spoke in a foreign language when he made most of his calls. She said that a swarm of Secret Service men or FBI agents had descended on the rooming house looking for any evidence they could find. We thanked the landlady for the information and headed for Irving, Texas. We were not looking for O.H. Lee but for Lee Harvey Oswald, the name of the recently captured suspect. I reloaded my cameras en route to Irving."

In Irving, thanks to Tommy Thompson's Texas accent and cordial manner, the LIFE team found the house of Michael and Ruth Paine, the latter of whom had become a friend of Marina Oswald and, in fact, in the brief time period before the assassination, was Marina's host. The Paines had lived in Irving since 1959, and Ruth had had an interest in the Russian language—so finding Marina in the area was a gift. Lee Harvey Oswald lived principally in the Dallas boarding house, but had called the Paine house often, and did stay there with his wife and daughters on November 21. The next morning he left for work with a large package he had earlier stored in the garage, a parcel now believed to have contained a 6.5-mm caliber Mannlicher-Carcano rifle.

Grant remembered that he and Thompson approached the Paines trepidatiously, and "when Tommy asked if [Ruth] believed Lee Harvey Oswald could have shot the President, a distraught looking elderly woman in a nurse's uniform with her stockings rolled down to her knees, sitting in a dark corner of the room, jumped up and said, 'Don't you think I should answer that question? I'm Lee's mother!' Tommy and I were astounded and moments later we got another shock. A very pretty and very pale young woman appeared in the doorway with a small baby in her arms and headed towards the kitchen. It appeared that we had stumbled onto the alleged assassin's family . . ." The photographs on these pages were made on November 22.

With the Oswalds in Irving

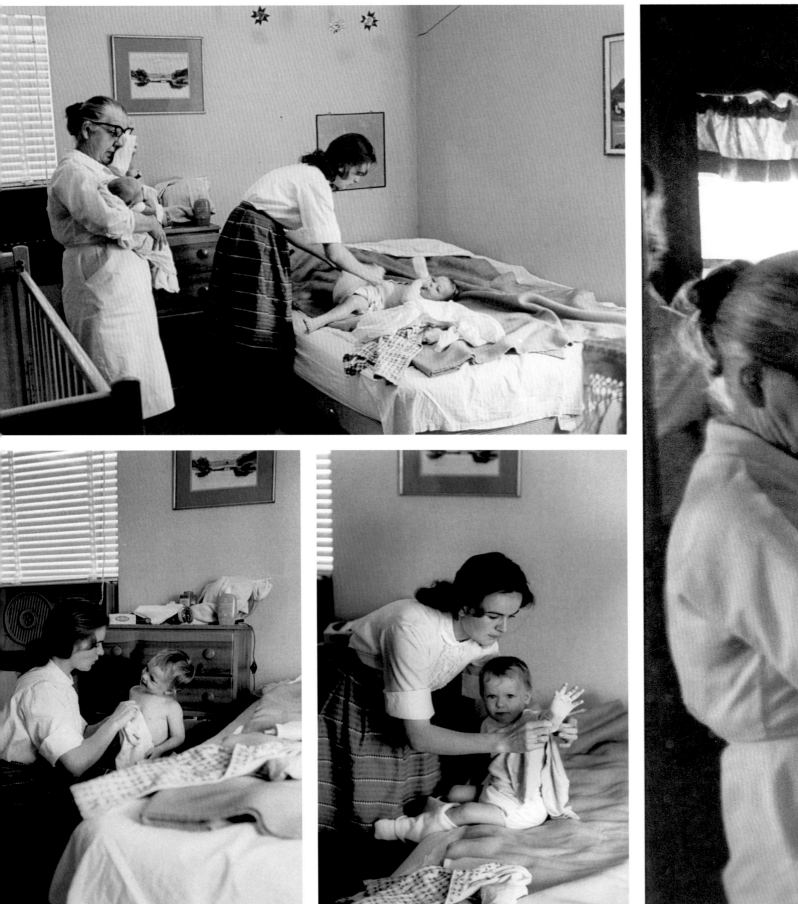

At the Paines' house in Irving, Grant and Thompson were a bit surprised although certainly pleased that the FBI or other authorities weren't present when they arrived. In fact, Marina and Marguerite Oswald had already reported to police headquarters in Dallas, and Marina had given an affidavit. In this domestic setting, Grant made the first of his memorable pictures of the Oswald family: Marina; Marguerite, her mother-in-law; her brother-in-law, Robert; and her two daughters (although the photographs wouldn't be deemed memorable for a good long while, as will be explained shortly). Afterward, he and Thompson stood watch outside in the street until the lights were turned off inside the home, hoping to protect the exclusivity of their story from other reporters who might show up. Then, as Richard Stolley has recounted earlier, they returned to their Dallas hotel, having put in place a plan to spirit the Oswald family from Irving into the city and to perhaps arrange a visit with Lee Harvey Oswald. Grant remembered: "Early Saturday morning,

November 23, we returned to the Paine house. There were freshly washed diapers drying in the sun and a suitcase waiting to be packed for the short trip to the Adolphus Hotel and then on to the Dallas county jail. Marina put a fresh diaper on her daughter June. Marguerite cradled young Rachel in her arms while wiping away some tears in anticipation of seeing her son in the Dallas jail and perhaps finally finding out from Lee Harvey what was going on . . . [Marina] continued with her chores. She had an inner peace that I thought might save her from being destroyed by this catastrophic event that eventually would take her husband from her just as swiftly as John Kennedy was taken from his family."

Into Dallas

In Dallas, the feds, who had called Stolley, finally entered this story, as Grant remembered vividly: "Shortly before noon we were startled by a loud knock on the door of our hotel suite. We quietly moved the family to one of the bedrooms and closed the door after locking it on the inside. The knock got louder and was followed by an announcement, 'This is the FBI open up now.' Tommy asked for some kind of identification to be slipped under the door. We were told that if we didn't open the door now we would be facing serious charges for 'harboring persons that may have been involved in a serious crime.' Tommy shrugged, opened the door slowly and peered over the shoulder of this tall, well-dressed man holding his FBI identification in his hand. It identified the man as a special agent for the FBI named Bardwell Odum." In the photographs opposite, at the hotel, Odum is accompanied by a dark-haired woman who had been retained by Grant and Thompson as a Russian interpreter.

Grant asked Special Agent Odum how he had found them. "'The same way you found out that they lived in Irving, Texas,' he answered, matter-of-factly. I asked if he would permit me to photograph his interrogation of Marina. 'It's your hotel room. Do what you have to.'

"I knocked on the bedroom door. Marguerite opened it. Marina was fixing her hair in the mirror, getting ready to visit Lee Harvey. Marguerite announced that she had made her own arrangements to see her son (evidently using her phone in the bedroom) with Captain Will Fritz of the Dallas Police Department, whom she said she saw on television. They said they would call her back at the Adolphus using the registered name Grant as a room number and confirm the arrangements for the visit for Marina, her two children and Oswald's mother, Marguerite, and his brother, Robert, and give them a scheduled time. Somewhat stunned by what Marguerite did, Tommy introduced the Oswalds to FBI Agent Odum, explaining that Marina spoke very little English and offering him our Russian interpreter." In the photograph opposite, bottom: Marina, the interpreter, Agent Odum, Marguerite and Robert Oswald.

Oswald's Funeral

DONALD UHRBROCK (4)

Now then: Why didn't Allan Grant's extraordinary photographs become famous in their time? Well, after the authorities moved the Oswald family to a secure location, Grant's work was done, and he returned to L.A. He recalled that on Sunday, after a fitful sleep, he was awoken by his fishing buddy Leo: "'Hey . . . what the hell are you doing home? I thought you'd still be in Dallas.'

"'Why, what's up?' I asked. 'Someone just shot Oswald!' he yelled, 'Turn on your damn TV set.' Two weeks later LIFE published one small picture of Marina Oswald from our exclusive story of the *other family*." Actually, LIFE published a picture of Marguerite, too, as you will see in the reprinted issue included with this volume, but Grant's point stands—and now, fittingly, the other pictures and story do appear exclusively in LIFE, 50 years after the fact.

Oswald had indeed been shot, and LIFE stayed on this story, with photographer Don

Uhrbrock picking up the assignment; his photographs of the funeral, on November 25 at Fort Worth's Rose Hill Cemetery, are seen here. As with so much that had happened and was continuing to happen, there was chaos and confusion at the scene. The minister who was scheduled to preside at the graveside ceremony failed to show, and Rev. Louis A. Saunders, executive secretary of the Fort Worth Area Council of Churches, was pressed into service. Above, left, and top right: Security was heavy at the cemetery's chapel, and members of the press corps volunteered as pallbearers. Above, right: The casket. The original gravestone bore the years of life and death, too, but it was later stolen. Today, a flat marker simply reading OSWALD marks the spot. Cemetery officials will not direct tourists to it. On the page opposite: Marina, Robert and Marguerite Oswald, with the children, June and infant Rachel, weep during the burial.

Some updates: Both Marguerite and Robert came to dislike the Paines, judging Ruth to be a publicity seeker in the aftermath of the tragedy; eventually Marina split from her, too. Today Ruth Paine lives in California, where she gives her time to her Quaker faith and various liberal organizations. Marina Oswald remarried in 1965, and she and her second husband, Kenneth Porter, raised the girls (and their own two sons) in the Dallas countryside, away from the glare. Marina became a U.S. citizen in 1989. The girls grew up as June and Rachel Porter, young Rachel discovering her birth father's history only when, as an adolescent, she stumbled on a box of telltale papers in the attic. Marina today professes her late husband's innocence (while never recanting her testimony to the Warren Commission), and the girls welcome any fresh probes of the evidence. Robert Oswald, 79, is a retired salesman in Wichita Falls, Texas.

Farewell

There would not be a funeral train as there had been with Abraham Lincoln and would be again with Bobby Kennedy. And yet the whole country came out and joined in, differently. There was television now, so there could be communal mourning. Parents explained to children what the images meant, and why the grandparents were crying. The Kennedy family stood tall and straight, though that surely took a mighty effort.

F EW EVENTS IN THE 20TH CENTURY—indeed, few in American history—were as universally experienced as the mourning for John F. Kennedy. The historian Martha Hodes has helped explain that in these pages, and a host of world citizens have testified to that fact. And now, here, these pictures from Washington, D.C., Arlington National Cemetery and elsewhere confirm what everyone knows: This was a seminal national moment.

But imagine, for a moment, what it was like on the inside—a grief no camera could capture. We all experienced the enormous tragedy as a stunning thing, but for the Kennedys it was the latest: This family simply could not escape the firm grip of fate. There were all the earlier disasters and adversities of the 1940s and '50s, already recounted. Since the great success of the 1960 election, there had been Joe, who had worked so vigorously and at times ruthlessly to see his sons triumph, having so little time to savor Jack's ascension before he had suffered a massive, disabling stroke that would leave him partially paralyzed if mentally lucid for the rest of his days. The grace of cognition would be its own curse: Before dying in 1969, Joe would bear near silent—but tear-stained—witness to the assassinations of two of his sons as well as the incident at Chappaquiddick and other sad events.

In August 1963, as we have briefly alluded to, Jackie gave birth to a second son, their fourth child by the family's reckoning—many were unaware that Jackie had given birth to a stillborn baby, a girl named Arabella, in 1956. The 1963 baby, Patrick Bouvier Kennedy, was born prematurely with a respiratory disease and lived less than two days. At the funeral, the presiding prelate had had to coax the heartbroken President away from the tiny casket. And then:

On November 22 of that same year, the sword of Damocles fell once more.

If, on the inside, this was the latest unfathomable affliction, on the outside this was the one we were compelled to share in. World leaders made their way to Washington; the man and woman in the street made their way to the Capitol rotunda. Everyone who couldn't pay respects in person gathered with friends or family around the television. At the time, this was the first great shared funeral (it predated Winston Churchill's by 14 months). Americans had been trained to come together for a space launch, and now there was this: We knew what to do, we knew how to enter the room. Also, the great advances in still photography had been achieved, and so we have a record unlike any other up to that point in historic time.

There is always one image, though. An entire war can be fought, and there is one image—or two or three or four—to symbolize it: a flag raised on Iwo Jima, a sailor kissing a nurse in Times Square. John F. Kennedy was killed, the entire world bade farewell, but we remember the President's son, saluting along with the military escort. It is a beautiful and painful image. It is from the outside, and from the inside.

ELLIOTT ERWITT/MAGNUM

HENRY BURROUGHS/AP

U pon landing at Andrews Air Force Base on November 22, President Johnson had asked for his countrymen's help in leading the nation. One who quickly offers assistance is the Republican Dwight D. Eisenhower, who only three years earlier had occupied the Oval Office (above). Johnson chooses to walk in the funeral procession, a gesture for which the widow Jacqueline Kennedy will thank him in a handwritten note. At left, members of the White House staff file past the flag-draped coffin, in which the late President is lying in repose (as opposed to the public "lying in state") in the East Room of the Executive Mansion for 24 hours before being transferred by horse-drawn caisson to the U.S. Capitol—proceeding, fittingly, through the daylong rain. Opposite: In the Capitol rotunda, Jacqueline and Caroline Kennedy kneel and pray as the casket rests on the Lincoln Catafalque, upon which America's first great martyr's coffin had lain.

President Kennedy had been killed on a Friday; his state funeral in Washington would last the following three days. On Sunday, hundreds of thousands of Americans stood patiently in line, day and night, outside the U.S. Capitol, waiting a turn to file past the coffin and say farewell. Former Presidents Truman and Eisenhower had visited in the East Room, and now the citizenry came forth. On Monday morning there was a Requiem Mass at the Cathedral of St. Matthew the Apostle on Rhode Island Avenue, several blocks from the White House. In the photograph at top, the caisson outside the church awaits the casket, and, at bottom, Mrs. Kennedy enters the cathedral with Caroline and John Jr. to attend the Mass; Senator Edward M. Kennedy of Massachusetts trails behind. Above, left: On the walk to St. Matthew's cathedral from the White House, a stroll Jackie and Jack used to take when attending Sunday Mass, the President's widow is accompanied on this day by (left to right) her brothers-in-law Stephen Smith (head down), Bobby Kennedy, Sargent Shriver (blue vest) and Ted Kennedy. More than 90 nations are represented by more than 200 dignitaries, including 19 heads of state at the Monday events, and Washington, so silent you can hear a pin drop, is as filled with witnesses as it might be for an inauguration.

The Funeral Procession

BETTMANN/CORBIS (2)

Above: Outside St. Matthew's cathedral, as the late President's casket is placed upon the caisson, Jackie, just a moment earlier, has urged her son—whose third birthday is today, November 25—to salute his father, and the boy's gesture is every bit as crisp as the color guard's. In world history, there has never been a more visually indelible or heartbreaking salute. Right: A sailor in the crowd of mourners is overcome. John F. Kennedy's war service in the Navy permeates the state funeral: A sailor bears the presidential flag; the Navy Hymn, "Eternal Father, Strong to Save," is played; separately, the Naval Academy Glee Club is enlisted for a requiem performance at the White House. An Army Special Forces unit has also been recruited by Robert F. Kennedy to attend the casket because Bobby knew of Jack's particular interest in the special ops. Opposite: After the Mass at St. Matthew's, the funeral cortege crosses the Memorial Bridge over the Potomac River to Arlington National Cemetery, where Kennedy will be buried. The riderless horse, Black Jack, symbolizes a fallen leader and trails the caisson carrying the casket—the same caisson that had borne the body of not only Franklin D. Roosevelt but also that of the Unknown Soldier. On the following pages: Meantime in New York City, a crowd assembles in Grand Central Terminal to watch a televised account of the proceedings. Some who were there remember that the great hall, with its cathedral-like vaulting and dim lighting, offered a proper, churchly atmosphere.

ELLIOTT ERWITT/MAGNUM (2)

AP

Three scenes from Arlington National Cemetery in Virginia, just outside the nation's capital, where John F. Kennedy is buried on November 25 with full military honors: His widow, Jacqueline, and brother Bobby (top); the coffin about to be lowered (bottom); and servicemen standing guard over the flower-banked grave at dawn on the 26th, a white picket fence enclosing the area where the President is buried. Events of the long Monday, a national day of mourning as declared by President Johnson, are witnessed by perhaps a million people in Washington and, it is thought, nearly the entire remaining American population on television. (Coverage of events prior to the coffin being borne into the cathedral is transmitted to 23 additional countries, including the Soviet Union, via satellite.) The three major networks share 50 cameras, so that nothing—from the pipers of the Scottish Black Watch to the riderless horse to the minute movements of Mrs. Kennedy—is missed. Johnson has been urged by aides not to march in the funeral cortege, for safety's

sake, but he does so nonetheless, falling in behind the caisson. In his memoirs he will recall that, as he walked, "The muffled rumble of drums set up a heartbreaking echo."

The limousine procession bearing foreign guests is so long from St. Matthew's to Arlington that burial services begin before the last car arrives. The reason there are no pictures

of the children at the graveside is because it had been determined by Jackie they were too young for that experience; they had said goodbye to their father shortly after John Jr.'s salute outside the church. Jackie herself lights the eternal flame that continues to burn at the grave, a flickering torchlight that meant so much to her during the remainder of her life (she died

in 1994 at age 64), as she told the writer Theodore H. White (please see page 153). At 3:34 p.m. the casket is lowered into the ground.

As mentioned, the 25th was John Jr.'s third birthday. Two days later Caroline would turn six. Their party was postponed by their mother until December 5—the Kennedys' last day in residence at the White House.

After a Death, the Birth of Camelot

LIFE's Teddy White (right) was no relation to the other T.H. White, the English novelist who wrote *The Once and Future King*, the novel on which the musical *Camelot* was based. But the American was able to conjure for a contemporary audience a place where, as the Briton had imagined it, all people might dream of "a new Round Table, which had no corners, just as the world had none—a table without boundaries between the nations who would sit to feast there." For his King Arthur and Queen Guenever he had the perfect 20th-century couple, Jack and Jackie, seen opposite with daughter Caroline on the day after his election in November 1960—just as they were laying claim to the castle.

WITH HIS PULITZER PRIZE–WINNING *THE Making of the President 1960* having cemented his stature among America's preeminent journalists, Theodore H. White joined LIFE in 1962. The presence of White—a scholar with experience as a shoe leather reporter—only added further heft to the already massively popular magazine.

On November 22, 1963, White was lunching with James Shepley, then an assistant publisher of LIFE, later the president of Time Inc. With the 1964 presidential election looming, White was already at work on the sequel to his groundbreaking bestseller, and Shepley was well-connected in Republican circles. But White had barely begun to pump Shepley for gossip when a waiter told Shepley that President Kennedy had been shot. White headed to LIFE's offices, where the editors had nearly closed that week's issue. As the editors began to get a grip on what was still a handful of facts inside a tide of questions, White barked, "This is my story." No one dared challenge him. Collecting cash from each of his colleagues—credit cards were rare in 1963 and ATMs of course nonexistent—he headed for the airport. He spent the next few days in Washington reporting and observing, finally filing a masterly piece, part eulogy and part analysis, a few short hours after John F. Kennedy was interred. Then he returned to New York.

The next two days, and then even Thanksgiving, passed in a dismal blur. On Friday, a gloomy, stormy day, White had scheduled that most banal of appointments, a dental check-up. He was in the chair and being examined when a receptionist announced that White had an emergency phone call. It was his mother. Jackie Kennedy telephoned, the elderly, excited Mrs. White reported. She said she needs you.

White ran home and called the former First Lady, who was in Hyannis Port. She had something she wanted LIFE magazine to tell the nation, she told him, and he must be the conduit. The Secret Service would furnish a car to bring him to her.

There followed an unceasing barrage of complications. White called LIFE, which had held the presses for more than two days waiting for his previous story as well as other copy and photographs, and told them that they would need to hold the presses again. He then called the Secret Service to arrange a car. Sorry, the Secret Service curtly informed him, Mrs. Kennedy isn't First Lady anymore; she can't authorize anything. White then tried to buy a ticket on a plane to Massachusetts, only to be told that all flights were canceled due to a storm whipping up the coast. He tried to charter a plane: no good, now that all the airports were closed. On the phone with a car service, he looked over to see that his mother was—literally—having a heart attack. With White torn between his duty to his mother and his summons from Mrs. Kennedy, White's wife, Nancy, took charge. She all but ordered the family doctor to leave his holiday weekend to attend to White's mother, and then dispatched White in a car service to Massachusetts.

He arrived just after eight p.m., and after ascertaining that his mother was stable and recovering, he finally sat down with Jacqueline Kennedy. "Composure . . . beautiful . . . dressed in black trim slacks, beige pullover sweater," his notes read. "Eyes wider than pools." They met alone, and in a calm, quiet voice, the 34-year-old widow, whose courage and dignity in the past week had impressed the world, proceeded to give what is considered in journalistic annals to be one of the most privileged interviews ever. Throughout the rest of her life, Jacqueline Kennedy talked for public consumption about the traumatic murder of her husband on a mere handful of occasions, and hardly ever at any length. But she spoke to White, in stunning detail, with the wounds still fresh—and in a way that she planned, this forever colored our view of her husband's presidency.

When she and White had talked on the phone, Jackie had complained about the "bitter people" who wrote history, specifically mentioning Arthur Krock and Merriman Smith, respected journalists with *The New York Times* and UPI, respectively, whose postmortems on the successes and failures of the Kennedy administration had struck Jackie as cold and clinical. In calling White, her intention was to make certain that their stark summations did not stand alone as the final word. For White's part, he confirmed, through his work, Mrs. Kennedy's good sense in summoning him. As he makes clear in his 1978 memoir, *In Search of History*, their conversation rambled and was full of digressions, and he subsequently rearranged his notes to enhance the clarity of their discussion. By the time White handed in his draft, there was no mistaking what Mrs. Kennedy wanted to say.

Before talking about the man she had known, she talked about his murder. You will shortly read the famous essay, but you won't read—there—a good deal of what Jackie said that day.

"They were gunning the motorcycles," she remembered, describing the motorcade. "There were these little backfires . . . I saw Connally grabbing his arms . . . Jack turned and I turned. All I remember was a blue-gray building up ahead. Then Jack turned back so neatly, his last expression was so neat . . . you know that wonderful expression he had when they'd ask him a question about one of the ten million pieces they have in a rocket, just before he'd answer. He looked puzzled, then he slumped forward . . . I could see a piece of his skull coming off . . . I can see this perfectly clean piece detaching itself from his head. Then he slumped in my lap, his blood and his brains were in my lap . . . All the ride to the hospital I kept bending over him, saying 'Jack, Jack, can you hear me, I love you, Jack.' I kept holding the top of his head down, trying to keep the brains in."

Mrs. Kennedy continued, in relentless and expressive detail. "Big Texas interns" in the hospital physically separating her from the President and leaving her in a corridor outside. Standing amid a turmoil of cops and aides and agents and doctors before a policeman thought to bring her a chair. Insisting, finally, on pushing back into the operating room and demanding to be with Jack when he died, with the President's personal physician, Rear Admiral George Burkley, asserting, "It's her prerogative. It's her prerogative," to the surgeon in charge. The tall bald doctor finally relenting when she said, "It's my husband, his blood, his brains, are all over me."

There was a hunt for a priest to administer the sacrament of absolution and extreme unction. "There was a sheet over Jack," she went on. "His foot was sticking out . . . whiter than the sheet. I took his foot and kissed it. Then I pulled back the sheet. His mouth was so *beautiful*." As the priest anointed the body, she held the President's hand. The blood on her gloves had stiffened, which kept her from removing them, so she held out her hand and a policeman pulled off the glove. Then she took off

her ring and placed it on Jack's hand. "Do you think it was right?" she wondered. "You leave it where it is," Jack's right-hand man, Kenneth O'Donnell, reassured her.

"But there's one thing I wanted to say," Mrs. Kennedy told White, taking her soliloquy in a new direction. "All I keep thinking of is this line from a musical comedy, it's been an obsession with me." She then described how Jack at bedtime liked to play records, and that his favorite song was the finale of the Broadway musical *Camelot,* which of course was about chivalry and King Arthur and his knights of the Round Table. The song's concluding lines: "Don't let it be forgot / That once there was a spot / For one brief shining moment that was known as Camelot."

"There'll never be another Camelot again," Jackie told White.

"History," she said, jumping again. "When something is written down, does that make it history? The things they say . . . For a while I thought history was something that bitter old men wrote." But then she married, and changed her mind when she saw how much her husband loved history. "For Jack, history was full of heroes." It was the source, she said, of his idealism. And "if it made him see the heroes, maybe other little boys will see." She was writing an early draft of history here with White, and she well knew it.

Her thoughts shifted back to Dallas. After her husband was shot, various people, including nurses and Lady Bird Johnson, whether acting out of solicitousness or a sense of propriety, asked Mrs. Kennedy if she "wanted to clean up." It would not be until she boarded Air Force One and stood in a washroom as Lyndon Johnson and the rest of the traveling party waited for her to join them for his swearing-in that she would wipe away the blood and hair that had splattered onto her face. Later she wondered to White, "Why did I wash the blood off? I should have left it there, let them see what they've done."

After about four hours, White concluded that he had enough to write. Ironically, though he'd sat mesmerized by her chilling descriptions, he used very little of her most striking testimony. Instead, he used more anodyne elements. He began his piece with the storm-tossed circumstances of their meeting, then shifted to her recollections of the sunny streets of Dallas and the heat of the motorcade, the sounds of motorcycle backfires and Connally being hit. Instead of describing the President's wounds, he allowed two blood-spattered roses that had been in her bouquet and that Dr. Burkley had retrieved for her to stand in for the more graphic imagery. He did recount the moment she transferred her wedding ring to his finger. White noted that she kissed his foot. You'll read all that shortly (or most of it, as we will explain in just a second), and you'll see how he wove in the Camelot concept: "There'll be great Presidents again—and the Johnsons are wonderful. They've been wonderful to me," he quotes Jackie saying (and an interesting aside: the editors would change his period after "are wonderful" to a comma), but "there'll never be another Camelot again." White used his final paragraphs to look ahead with Jackie: her intention to raise her children in America, her hope that people will continue to associate her husband with space exploration, her satisfaction that his grave was marked with an eternal flame that can be seen "for miles and miles away."

White finished his draft at about two a.m., and phoned it in to editors Ralph Graves and David Maness, who were waiting in New York, holding the presses at a cost of $30,000 an hour. He also gave a copy to Jackie to read. The editors cut his rainy opener, and also struck the mention of Jackie kissing her husband's foot as too personal. Those who wondered why White left in his notepad all of Mrs. Kennedy's most intense revelations should consider his editors' judgments: Nothing that might have made readers too uncomfortable would have gotten past them, which probably explains why White ignored most of Jackie's flesh-and-blood memories while keeping testimony that reinforced the image of the President as an idealistic churchgoing family man.

Over the phone, Maness noted to his writer that there was an awful lot of Camelot in the story. "Mrs. Kennedy had come in at that moment," White recalled in his memoir. "She shook her head. She *wanted* Camelot to top the story." White pushed back against his colleagues in New York. Something in his tone roused Maness's suspicions.

"Hey, is she listening to this now with you?" Maness asked.

It was late. The editors capitulated. And thus Jacqueline Kennedy's idea of countering the judgments of bitter old men with the romantic conception of Camelot on the Potomac rolled off those long-delayed presses and, once read by millions upon millions of Americans, came vibrantly to life. The idea acquired a cultural currency not even Mrs. Kennedy could have imagined.

Interestingly, in the years to come, White dismissed the idea of equating the Kennedy years with a mythic Camelot. "A misreading of history," he said. Jackie herself reportedly admitted to friends that the comparison was a little overwrought. But thanks to her original impetus, the man she loved acquired a mythic luster, and 50 years after his death is still revered by many.

JAMIE MALANOWSKI has been a writer and editor at *Time, Esquire* and *Playboy* magazines. Recently he contributed several of the historical accounts focusing on the Civil War in *The New York Times*'s "Disunion" series.

On January 20, 1961, at the White House on inauguration day, Jackie beams as the incoming and outgoing Presidents, John F. Kennedy and Dwight D. Eisenhower, are seen just to the right. Heavy snow had fallen in Washington the night before, but it was decreed the ceremony would go forth. The Kennedys attended Holy Trinity Catholic Church in Georgetown that Friday morning, then joined Eisenhower to travel to the Capitol. In his now-famous address that day, President Kennedy sounded very much like a latter-day Arthur.

The stirring rhetoric—"Ask not what your country can do for you, ask what you can do for your country" the best-remembered exhortation, as said earlier in our pages—was evident from the start: "The world is very different now. For man holds in his mortal hands the power to abolish all forms of human poverty and all forms of human life. And yet the same revolutionary beliefs for which our forebears fought are still at issue around the globe—the belief that the rights of man come not from the generosity of the state, but from the hand of God."

FOR PRESIDENT KENNEDY An Epilogue

by Theodore H. White

Hyannis Port

SHE REMEMBERS HOW HOT THE SUN was in Dallas, and the crowds—greater and wilder than the crowds in Mexico or in Vienna. The sun was blinding, streaming down; yet she could not put on sunglasses for she had to wave to the crowd.

And up ahead she remembers seeing a tunnel around a turn and thinking that there would be a moment of coolness under the tunnel. There was the sound of the motorcycles, as always in a parade, and the occasional backfire of a motorcycle. The sound of the shot came, at that moment, like the sound of a backfire and she remembers Connally saying, "No, no, no, no, no . . ."

She remembers the roses. Three times that day in Texas they had been greeted with the bouquets of yellow roses of Texas. Only, in Dallas they had given her *red* roses. She remembers thinking, how funny—red roses for me; and then the car was full of blood and red roses.

Much later, accompanying the body from the Dallas hospital to the airport, she was alone with Clint Hill—the first Secret Service man to come to their rescue—and with Dr. Burkley, the White House physician. Burkley gave her two roses that had slipped under the President's shirt when he fell, his head in her lap.

All through the night they tried to separate him from her, to sedate her, and take care of her—and she would not let them. She wanted to be with him. She remembered that Jack had said of his father, when his father suffered the stroke, that he could not live like that. Don't let that happen to me, he had said, when I have to go.

NOW, IN HER HAND she was holding a gold St. Christopher's medal.

She had given him a St. Christopher's medal when they were married; but when Patrick died this summer, they had wanted to put something in the coffin with Patrick that was from them both; and so he had put in the St. Christopher's medal.

Then he had asked her to give him a new one to mark their 10th wedding anniversary, a month after Patrick's death.

He was carrying it when he died and she had found it. But it belonged to him—so she could not put *that* in the coffin with him. She wanted to give him something that was hers, something that she loved. So she had slipped off her wedding ring and put it on his finger. When she came out of the room in the hospital in Dallas, she asked: "Do you think it was right? Now I have nothing left." And Kenny O'Donnell said, "You leave it where it is."

That was at 1:30 p.m. in Texas.

But then, at Bethesda Hospital in Maryland, at three a.m. the next morning, Kenny slipped into the chamber where the body lay and brought her back the ring, which, as she talked now, she twisted.

On her little finger was the other ring: a slim, gold circlet with green emerald chips—the one he had given her in memory of Patrick.

THERE WAS A THOUGHT, TOO, that was always with her. "When Jack quoted something, it was usually classical," she said, "but I'm so ashamed of myself—all I keep thinking of is this line from a musical comedy.

"At night, before we'd go to sleep, Jack liked to play some records; and the song he loved most came at the very end of this record. The lines he loved to hear were: *Don't let it be forgot, that once there was a spot, for one brief shining moment that was known as Camelot.*"

She wanted to make sure that the point came clear and went on: "There'll be great Presidents again—and the Johnsons are wonderful, they've been wonderful to me—but there'll never be another Camelot again.

"Once, the more I read of history the more bitter I got. For a while I thought history was something that bitter old men wrote. But then I realized history made Jack what he was. You must think of him as this little boy, sick so much of the time, reading in bed, reading history, reading the Knights of the Round Table, reading Marlborough. For Jack, history was full of heroes. And if it made him this way—if it made him see the heroes—maybe other little boys will see. Men are such a combination of good and bad. Jack had this hero idea of history, the idealistic view."

But she came back to the idea that transfixed her: *"Don't let it be forgot, that once there was a spot, for one brief shining moment that was known as Camelot*—and it will never be that way again."

AS FOR HERSELF? She was horrified by the stories that she might live abroad. "I'm *never* going to live in Europe. I'm not going to 'travel extensively abroad.' That's a desecration. I'm going to live in the places I lived with Jack. In Georgetown, and with the Kennedys at the Cape. They're my family. I'm going to bring up my children. I want John to grow up to be a good boy."

As for the President's memorial, at first she remembered that in every speech in their last days in Texas he had spoken of how in December this nation would loft the largest rocket booster yet into the sky, making us first in space. So she had wanted something of his there when it went up—perhaps only his initials painted on a tiny corner of the great Saturn, where no one need even notice it. But now Americans will seek the moon from Cape Kennedy. The new name, born of her frail hope, came as a surprise.

The only thing she knew she must have for him was the eternal flame over his grave at Arlington.

"Whenever you drive across the bridge from Washington into Virginia," she said, "you see the Lee Mansion on the side of the hill in the distance. When Caroline was very little, the mansion was one of the first things she learned to recognize. Now, at night you can see his flame beneath the mansion for miles away."

She said it is time people paid attention to the new President and the new First Lady. But she does not want them to forget John F. Kennedy or read of him only in dusty or bitter histories:

For one brief shining moment there was Camelot.

Reprinted from the LIFE issue of December 6, 1963

The resplendent First Lady is being seated at a dinner at the Breakers estate in Newport, Rhode Island, on September 14, 1962 (opposite). Above: Jack and Jackie, along with 1,700 invited children from child-care agencies, are on the White House lawn on November 13, 1963, reviewing a performance by the Royal Highland Regiment, The Black Watch—an ancient version of which might have entertained Arthur and Guenever at Camelot. Precisely 10 days after this photograph was made, a subheadline in the *London Herald* would read, even in advance of the publication of Theodore H. White's piece: AMERICA MOURNS CAMELOT DREAM.

Was There a Conspiracy?

According to more than one poll, a great majority of Americans still feel that Lee Harvey Oswald didn't act alone. J.I. BAKER explores, with the help of an expert panel, the top 10 theories of those who would investigate further.

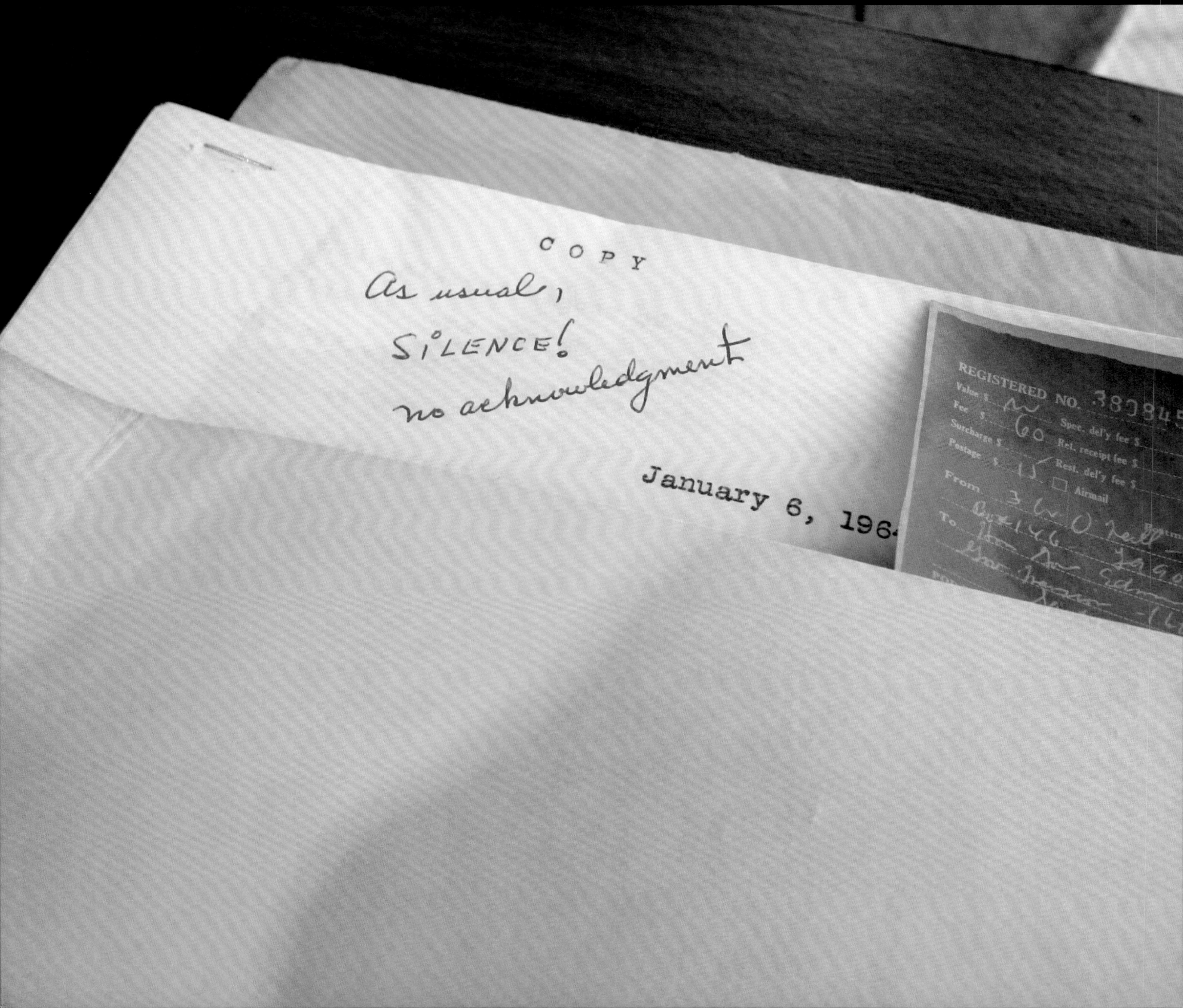

COPY
As usual,
SILENCE!
no acknowledgment
January 6, 196
REGISTERED NO. 38984
Value $
Fee $
Surcharge $
Postage $
Spec. del'y fee $
Ret. receipt fee $
Rest. del'y fee $
Airmail
From
To

SOON AFTER THE ASSASSINATION—IN AN ISSUE DATED December 6, 1963—LIFE published an article entitled "End to Nagging Rumors: The Six Critical Seconds." In it, the journalist Paul Mandel tried to quell the speculation that, even then, swirled around the President's death. Did Oswald have help? Did he really shoot the President? LIFE's answer: He acted alone. But the attempt to defuse the conspiracy theories ironically inflamed them—because Mandel claimed that, according to "a Dallas doctor," one bullet had entered the President's throat. How could that have happened if shots weren't coming from the grassy knoll to the side of the President, in addition to the Texas School Book Depository behind him? Well, Mandel claimed the Zapruder film showed the President turning back toward the Depository, presenting his throat as a target.

By all subsequent accounts Paul Mandel's was a simple, not a sinister, mistake. "But even if that piece had been wholly accurate," says Gerald Posner, author of *Case Closed*, "the conspiracy theories would have spread—for two main reasons. First, this was the first time in U.S. history where a high-profile case involved an assassin we didn't see at the scene of the crime. It fit all our Hollywood visions of a professional hit. And then Ruby killed Oswald, which looked like the silencing of a guy the crime was being pinned on."

To this day, despite reams of analysis, no one seems to agree whether there was a conspiracy or, if there was, who drove it. Authors on both sides of the fence slant facts and attribute evidence that doesn't fit their theories to witnesses who may have been confused or unreliable— but then use as gospel the testimony of similarly compromised witnesses who support the authors' claims. They also employ tautologies: "Because we know *x* it follows that *y* . . ."

But do we really know *x*? Do we in fact know *anything*? "You look at some evidence and say, 'This provides incontrovertible proof that there was only one gunman,'" says the documentary filmmaker and author Errol Morris, whose short film *The Umbrella Man* deals with the assassination. "And then you look at other stuff and say, 'Well, there had to have been *more* than one.' There's a line I've always loved from a woman in the Zoar religion who on her deathbed said, 'Think of all those religions—they can't all be right. But they could all be wrong.'"

It's not possible to do justice to the case's complexities here, but we've tried to present a range of contradictory viewpoints—from seven experts—regarding 10 of the most lasting, vexing and controversial conspiracy theories in this eternally elusive and divisive case.

At left is an intriguing document taken by a news photographer concerning the assassination that was kept with old papers in a courthouse safe by the Dallas County district attorney's office until 2008. It illustrates the never-ending nature of this story, and do not think for a minute that something new won't be uncovered this year or next. Above, on September 24, 1964, President Lyndon Johnson accepts from U.S. Chief Justice Earl Warren the hefty report of his commission's investigation of the assassination—a report that, along with the Zapruder film, is the starting point of a thousand alternative theories.

The Single-Bullet Theory

THE SO-CALLED SINGLE-BULLET THEORY has sparked more controversy than perhaps any other element of the assassination—and that's really saying something. Allegedly fired from Oswald's $21 mail-order Mannlicher-Carcano rifle, the so-called Magic Bullet—Warren Commission exhibit CE 399—struck Kennedy in the back, exited through his throat, struck Governor Connally's back, exited his chest and went through his wrist, and finally ended up in the governor's thigh. It was eventually found on the gurney that carried Connally into the Parkland operating room.

The crux for conspiracy theorists: After traveling through both men, the bullet seemingly remained intact. "How can a bullet do all that and emerge with its only deformity at the base from the impact of the firing mechanism?" asks Dr. Cyril Wecht, who was the lone dissenting member of the forensic pathology panel that reexamined the murder for the House Select Committee on Assassinations (HSCA) in the late '70s. The other eight HSCA panelists upheld the Warren Commission's conclusion. "It is a damaged bullet that is flattened on one surface," says the forensic pathology panel's chief, Michael Baden. "It is thicker and stronger than most jackets."

Theorists also claim the bullet defied the laws of physics, as it seemingly made an abrupt turn in midair. But Vincent Bugliosi, author of *Reclaiming History,* says, "If you look at the Zapruder film, you see Connally and Kennedy reacting at almost the same time. If the bullet that hit Kennedy did not hit Connally, there must have been a second gunman because Oswald couldn't have fired two shots within a split second of each other." And theorists, Bugliosi suggests, improperly place Connally in a direct line in front of Kennedy in the presidential limo, rather than slightly to the left and turning to the right. An alleged second bullet was never found. "If we're to believe the conspiracy theorists, after the bullet exited the front of Kennedy's throat, it may as well have vanished without a trace into thin air," Bugliosi says. "And that's a whole other kind of magic bullet."

Still, three of seven Warren Commission members disputed the single-bullet theory and wanted their objections noted in the Warren Commission report, and a fourth didn't want to sign if it stated that there was no doubt that they were hit by the same bullet. But—another conspiracy?—those objections too went missing. Anthony Summers, author of *Not in Your Lifetime,* reports that commission member Senator Richard Russell told Lyndon Johnson: "I don't believe [the commission's theory]." Johnson responded: "I don't either."

CE 399

WARREN COMMISSION/NATIONAL ARCHIVES

MONDADORI/EVERETT

Above is the bullet found on the stretcher in Parkland Hospital and said by the Warren Commission and the House Select Committee on Assassinations to have wounded President Kennedy and Governor Connally (the nickel is only for size comparison, not part of any theory). Right: Investigators and an unidentified man (squatting) searching for evidence in Dealey Plaza. Opposite: President Kennedy's suit coat, with bullet hole indicated. The single-bullet theory, credited largely to the young Warren Commission staff member Arlen Specter, who would go on to a career in the U.S. Senate, representing Pennsylvania, was not subscribed to by all commission members in the final report, but the commission finally decided that despite a "difference of opinion" there was "persuasive evidence from the experts" that one bullet had struck both Kennedy and Connally.

VIEW OF THE BACK OF PRESIDENT KENNEDY'S
SUIT COAT SHOWING BULLET ENTRANCE HOLE.

EXHIBIT
59

The Mysterious Deaths

DAVID WOO/THE DALLAS MORNING NEWS

EDITOR PENN JONES JR. EARLY ON SUGGESTED that people who allegedly knew too much about the assassination were systematically murdered themselves. (The idea was popularly treated in the 1973 film *Executive Action* and, later, in Oliver Stone's 1991 film, *JFK.*) Some of the people on the putative lists clearly died under less-than-sinister circumstances. (Paul Mandel, for instance, died of skin cancer.) Other stories are, if not evidence of conspiracy, admittedly unsettling.

The first "hit" on Jones's list, the actress Karyn Kupcinet, is alleged to have called an operator just before the assassination to claim that JFK was going to be murdered. Six days afterward, she was strangled in her Hollywood apartment. (Her killer was never identified.) Some suggest that Kupcinet, known to be unstable, was killed because she knew about a conspiracy from her father, the famed Chicago columnist Irv Kupcinet. But if that was true, why wasn't Irv killed?

Anthony Summers acknowledges that the mysterious death of Rose Cheramie, who also claimed to know about the assassination before it happened, remains intriguing. She died in Texas in September of 1965 after a car accident, according to the official report. The rumor is she had been shot. And there are others. But a researcher for the House assassinations committee found that "the available evidence does not establish anything . . . which would indicate that the deaths were . . . caused by the assassination of President Kennedy or by any aspect of the subsequent investigation." And Posner correctly stated that "no major writer or investigator on the case—even those trying to expose dangerous conspiracies—has died an unusual death." Oliver Stone is, for instance, still alive. As of this writing.

Oliver Stone boosted the disappearing witnesses theory with his film *JFK,* which in the top photo is filming on April 15, 1991 (a reenactment of the motorcade on Elm Street). Above: Strange deaths after the assassination began with Oswald's, of course, and here folks line up for Jack Ruby's trial.

Oswald's Murky Past

CORBIS (3)

I N 1958, OSWALD WAS A MARINE ASSIGNED TO EL TORO MARINE CORPS
Air Station in California, where he said he was a Russophile studying the Russian
language at the height of the cold war. He was known as "Oswaldskovich." In 1959,
he was an American defector to the Soviet Union. And although he had worked on a
base used for the U.S.'s CIA U-2 spy plane and, some believe, may have shared secret
information with the Soviets, he managed to return to the U.S. In 1963, he set up a pro-
Castro Fair Play for Cuba Committee in New Orleans, of which he was the only member.

Some suggest that this all points to Oswald being linked to Castro, the communists,
the FBI or the CIA. But, Vincent Bugliosi asks, "if you're hiring someone to kill the
President, do you really want a bad marksman with a [cheap] mail-order rifle who was
notoriously unstable? A man who defects to the Soviet Union pre-Gorbachev, tries to
become a citizen, turns them down, then slashes his wrist and attempts suicide?" In addition, he says, "there is no evidence that Oswald had any association whatsoever with any
of the groups that the conspiracy theorists claim were behind the assassination."

Summers, for one, disagrees: Any serious study of the Kennedy case must confront
the possibility—some would say probability—that "at some point Oswald was manip-
ulated, unwittingly or otherwise," by some branch of U.S. intelligence. He notes,
though, that there is no evidence that any U.S. intelligence agency, as an agency, was
complicit in the assassination.

U.S. government organizations may not have orchestrated the President's death,
but their mistakes have fueled the conspiracy theories, Gerald Posner says. FBI agent
James Hosty was, for instance, investigating Oswald and his Russian wife, Marina,
just before the assassination. "The FBI was afraid that somebody would point the
finger at its agents, saying, 'You were aware of all this,'" Posner says. "They had to
back off Oswald as fast as they could. The CIA was terrified someone would stumble
into their plots with the mob to kill Castro. So there *was* a cover-up—of bureaucratic
reputations—and people picked up bits of that."

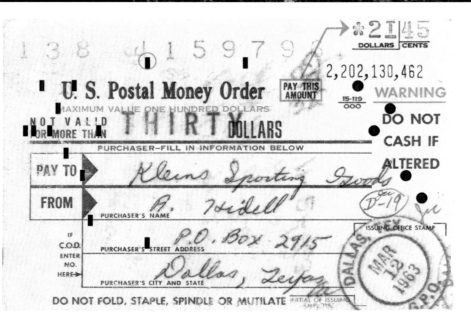

Top: Oswald had quite a collection of political literature when his family
was found at the Paine residence in Irving, Texas, on the day of the
assassination, and his wife and her host, Ruth Paine, were quick to turn
it over to authorities. Above: A money order for $21.45 for the rifle and
telescopic sight that were allegedly used to kill President Kennedy. The
pseudonym "A. Hidell," used by Lee Harvey Oswald, is handwritten in
the purchaser's name box.

The Double Oswalds

CONSULADO DE CUBA, MEXICO, D.F,

(foto)

Solicitud de visa No.: __779__

Fecha: 27 de septiembre de 1963.

Nombre: Lee Harvey Oswald

Ciudadanía norteamericana

Fecha y lugar de nacimiento: Octubre 18, 1939 en New Orleans, U.S.A.

Pasaporte No. D-092526

Dirección permanente: 4907 Magazine St. New Orleans, La., U.S.A.

Ocupación (expresando empresa para la que trabaja) Fotógrafo Comercial

Estancias anteriores en Cuba ---

Motivos de las estancias anteriores ---

Familiares o personas conocidas residentes en Cuba ---

10 OCT. 1963

Ha sido invitado desde Cuba? (Sí:) (No:)

Con que objeto? ----

Cual es el motivo del viaje propuesto viaje en tránsito para la Unión Soviética

mismo 2 semanas y si es posible mas tiempo.

Fecha propuesta de llegada a Cuba septiembre 30 de 1963

Dirección en Cuba:

Lee H. Oswald
(firma del interesado)

PARA USO DE LA MISION

OBSERVACIONES El solicitante dice ser miembro del P.C. Norteamericano y Secretario en New Orleans del Fair Play for Cuba Committee. Y que vivió en la Unión Soviética desde Octubre de 1959 al 19 de junio de 1962; que allá se casó con una ciudadana soviética. Mostró documentación que lo acredita como miembro de las dos organizaciones mencionada y acta de matrimonio. Se presentó en la Embajada de la URSS en esta ciudad pidiendo que su visa sea enviada a dicha Embajada en Cuba. Nosotros llamamos al Consulado de la URSS y nos contestaron que ellos tenían que esperar la autorización de Moscú para dar la visa y que tardaría alrededor de 4 meses.

This is a copy of Lee Harvey Oswald's visa application, released by the Cuban government in 1978. Sometimes controversies and theories demand, over time, the disclosure of documents—birth or death certificates, wedding licenses, travel receipts—that otherwise would have moldered in the files.

SEVERAL SOURCES CLAIMED that they saw more than one Oswald before and after the assassination. At times, a given "Oswald" seemed to be doing things (or appearing in places) that don't fit the profile or whereabouts later established for "Lee Harvey Oswald" by the Warren Commission.

Many of these Oswald-doppelgänger scenarios are unalloyed nonsense; others are intriguing. One looms larger than the rest—and it involves Oswald's controversial visit to both the Cuban consulate and the Soviet embassy in Mexico City over a few days in the fall of 1963. (He was ostensibly attempting to travel to Cuba en route to the Soviet Union.) The stories and counter-stories are too complicated to explain here, but the bottom line is that controversy exists over whether or not both Oswald *and* an Oswald double were in Mexico. In a phone conversation held just after the assassination, FBI director J. Edgar Hoover told President Johnson, "We have up here the tape and the photograph of the man who was at the Soviet embassy, using Oswald's name. That picture and the tape do not correspond to this man's voice, nor to his appearance. In other words, it appears that there is a second person who was at the Soviet embassy."

In their books, Bugliosi and Posner attempt to systematically discredit the multi-Oswald scenarios, but the real sticking point is: Why would anyone have wanted an Oswald double? If an Oswald clone was in fact in Mexico City in 1963, as Hoover asserted, why was he there along with Oswald himself? Author John Newman's explanation: "Someone wanted to make sure that Oswald's Cuban and KGB contacts in Mexico were fully documented . . . [to establish] evidence of an international communist conspiracy" behind the President's impending murder.

Maybe, but since Oswald himself was in Mexico City, the need for a double—if there was one—remains unclear. This is one more instance where there's so much smoke that we can't be sure if it means fire, or if it is just obscuring reality.

Jack Ruby

LAWRENCE SCHILLER/POLARIS COMMUNICATIONS/GETTY

I F OSWALD HAD NOT BEEN ASSASSINATED BY JACK Ruby, Posner suggests, much of the hysteria surrounding "the conspiracy" would not exist: We'd no longer believe that someone in the chain was hired to silence Oswald after Oswald had played his part in the larger, nefarious plan. But others believe that's exactly what Ruby was hired to do, citing a number of mysteries and irregularities. How, primarily, was it possible that Ruby could just walk up and shoot the most-wanted man in the world in the basement of the Dallas police headquarters during Oswald's transfer?

The late journalist Seth Kantor, who was in one of the JFK motorcade's press buses and was later interviewed by the Warren Commission, makes the case in his 1978 book, *Who Was Jack Ruby?*, for Ruby's being a hitman with Mafia connections. This is dismissed by Posner and Bugliosi, who portray Ruby as a volatile, unintelligent man who desperately wanted to belong and be famous. Says the colorful Bugliosi: "If the mob could rely on Oswald and Ruby to do their bidding they may just as well have gone down to Disneyland to get Donald Duck and Mickey Mouse to do their bidding, too."

Yet Ruby himself appeared before the Warren Commission and his testimony remains tantalizingly cryptic. "I have been used for a purpose," He said. "I am used as a scapegoat." In language Bugliosi might applaud, he added: "Now it is the most fantastic story you have ever heard in a lifetime, the most dastardly crime that has ever been committed."

JOHN DURICKA/AP

Above: Ruby loved the night life and he loved his Dallas club. Was he mobbed up? Did the mob want JFK dead? Or Oswald? That web can be spun on and on. Kennedy was close to Frank Sinatra, who had ties to organized crime; JFK had had an affair with Judith Exner, who also was "friends" with Sam Giancana; and the mob was no doubt angry with the Kennedys because they had hounded them after Giancana had helped the cause in the 1960 West Virginia primary. Various investigators have gone down that road through the years; at left, Mafia boss Santo Trafficante takes his seat before the House assassinations committee, then clears his throat and says he has been misunderstood about maybe knowing in advance of the murder of John F. Kennedy. "Absolutely not," he asserts. "No way."

The Umbrella Man

ONE OF THE MOST INTRIGUING ASPECTS OF THE ASSASSINATION is the odd cast of characters who are (supposedly) attached to it—from the Three Tramps (transients who were arrested after the assassination, identified on occasion as various luminaries, including E. Howard Hunt, of the CIA and Watergate-break-in fame, and Woody Harrelson's father) to the Babushka Lady to the Black-Dog Man. You can look them up, should you choose.

Chief among these bit players is the so-called Umbrella Man. The man was standing on the sidewalk as the motorcade passed, carrying an umbrella on a sunny day. He was the only one. Not only that, but, for no apparent reason, as the President approached and passed, the Umbrella Man opened and lifted the umbrella above his head, then turned it clockwise. After the assassination, the man sat on the sidewalk before getting up and walking toward the Texas School Book Depository.

Was the umbrella a signal? Did it conceal some kind of weapon? In 1978, after public appeals from the HSCA, a man named Louie Steven Witt identified himself as the Umbrella Man. He told the committee that his umbrella was a protest against JFK's father's support of Neville Chamberlain's appeasement policies before World War II. (Chamberlain famously carried a black umbrella.)

In Errol Morris's film, Josiah "Tink" Thompson, author of the 1967 book *Six Seconds in Dallas,* sees the whole scenario as evidence that "if you put any event under a microscope, you will find a whole dimension of completely weird, incredible things going on." Others believe there was nothing at all weird about it: Either Witt wasn't the real Umbrella Man, or he wasn't telling the truth. A protest harkening back to pre–U.S. involvement in World War II staged in Dallas in 1963? A symbolic act so subtle that the folks in Texas were required to know that Neville Chamberlain was prone to carry a black bumbershoot?

If you were in Dealey Plaza that day, you became part of the story; if you so much as sneezed, you became a player in a theory. At top: On November 22, 1963, three men who were in the area are being taken in for questioning. The Dallas Police Department records that they are transients and gives their names as (back to front) Gus Abrams, John Forrester Gedney and Harold Doyle. They are detained briefly and disappear after release, leading to conjecture by conspiracy theorists about their "true" identities. Above: The Zapruder film has been hyper-analyzed frame by frame to nail down the actions of the Umbrella Man (center, at bottom of photo) and others.

The Head Shot (Zapruder Film Frame 313)

YOU KNOW MUCH OF THIS ALREADY FROM these pages, if not elsewhere: Dan Rather, then a little-known CBS southern bureau chief, was the first to talk about the Zapruder film on television. He claimed that, in the film, the President's head could be seen to "move violently forward" when the supposed third bullet struck the back of his head. But the head clearly jerks backward and to his left. For some conspiracy theorists, this indicates that the head shot came from the grassy knoll to the side of the President, rather than from the Texas School Book Depository, which the motorcade had just passed.

"Each frame of the Zapruder film is about an 18th of a second," Bugliosi says. "At Frame 312, the President's head is okay. At 313, the all-important moment of impact, you see the explosion and his head being pushed not to the rear, but

ZAPRUDER FILM © 1967 (RENEWED 1995) THE SIXTH FLOOR MUSEUM AT DEALEY PLAZA (2)

forward—about two or three inches—indicating that the bullet came from the President's rear. In Frames 314 to 321, a so-called neuromuscular reaction causes the head snap to the rear."

Josiah Thompson, a former LIFE magazine consultant who had early access to the Zapruder film (and is not to be confused with the editor and writer Tommy Thompson, who played a large part in Richard Stolley's and Allan Grant's reminiscences earlier in these pages), says he was the first to identify the slight forward motion. "But I made an error," Thompson says today. "There is no movement of the head forward between those two frames that's significant. Since then, everyone—critics and supporters of the Warren Commission—has accepted this as truth, but I'm the guy who found it, and I have to say, 'I screwed up.' What I measured wasn't the movement of Kennedy's head but the movement of Zapruder's camera." He rejects the "neuromuscular reaction" explanation, citing the gunshot experiments that the Warren Commission relied on, which had been done on goats years earlier. However, the explanation convinced the forensic panel of the HSCA.

"You would think the Zapruder film would provide the answers we're searching for," says the documentarian Morris, who knows this territory very well. "But what we've learned about images in general is that they just defer the question. So we read endless debates about what individual frames mean, what they show, whether or not the film itself is real. Every argument about the nature of film—and its relationship to the reality it records—can be found in the discussions of the Zapruder film."

Perhaps no single piece of hard evidence has been more responsible for the multiplicity of theories about a second shooter than the Zapruder film's Frame 313, left, which is indisputable in its authenticity (says LIFE) but as varied in its interpretation as a poem by T.S. Eliot or a symphony by Shostakovich. Below: During testimony before the House Select Committee on Assassinations in Washington on September 9, 1978, ballistics expert Monty C. Lutz holds the Mannlicher-Carcano rifle believed to have been the weapon used in the assassination of President Kennedy. This remains the only weapon ever linked to the crime.

JOHN DURICKA/AP

The Warren Commission

The CIA, the FBI, the mob, Cuba, Johnson and the Soviets: Those are the big suspects in most of the theories that run counter to the findings of the Warren Commission. Would Fidel Castro have wanted Kennedy dead? Yes—after the U.S.-sponsored Bay of Pigs invasion sought to depose or kill him. Above, in Havana in April of 1961, the Cuban leader, cigar in place, enters a public trial for captured members (seated) of the failed invasion.

What the commission looked at, counterclockwise from below: The shirt worn by Kennedy on the day of his assassination (the initials JFK are embroidered on the left sleeve); Lee Harvey Oswald's palm print, taken on November 22; an FBI and Secret Service reenactment of the assassination in May 1964, with two unidentified FBI agents sitting in the exact spots that Kennedy, left, and Connally, right, were in when struck; and a man pointing the alleged murder weapon from the sniper's nest in the same reenactment.

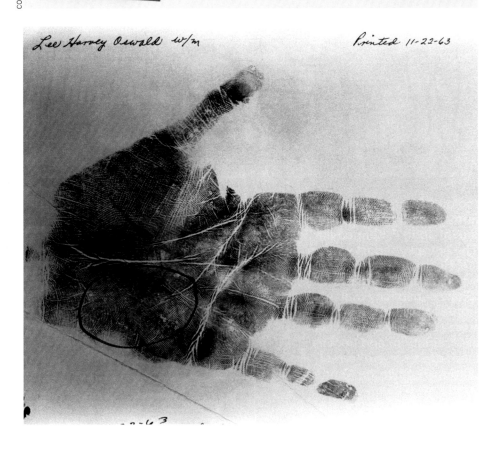

THERE ARE MANY REASONS WHY THE CONCLUSIONS OF THE Warren Commission—its report and 26 volumes of testimony and evidence—remain controversial. For one thing, J. Edgar Hoover withheld information and pressured commission members to parrot his point of view. "[The FBI] would have us fold up and quit," General Counsel J. Lee Rankin said in 1964. "They found the man [Oswald]. There is nothing more to do." And commission member Allen Dulles, who as a former CIA director was well versed in secret details of the agency's involvement in Cuba (the Bay of Pigs invasion; mob-connected Castro assassination attempts), never divulged all that he knew to the commission. His insights would have been nothing if not pertinent, given Oswald's possible Cuban connections.

Since President Lyndon Johnson had established the Warren Commission to investigate the death, reporters didn't dig deep on their own—there was no equivalent of Woodward and Bernstein on this story in 1963. "One reason the field was left clear for the most baseless of the conspiracy theories is that few reporters worth their salt pursued the story in the '60s," says Summers. "Precious few have done so since."

The many and diverse conclusions of the theorists, combined with the fact that the Warren Commission had no way to address its critics or any of the metastasizing theories, helped fuel the American public's increasing mistrust of not only the assassination investigation but of the government itself. This relatively new dynamic was reinforced by lies disseminated during the Vietnam War, the Watergate saga and the Iran-contra affair. Finally, many people were left to believe: The government always covers up, it's been covering up since the Kennedy assassination. "In a reality TV society, where many people think that our own government took down the World Trade Center, the idea of seven middle-aged white men telling the world how the President was murdered in a book whose supporting documents were not disclosed is pretty much unthinkable," Posner says.

To some close to the case, it was unthinkable even at the time. President Johnson himself privately disbelieved some of the commission's conclusions, which of course were made at the behest of his administration.

The Missing Brain

THE PRESIDENTIAL AUTOPSY WAS HOPELESSLY botched. The Secret Service agents removed the President's body from Dallas by holding both the Dallas medical examiner and a justice of the peace not only at bay but at gunpoint. Their mission? To take the body to Bethesda, Maryland, where the government could presumably exercise greater control. But there, at Bethesda Naval Hospital, the autopsy was performed by people who had never carried out a gunshot autopsy before—"and they made a lot of mistakes," says House assassinations committee pathology chief Michael Baden.

The doctors in Maryland didn't follow standard procedures. The head wasn't shaved (some say because the Kennedy family wanted the President to look good—a virtual impossibility—if an open casket was an eventual part of his funeral services). Certain routine procedures were also prohibited by the family, say the conspiracy theorists, because the Kennedys didn't want the public to know the President had suffered from Addison's disease. Although the brain was fixed in formaldehyde, which firms it for dissection, the doctors failed to section it to track the bullet.

But worse: The brain itself disappeared.

Baden originally believed the brain, the microscopic slides, the paraffin blocks and tissues from the autopsy were placed in a steamer trunk and given to the National Archives. But after his HSCA forensic pathology panel received permission from the Kennedy family to open the trunk in 1979, it discovered that the brain and all the tissues were missing. "We interviewed anybody who had anything to do with the brain at the hospital and in the pathology department," Baden says, "and all the grave diggers who had anything to do with burying the President. But we could not track down what had happened."

Some suggest the brain was appropriated by Bobby Kennedy to prevent it from becoming part of any kind of assassination sideshow (although it surely would have been safe in the steamer trunk). Baden, for his part, is convinced its disappearance was not nefarious: "Some people have said 'Oh, there was another bullet in the brain,' but X-rays were taken to show this wasn't true."

Of course, there are controversies about the X-rays, too. With Dr. Cyril Wecht as the sole exception, the HSCA forensic panel decided that the President was shot twice—and only twice—both times from behind. "Since then no new scientific evidence has changed our interpretations of each wound, the [bullet] that missed, the ones that struck and the damage that was done," Baden says. His opinion does not satisfy all.

Top left: U.S. Army colonel Pierre Finck was a member of the three-man team that performed the autopsy on President John F. Kennedy in Maryland. Above: The autopsy report written at the Bethesda Naval Hospital. The photograph of Finck was taken when he appeared as a witness in the Clay Shaw conspiracy trial in New Orleans, on February 24, 1969. The businessman Shaw was the only person ever prosecuted in the assassination, and he was acquitted—a result that does not put to rest any of the debates about whether the Kennedy autopsy should properly have been performed in Dallas, or whether the medical work in Maryland was conclusive.

The Grassy Knoll

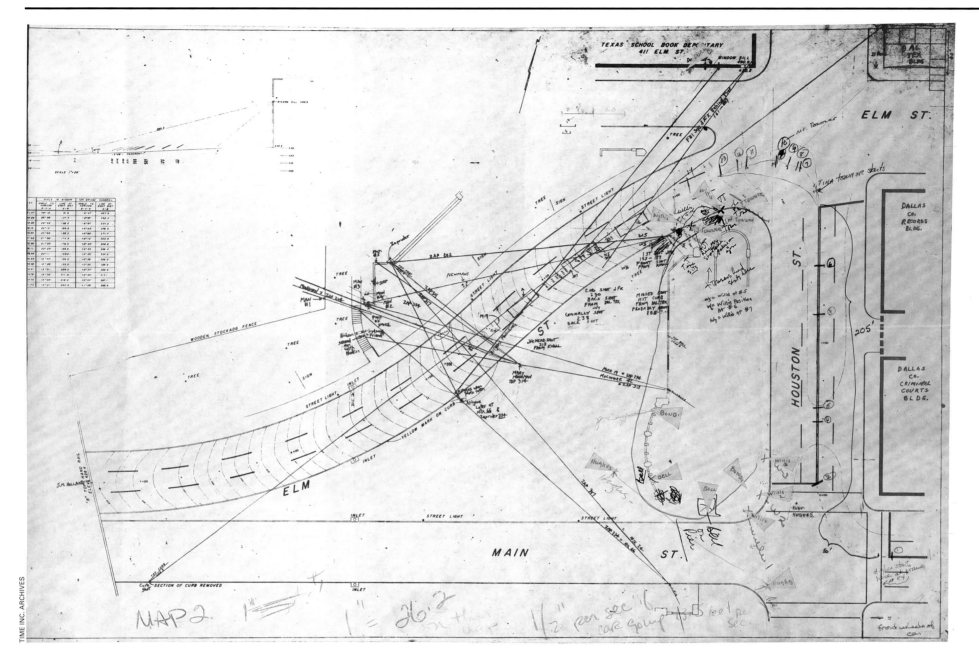

WAS A SECOND GUNMAN STATIONED ON THE GRASSY KNOLL to the side of the motorcade? Twenty-one of 178 witnesses surveyed believed they heard shots coming from the area. In addition, author Anthony Summers reports, of the seven known people standing on the knoll that day, "almost all of them believed some of the gunfire came from behind them." Kennedy aide David Powers, who was in the car behind the presidential limo, believed that he heard gunfire coming from the front.

While some, including Posner, credit all ear-witness confusion to the odd acoustics in Dealey Plaza—it is indeed a small bowl of a place, where sounds might rebound—in 1978, audio evidence retrieved from a Dallas Police Dictabelt led three acoustics experts to conclude that a fourth shot had come from the grassy knoll. At the 11th hour of its investigations, this testimony was one of the things that led the HSCA to conclude that there was a high probability of a conspiracy.

But then, three years later, the National Academy of Sciences said that the HSCA's findings regarding acoustics were wrong.

What does this all boil down to—and by "this" we don't mean simply theory number 10 regarding the grassy knoll? "We're 50 years after the fact and not one credible word, not one credible syllable, has come out indicating that there is a conspiracy," Vincent Bugliosi says. Summers counters that in some respects the evidence suggesting the possibility of conspiracy remains as strong as ever, if not stronger.

Whether or not Oswald acted alone, Summers adds, "Most people think they haven't been told the whole truth about the Kennedy assassination, and I think that's true." It seems more Americans agree with him than not.

Writer and editor **J.I. BAKER** is the author of *The Empty Glass*, a fictionalized account of the death of Marilyn Monroe, which is being turned into a film.

Top: A map of Dealey Plaza with possible bullet trajectories drawn. Above: Bill Newman (far left) and his wife, Gayle, and their children dive to the ground for cover on the grassy knoll as news photographers take pictures of the scene moments after the shots have rung out in Dealey Plaza.

The Kennedy Legacy

There is a phrase: "He lived on after his time." Rarely has this been more applicable than to John F. Kennedy. He had already achieved much in his cut-short life, and it was almost as if everyone—his successor, his former colleagues, his brothers, his sisters, his children, his countrymen—felt duty-bound to honor his wishes and thereby his memory.

LEGACIES CAN BE MEASURED IN BRICK and mortar, in flesh and blood, in spirit and inspiration. The first equation is the easiest to quantify. There are dozens—scores, *hundreds*—of John F. Kennedy schools in the United States, including one in Montana and another on Long Island that were renamed the very week after his death. There are a dozen Kennedy schools in the Netherlands. There are airports and plazas around the world, and Kennedy streets in Lebanon and Israel. In France there are two dozen Kennedy avenues, boulevards and rues, plus at least one corniche and one *cours*.

He left a legacy of family: Jackie, Caroline and John Jr. went on in life, accomplishing much, each of them contributing. Jackie died too young, of cancer, and John died much too young in an airplane crash. More Kennedy tragedy. Caroline continues today as she always has: a beacon of intelligence and diligence, doing the family—and the nation—proud. Her kids, a son and two daughters, are strong young adults now.

We know what happened to Jack's brothers, of course, and it would be impossible in this space to delineate, even briefly, what happened to all of their various offspring. If these myriad personal histories of the newest generation needed a solid bookend, it has one now in Joe Kennedy III, who in 2012 won his race for Massachusetts's 4th district congressional seat. And so, after a very brief hiatus, a Kennedy is back in Washington. Who knows how many more might be forthcoming?

Who knows, indeed, what might be next for this family, or what might still be accomplished in America and throughout the world thanks to the words that John F. Kennedy spoke, and the initiatives he undertook, more than a half century ago? There are still young people (and older) in the Peace Corps today, doing good works globally. The cold war did end, eventually, without any kind of general annihilation; the Soviet Union came apart, and Kennedy surely contributed to that. The Johnson administration had tremendous successes with civil rights initiatives, always pushing them forth by insisting that this is what JFK wanted. All of its other Great Society policies—the most progressive social agenda fulfilled since the New Deal—was pushed in the spirit of Kennedy. Those policies have their detractors today (and so does Kennedy and so does Johnson). But when we're discussing legacies, we're discussing results: the actual, the tangible—an influence felt all the way to the present day. And Kennedy left all manner of legacy.

Presidents who came after, men of both parties, have said they were inspired by him. Awards, which are based upon achievements that in turn are based upon words and actions, have been given out to the next generation's best and brightest in his name. No President who lived such a short time in office has persevered so durably in his American afterlife.

It is a cliché to say that "society changed in the 1960s." Within the cliché, we see fire hoses, hippies, Vietnam protests, riots. Society, however—and everything—had changed earlier than that, with Kennedy, the transitional figure: a hero of World War II, a member of the Greatest Generation, a man never seen in anything but a suit or, at Hyannis Port, a polo shirt. But new and different and young.

Fifty years after his death, we still yearn for his presence.

DENNIS STOCK/MAGNUM

At left, respects are paid during an exhibition remembering JFK at the IBM Building in New York in 1964. Opposite: After a surprise snowstorm in early September 2007, President Kennedy's eternal flame (slightly right of center) takes on added serenity. The part of the Kennedy legacy that would be most consequential for millions of people would be the legislation that was enacted across the Potomac in Washington, during the tenure of his successor Lyndon Johnson. A master politician—and a master manipulator—Johnson accomplished things by leaning on perceived debts owed to Kennedy that JFK himself probably could not have pushed through. The greatest triumphs were the Civil Rights Act of 1964 and the Voting Rights Act of 1965. Mark Updegrove, Johnson biographer and director of the late Texan's presidential library, says, "Kennedy couldn't have gotten those done. Johnson could and did. He leveraged tragedy to get those crucial laws passed."

GLOBE/ZUMA

I f we look at über-famous American women of the 20th century, we find such as Eleanor Roosevelt and such as Grace Kelly, and then we have Jackie, indisputably an icon, a combination of both, singular. In the aftermath of the President's death, no one assumed she was done—and she wasn't. In the public realm she spearheaded cultural initiatives like the restoration of New York City's Grand Central Terminal that reminded all of her work at the White House, and personally she found an edifying profession as a book editor. She was active in tributes to her late husband, be they the John F. Kennedy Presidential Library and Museum in Boston, the John F. Kennedy Center for the Performing Arts in Washington or others in between. (Above, in 1967, she and John Jr. look on gleefully as Caroline christens the Naval aircraft carrier *John F. Kennedy.* On

the opposite page, top right, she is escorted by Roger Stevens, then chairman of the board of the Kennedy Center for the Arts, to a 1971 performance of Leonard Bernstein's *Mass,* a work dedicated to her late husband.) By any estimation, Jackie was a fine and hands-on parent, the proof being the solid young adults her two children became.

She asked for privacy, a request not granted; in a contest without a winner, she was probably the world's greatest celebrity. She had told LIFE's Theodore H. White that she had no intention to leave America and raise her children elsewhere, and she did not in fact leave, making New York City home. But she did marry Aristotle Onassis, the phenomenally wealthy Greek shipping magnate (seen opposite, top left, on their wedding day, October 20, 1968, on the Greek

island of Skorpios). Jackie overnight became Jackie O in the tabloids and magazines, and if she had thought or hoped this second marriage might distance her somewhat from the spotlight, it served no such purpose.

She was diagnosed with non-Hodgkin's lymphoma in early 1994 and the end was relatively quick; she died in her sleep on May 19, 1994, and the next day John Jr. issued a statement: "My mother died surrounded by her friends and her family and her books, and the people and the things that she loved. She did it in her own way, and on her own terms, and we all feel lucky for that." In the photograph opposite, bottom, John touches the gravestone of his father at Arlington National Cemetery on May 23 as his mother's casket sits beside the eternal flame during burial services.

HELLAS/CAMERA PRESS/REDUX

BETTMANN/CORBIS

GARY HERSHORN/REUTERS

With Jack's generation of Kennedys, each of those who were left—his widow, his brothers and sisters—had to eventually think: What is next for me? What part of the legacy is bequeathed? Do I go my own way? Do I follow Jack's path? For Bobby, certainly, the question was: Do I pick up the torch? He was the next brother in line. When Joe Jr. had been killed, Jack had carried on. Would Bobby do—or attempt to do—the same?

He did, in his way. He ran for the Senate from New York and won, overcoming charges of carpetbagging, charges that are part of the game in New York (see: everyone from James L. Buckley to Hillary Clinton). His appeal to the young was stunning; the term "rock star" wasn't on the table when Jack had been President, but now it was, and Bobby was a rock star, just as his brother had been (opposite, top: Outshining the New York congressional candidate for whom he is campaigning in November 1966).

The big question as 1968 approached and Lyndon Baines Johnson was increasingly engulfed by a progressively unpopular war in Vietnam: Would Bobby run for President? Would he challenge Jack's former Vice President, whom Bobby, in particular, had always detested?

He seemed reluctant, but LBJ was discouraged early by the New Hampshire primary results, and announced that he would not run again. Bobby did enter the race (opposite, bottom: With brother Ted during a campaign strategy session at Bobby's house, the storied Hickory Hill, in Virginia) and his campaign started to steamroll, fueled by a youthful energy. He was in the midst of his greatest-yet victory in the California primary on June 5, a win that would surely catapult him to a general election showdown with none other than Richard Nixon, when he was assassinated at the Ambassador Hotel in Los Angeles by Sirhan Sirhan. In the famous photograph at right, taken that night by LIFE's Bill Eppridge, who had been with the campaign from the start, the busboy Juan Romero cradles the stricken senator's head.

Below: Two days later, during funeral services at St. Patrick's Cathedral in New York City, John F. Kennedy Jr. is seen turning as he walks next to his sister, Caroline. They are in the midst of a sea of

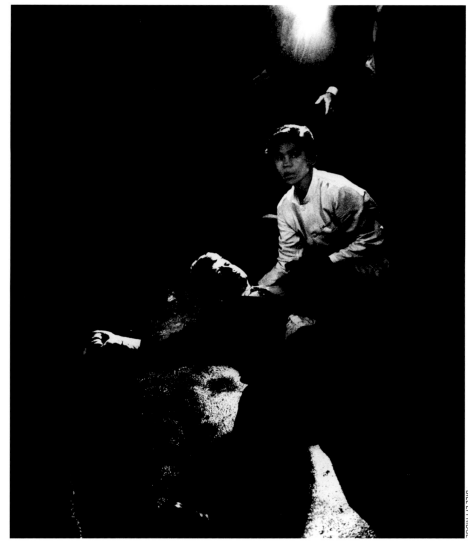

Kennedy cousins (Bobby and Ethel already have 10 children and Rory is, at this time, on the way).

Now, by 1968, the idea is becoming part of the culture: that from this extraordinary American family, to which so much had been granted, much is being exacted.

The Youngest Brother
Teddy

GEORGE TAMES/THE NEW YORK TIMES/REDUX

JOHN LANDERS/BOSTON HERALD/POLARIS

DARRYL HEIKES/BETTMANN/CORBIS

He certainly was to the manner born, and when Ted was tapped by the family to run for the Senate seat vacated by his brother Jack upon being elected President, he did as instructed—just as soon as he was legally able at age 30. Dick Donahue has told us already in these pages about the feuding within the Massachusetts Democratic party between the McCormacks and the Kennedys, and this was renewed in 1962 when the experienced war veteran Eddie McCormack vied for the seat with peach-faced Teddy Kennedy (left, campaigning at Coolidge Corner in Brookline that August) and quickly brought the race down to good old-fashioned bare-knuckles Massachusetts standards: "I back Jack, but Teddy ain't ready," said McCormack, and "The office of United States senator should be merited, and not inherited." He declared snidely during a debate, that if his opponent's name was Edward Moore instead of Edward Moore *Kennedy,* his candidacy "would be a joke." Yes, but his name *was* Edward Moore Kennedy, and he defeated McCormack two-to-one in the primary, which was a de facto election (he brushed aside the Republican surnamed Lodge in the general contest). Ted Kennedy proceeded on a nearly 47-year career in the U.S. Senate (fourth-longest ever), with many legislative triumphs and exemplary bridge-building across the aisles, certainly one of the most distinguished congressional careers in U.S. history.

He might have been President (above, with his first wife, Joan, at the 1980 Democratic convention in New York City, when he had failed in his attempt to unseat Jimmy Carter but had nonetheless delivered one of the most stirring speeches of his life). Yes, he might well have been President, but there had been an incident in July 1969: After a party to thank his brother Bobby's former staff on the island of Chappaquiddick off Martha's Vineyard, Kennedy drove off the Dike Bridge. He survived, but his passenger, Mary Jo Kopechne, drowned inside the overturned car. Kennedy gave a statement saying he had accidentally taken a wrong turn (left, bottom, he appears at Edgartown District Court on Martha's Vineyard to plead "not guilty" to motor vehicle violations) and received a suspended sentence—which was not suspended the least bit in the court of public opinion.

With Jack and Bobby—not to mention both Joe Sr. and Joe Jr.—gone, Ted assumed the role not only of the last Kennedy lion in Washington, but of the family patriarch, which took some growing into. His nephew William Smith had legal trouble in Florida, and it turned out his patron at the Au Bar in Palm Beach earlier in the evening had been Uncle Ted. (Smith was acquitted of rape.) But Ted did right his ship (a metaphor he, an inveterate recreational sailor, would have appreciated), and with his second wife, Victoria Reggie, enjoyed a celebrated twilight. He would be the one to preside at weddings and wakes in these years (opposite, top right: He and Caroline make their entrance into the church on her wedding day, July 19, 1986; he would eulogize her brother when he died in 1999). And he became an ever better father (opposite, top left: In Moscow, at the Kremlin—of all places!—in 1974, with his son Edward Jr., who has lost a leg to cancer; Teddy Jr.'s farewell remarks to his dad at the Boston funeral in 2009 were as eloquent and memorable as his father's had been for John Jr.). In the photograph at bottom, Edward M. Kennedy's casket is carried by an honor guard to a hearse at the Kennedy compound in Hyannis Port on August 27, 2009, after he has died at home at age 77 after a yearlong struggle with brain cancer.

KEN REGAN/CAMERA 5

STEVE LISS

STEW MILNE/AP

After the pop anthem "Sweet Caroline" enjoyed a second life as the unofficial theme song of the Boston Red Sox during their very successful run in the new millennium, the singer and songwriter Neil Diamond disclosed that indeed, back in the '60s, he had written the jaunty tune in honor of the late President's daughter. Everyone was delighted by the disclosure, because no one has ever thought ill of Caroline—a rare circumstance with a Kennedy. And why would anyone? She was, from the very first time we met her when she was a child, bright, engaging and pointed in all the right directions. You might even say that she, too, could have been President, but that really wasn't the case; when she floated her trial balloon for Hillary Clinton's vacated U.S. Senate seat in December 2008, it very quickly popped. She didn't have that Kennedy *thing* for politics. But she had everything else, and now, at 55 years old, she—a lawyer and a writer and editor like her mother, a keeper of the flame—is among the most admired of Americans. On these pages are three pictures of Caroline—two of them sweet, one painful—clockwise from left: On the day she weds Edwin Schlossberg on July 19, 1986, at Our Lady of Victory Church in Centerville, Massachusetts, in a picture made for LIFE by Harry Benson; with her brother during the Profile in Courage Award ceremony at the Kennedy Library in 1995; at the same event in 2000, with her brother's seat empty for the first time, as he, who had attended all of these awards programs since their inception, has died.

John Jr.

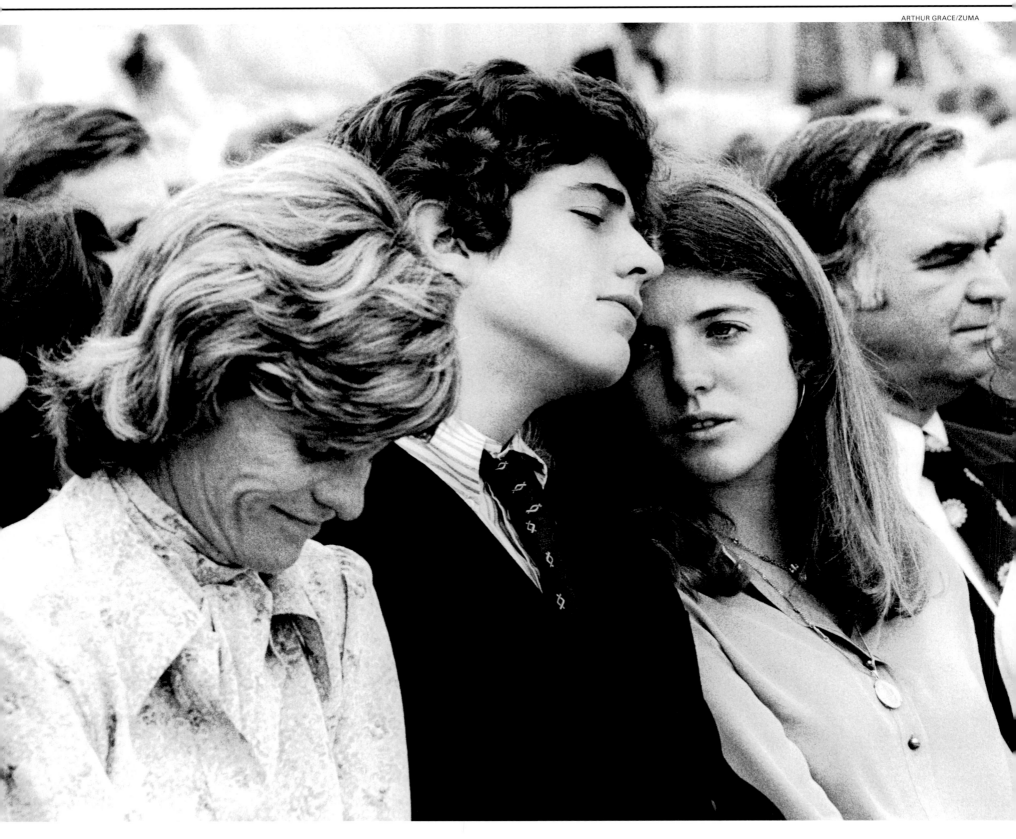

He was the baby born into the White House, and as John-John (not ever his nickname when a child, and one he didn't love later), he became America's favorite kid, not least because his father happily—and to Jackie's dismay—welcomed the press in to photograph his cute little boy and girl. After President Kennedy was killed, his widow proceeded differently, shielding her children as best she could from the glare. Since John and Caroline were the most famous of all the multitudinous Kennedy kids, we did know what was going on with them—which schools, what drama productions, what ski vacations— but we didn't know much else. We were able to figure that they were not falling prey to the difficulties (drugs and such) faced by some of Bobby's children, and so we felt well for them. When nice photos did circulate, like the one above of John and Caroline at the dedication of the Kennedy Library in Boston in 1977, we smiled.

John graduated from Brown University in 1983 and later got his law degree from New York University; he served as a prosecutor in the Manhattan district attorney's office for four years. He could not help but become a public figure. Was he even more handsome than his father, or the uncle he never knew, Joe Jr.? Perhaps; quite possibly. In the judgment of the modern age, he was *People* magazine's Sexiest Man Alive in 1988.

Because Jackie kept the kids under wraps, the public thirsted for any news or pictures of them. One of John Jr. in the attitude that he made a signature in the 1990s is seen opposite, left, hat on backward, but it was made in a reflective moment: His grandmother Rose Fitzgerald Kennedy, matriarch of the family, has died the day before—January 22, 1995—at the compound in Hyannis Port. To counterbalance all these premature Kennedy deaths we are dealing with in these pages, we are happy to note that Rose was 104 years old.

That same year, 1995, John presides at the launch of his new

BRIAN SNYDER/REUTERS

MARK CARDWELL/REUTERS

TYLER MALLORY/LIAISON/GETTY

political magazine, *George,* in New York City (above, right). It is an audacious effort and, for a time, an exciting and lively journal. It will not pan out for the long haul, but it gets everyone thinking again: Where is this Kennedy headed? Could he be headed for . . . ?

Meanwhile, John is taken off the "available" list when he weds Carolyn Bessette on September 21, 1996. They are seen at right, as John gives her a kiss on the cheek during the annual White House Correspondents' dinner in Washington in May 1999. Two months later—on July 16—John, who has a proper license, will choose to pilot a small plane from New Jersey to Martha's Vineyard, on their way to his cousin Rory's wedding on the Cape; he, his wife and one of Carolyn's two sisters, Lauren, will be killed when the plane disappears into the Atlantic. John is 38.

Many of the Kennedy deaths have been tragic and certainly all of them have been sad. This might be the saddest.

With the Kennedys it can be said: It's always about family, it's often about politics, it's all about the past and it's all about future—it's all about the last generation, the current generation and the next one. It's all about heritage and, again, family.

People who touch so many eras of this extraordinary saga are seen in the photograph at left, made in 1965 in Hyannis Port, in which the ailing Joe Kennedy Sr. poses with his grandchildren—the offspring of Jack, Eunice, Patricia, Bobby, Jean and Teddy, the Greatest Generation. These children's own children are now growing up, and some of them have made or will soon make the decision as to whether they should enter the family business. After Ted Kennedy died and then his son, Rhode Island congressman Patrick Kennedy, decided not to run for reelection to the House of Representatives in 2010, much was made of the fact that, for the first time in half a century, there was not a Kennedy in Washington. But now there is again. Joseph P. Kennedy III, whose father, Joseph P. Kennedy II, has also spent time in the House, won election in 2012 to represent Massachusetts's 4th district. (He is seen at right getting a hug from Dad.) Joe is a grandson of Bobby and Ethel Kennedy. Jack and Jackie, were they alive today, would have three grandchildren— Caroline's daughters, Rose and Tatiana, and her son, Jack. Jack is seen in the photograph at bottom at the Kennedy Library in Boston in May 2011, doffing a USS *John F. Kennedy* aircraft carrier cap in front of a picture of patrol boat skipper John F. Kennedy. It is worth noting that young Jack, Tatiana and Rose are all smart kids—and so is Joe III. They're good-looking, too, in the way of Kennedys.

Where are they headed? That question, asked many times before about many a Kennedy, is being asked again.

NASA

CHARLIE GRAY/CAMERA PRESS/REDUX

He said we should go to the moon before the decade was out, and we did (opposite: Buzz Aldrin's boot touching down, after Neil Armstrong's already has, on July 20, 1969). He said we should engage with the rest of the world in the postwar era—that the United States now had to assume such a leadership role—and we did (above: The John F. Kennedy Memorial to the Dead in the Orient, a tribute to French and Algerian soldiers, in Marseille, France). He said we should ask not for favors, but should ask how we might contribute to the greater societal good. He said much that will live down the decades and even centuries, and then he was cut down—in his prime, as they say. That was 50 years ago.

Today, he rests in peace in Arlington National Cemetery, where the plaque on his grave is simple and stark.

As this anniversary of his death confirms for us all: He will never be forgotten.

PAOLO PELLEGRIN/MAGNUM

Today in Dallas

In a photograph from 2010, the strange shapes of one of the peristyles in Dealey Plaza, near where people scrambled or cowered after the shots rang

out. Today, the structure gleams brightly in the sun.

OVER TIME I'VE HAD VARIOUS OCCASIONS TO TAKE VISITORS TO the place in Dallas where President Kennedy was murdered. I always park several blocks away and then, without saying that I'm doing so, walk the route of the motorcade. We head west down Main Street, turn right onto Houston, and proceed toward the Texas School Book Depository, which stands at the next corner. If not for its place in history, this blocky, unremarkable building would have been torn down long ago. In fact the Depository is so bland that the visitor and I are usually at the corner of Houston and Elm waiting for the light to change before my visitor lets out a surprised, "Oh, my God! That's it!" I watch as without fail the visitor's eyes search out the sixth floor window where Oswald had his sniper's nest and then go from there down to the street and then back up to the window again. And that's when my visitor will says something like, "It's not that far."

No, it's not. And although the trees are larger today than they were 50 years ago, their branches still don't interfere with the line the fatal bullet took that day. I doubt that any busy corner in any American city has changed so little in the last half century. Anyone who has read or watched anything about the assassination finds the rest of the landscape by the Depository so familiar it can be eerie. Everything is still there more or less just as it was—Elm Street curving slightly downhill away from the Depository; the grassy knoll leading up to the white, cement pergola with its shafts and ledges; the stockade fence; the open space across Elm from the knoll; and the triple underpass a short way down the road. These landmarks all have their important places in the mythology that has grown up year after year around the assassination. You can even make your way behind the grassy knoll to the stockade fence, concealed behind trees, where some conspiracy theories have placed a second assassin. The wooden stockade is covered with poems, sayings, drawings and tributes—and not just for JFK; there are a few sympathetic phrases for Lee Harvey Oswald as well. Some of the slats are broken off, presumably by souvenir hunters. The fence looks authentic, but it's not. The pickets have to be replaced every couple of years.

There is little else besides the graffiti to help the visitor know where he is—that he is, in fact, there. One small plaque in the ground says that this site has been commemorated by the federal government, but it doesn't say what for. Some local folks think that kind of willful obfuscation is nonsense, and others think it's for the best.

In front of the Depository and along both sides of Elm, there are usually knots of curious people poking around. They wander here and there taking photographs and pointing. Occasionally, though less often now than in the past, you can still see dogged conspiracy researchers bustling about importantly making measurements or lying on their backs to take a picture of the Depository from a particular spot at a particular angle. And then there are the hawkers selling grisly newsprint publications or books or DVDs about the assassination, complete with photographs of the autopsy. These blots on the landscape are generally loquacious, friendly men—sometimes a bit too friendly—whose tawdry presence around the Depository drives official Dallas crazy. The deans of this ragged group are Robert J. Groden and Don J. Miller. Since he arrived from the East Coast in 1995, Groden has been ticketed over 80 times for various minor offenses and has beaten every charge. Peaceful free speech and the right not to be harassed are his defense. On the other hand, Don J. Miller, who describes himself as a historian, has been coming to Dealey Plaza to sell his wares for as long as Groden and has never been ticketed. He says Groden, as an East Coaster, just doesn't know how to handle the typical Dallas policeman.

Groden, Miller and their lesser rivals around Dealey Plaza are an annoyance to proper Dallas because they are a reminder of what Dallas feared the site would become: a cheap, sensational tourist attraction. Then again, Dallas might have worked against that with some kind of substantial monument. But that wasn't going to happen, at least not out of doors. In the stunned aftershock of the event, Dallas was blamed for the assassination as much as Oswald was. The city leaders, a paternalistic and exclusive crowd in those days, knew that any hint that the city was trying to exploit this tragedy would doom the city's reputation forever. They commissioned Philip Johnson to create a memorial to President Kennedy on a site a couple of blocks from the School Book Depository. Unfortunately, it turned out to be bare, passive and emotionless—as well as in the wrong place.

They were always able to squelch any dubious plans for Dealey Plaza itself. The Texas School Book Depository changed hands a few times until Dallas County acquired the building in 1977 and renovated the bottom five floors for county offices. The sixth and seventh floors were preserved, and this made some folks curious, even wary. They were transformed into a museum, which opened in 1989,

The *X* (opposite) does indicate where Kennedy's car was when he was mortally wounded, but it is a highly unofficial marking, put in place and maintained by the people who work in the area as unaffiliated guides.

Above: In The Sixth Floor Museum at Dealey Plaza, the most poignant display is certainly the sniper's nest, where Oswald took aim, recreated just as it was when the investigators found it.

and this upset some people. The old railroad yards next to the Depository were paved over to make part of it a parking lot, the only really substantial change in the appearance of the area since 1963.

Called simply The Sixth Floor Museum at Dealey Plaza, it presents the events of the President's visit to Texas, the motorcade, the murder and the aftermath, clearly and without embellishment. There is also a savvy presentation of the cultural context of the early 1960s, an era that saw the appearance of music and literature that, like the assassination itself, remain important today: *Silent Spring*, *The Fire Next Time*, *The Feminine Mystique*, *The Freewheelin' Bob Dylan*, *One Flew Over the Cuckoo's Nest*, *Who's Afraid of Virginia Woolf?* and *To Kill a Mockingbird*. Oswald's sniper's nest is reconstructed exactly, although it's protected by walls of glass. Interior walls enclose a small room where black-and-white newsreels of the funeral play continually. Some moments like the riderless horse with the boot stuck backward in its stirrup and young John Kennedy making his salute to his father's casket stir the heart even after 50 years.

The seventh floor is also part of the museum. It's simply a large, open space used for meetings, lectures and other events. Most of the time, however, it's empty and a visitor can wander up there and stand solitary and uninterrupted at the corner window right above the sniper's nest below on the sixth floor and look down, much as Oswald must have done, on Elm Street and the grassy knoll and the triple underpass. Even before November 1963, Dealey Plaza was an odd little corner of Dallas. Right on the western edge of downtown and near land

that was used for the Dallas County Criminal Courts Building and other official structures, it was nevertheless unsuitable for development and historically subject to floods from the Trinity River, which flows through Dallas. But George B. Dealey, one of the leading citizens of early 20th-century Dallas, thought this area could become a stirring entranceway to the city and began buying parcels of land that he hoped would become a massive city park. The triple underpass was originally conceived as the gateway into that park, which would both awe and welcome visitors to Dallas. During the '30s a reflecting pool, some planter boxes and the pergola got built, and in 1949 a statue of Dealey was erected looking inward toward Dallas rather than outward toward the west. But otherwise his project languished, perhaps from simple lack of interest. And in time, Dealey's grand vision gradually transformed into a peculiarity. What was that reflecting pool doing on the edge of Dallas? Why was that odd pergola standing next to a warehouse full of schoolbooks? By November 1963, Dealey Plaza was just the visible remnant of a failed dream. For the Kennedy motorcade it was just a way of getting from here, Main Street, to there, the Trade Mart, where a luncheon would be held. After November 1963, Dealey Plaza became and still remains the unchanging setting for a tragedy of many, many other lost dreams. Almost hidden away, there is a museum, a very good one, that tells the stories.

GREGORY CURTIS, a native of Corpus Christi, Texas, and former editor of *Texas Monthly* magazine, is the author most recently of the book *The Cave Painters*.

Today in Dallas
Words Unsaid

Few museums in the world are as hushed as The Sixth Floor Museum at Dealey Plaza. Places that commemorate the Holocaust, certainly, and spaces in lower Manhattan preserving the memory of what happened on September 11, 2001. Exhibits in Normandy remembering D-Day.

Here, too, in The Sixth Floor Museum, everyone seems to realize the focus is on a tragic act. There is audio that takes us back to the day, and there are docents to explain things. But time and again, as you round a turn on your inevitable way to the sniper's nest, you quietly come across something that gives you pause, or even makes you draw a deeper breath.

On these pages, items associated with the final appearance on the Dallas schedule—the lunch that didn't happen. Counterclockwise from right: Stephen Kahn and 2,599 others were invited to the event in the cavernous courtyard of the Trade Mart, where Kennedy was due to enjoy lunch and give a speech; the President's unused place setting; his never-to-be-delivered remarks. Among the things he would have said: "There will always be dissident voices heard in the land, expressing opposition without alternatives, finding fault but never favor, perceiving gloom on every side and seeking influence without responsibility. Those voices are inevitable.

"But today other voices are heard in the land . . ."

The Dallas Citizens Council
The Dallas Assembly
The Science Research Center

request the pleasure of

the company of

Stephen Kahn

at a luncheon in honor of

The President and Mrs. Kennedy

The Vice-President and Mrs. Johnson

The Governor and Mrs. Connally

Friday, the twenty-second of November

at twelve noon

The Trade Mart

The Unspoken Speech
of
John F. Kennedy

at Dallas

November 22, 1963

Postmortems and Condolences

The afternoon had already been long when Dr. Robert N. McClelland, who had presided in Trauma Room One after Kennedy had been admitted to Parkland Memorial Hospital at 12:38 p.m., signed off on the Admission Note below. He and his colleague surgeons had known immediately upon examining the President that he was going to die. "[H]is head was . . . so greatly damaged," McClelland later told the Warren Commission. After death was officially pronounced, all of the other drama that ensued at Parkland—the fight over the right to do the autopsy, the Kennedy faction's successful scuffle for quick possession of the body—was all finished well before the Admission Note was clocked at 4:45; in fact the body was already being flown east. Back there would come the memorial services, the opening of thousands of letters of sympathy, the sending out of gracious notes of thanks in Jackie's name (opposite). It was over, except for the writing and remembering of it, things that continue a half century later.

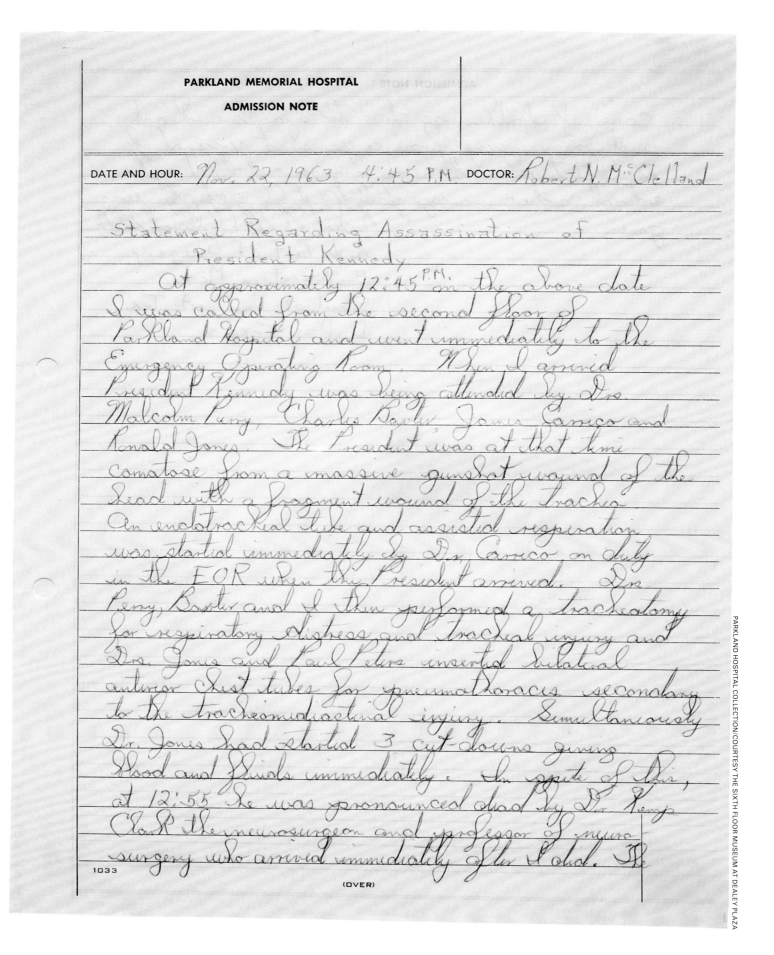

PARKLAND HOSPITAL COLLECTION/COURTESY THE SIXTH FLOOR MUSEUM AT DEALEY PLAZA

JOHN FITZGERALD KENNEDY
President of the United States
May 29, 1917 – November 22, 1963

✝

Dear God,

Please take care of your servant

John Fitzgerald Kennedy

ᔕ   ᔕ   ᔕ

Now the trumpet summons us again—not as a call to bear arms, though arms we need—not as a call to battle, though embattled we are—but a call to bear the burden of a long twilight struggle, year in and year out, "rejoicing in hope, patient in tribulation"—a struggle against the common enemies of man: tyranny, poverty, disease and war itself . . .

In the long history of the world, only a few generations have been granted the role of defending freedom in its hour of maximum danger. I do not shrink from this responsibility—I welcome it. I do not believe that any of us would exchange places with any other people or any other generation. The energy, the faith, the devotion which we bring to this endeavor will light our country and all who serve it—and the glow from that fire can truly light the world . . .

With a good conscience our only sure reward, with history the final judge of our deeds, let us go forth to lead the land we love, asking His blessing and His help, but knowing that here on earth God's work must truly be our own.

Mrs. Kennedy is deeply appreciative of

your sympathy and grateful

for your thoughtfulness

One More Artifact

WE HAVE ALREADY TRAVELED BACK IN TIME IN THESE pages and often then have brought things up to date. Fifty years ago, Dealey Plaza had little to do with John Fitzgerald Kennedy—a town square through which the motorcade passed on its way to the Trade Mart—and today it has everything to do with him, and the artifacts you have seen on the previous pages rest there, visited daily by people who are captivated by history or by the man himself.

One of the reasons we pay such attention 50 years later is because of the riveting impact Kennedy made on the national consciousness when he came on the scene. Rarely do things change overnight with the election of a politician, but *something*—not necessarily policy, not necessarily anything tangible—changed overnight when Kennedy became our leader. When, during that 14-minute inaugural address, which we visit one last time in the picture on this page, he challenged us to "Ask not . . . ," many listeners were instantly energized, and somehow all of us became younger. Kennedy allowed us to feel that way until the day of his death.

There is one final artifact we put before you in this book, and it in no way brings the story up to date but is here to take you back to that November. It is a replica of the issue of LIFE you have read about more than once in previous pages. By now you know that our printing plants were in Chicago; that we rushed an edit team from New York to the Midwest; that we halted the presses and scrapped the Roger Staubach cover; then halted them again when Oswald was killed and Thomas Thompson could put a new conclusion on his story; and that Theodore H. White's first dispatch from Washington was featured. The version of the magazine reprinted here is the final one. You will notice, in other features within the magazine and in the advertisements, reminders of an entirely different era: casual sexism in selling products, LIFE's use of the term *negro*. To remove them would have been not only misleading but, we think, dishonest. The entire point of including the issue—and indeed, the overarching goal of our book—is to bring us all back and examine once more that terrible day, just as it was.

The day Kennedy was killed.